The Essential Guide
to the
New Adolescence

ALSO BY AVA L. SIEGLER

What Should I Tell the Kids?
A Parent's Guide to Real Problems in the Real World

The **ESSENTIAL** GUIDE to the New ADOLESCENCE

HOW TO RAISE AN EMOTIONALLY HEALTHY TEENAGER

Ava L. Siegler, Ph.D.

A DUTTON BOOK

DUTTON
Published by the Penguin Group
Penguin Putnam Inc., 375 Hudson Street,
New York, New York 10014, U.S.A.
Penguin Books Ltd, 27 Wrights Lane,
London W8 5TZ, England
Penguin Books Australia Ltd, Ringwood, Victoria, Australia
Penguin Books Canada Ltd, 10 Alcorn Avenue,
Toronto, Ontario, Canada M4V 3B2
Penguin Books (N.Z.) Ltd, 182–190 Wairau Road,
Auckland 10, New Zealand

Penguin Books Ltd, Registered Offices:
Harmondsworth, Middlesex, England

First published by Dutton, an imprint of Dutton Signet,
a member of Penguin Putnam Inc.

First Printing, October, 1997
10 9 8 7 6 5 4 3 2 1

LIBRARY OF CONGRESS CATALOGING-IN-PUBLICATION DATA:
Siegler, Ava L.
    The essential guide to the new adolescence : how to raise an
emotionally healthy teenager / Ava L. Siegler.
        p.   cm.
    Includes index.
    ISBN 0-525-93970-9
    1. Teenagers—United States.   2. Child rearing—United States.
3. Adolescent psychology.   I. Title.
HQ796.S4585   1997
649'.125—dc21   97-15188
                                                              CIP

Printed in the United States of America
Set in New Baskerville

The case studies presented in this book are composites of more than one real
person. The actions and statements ascribed to each case study is a combination
of the actions and statements of the individuals on whom that characterization
is based.

This book is printed on acid-free paper. ∞

For Bobby, again

ACKNOWLEDGMENTS

I would like to acknowledge the debt that I owe to my parents, Charlotte Gunsberg Heyman and Phillip Heyman, whose lives were too short in reality, but very long in memory, and my sisters, Saida Heyman Baxt, M.D., and Adria Heyman Hillman, Esq., who have been such loyal and true friends.

I thank my colleagues at the Institute for Child, Adolescent & Family Studies, who have contributed their collective wisdom and support to these efforts, my agent, James Levine, whose acute intelligence and boundless enthusiasm have always pointed me in the right direction, and my editor, Deborah Brody, whose patience, sensitivity and skill have kept me properly focused.

I am pleased to be able to count on Arnold Dolin, Associate Publisher of Dutton, as a cherished and respected friend, and, of course, where would I be without my assistant, Rose Marie Horvath, who, with lasting good humor, labored day after day by my side.

I particularly want to thank my sons, Jess and Dan Siegler, who taught me so much about adolescence. And of course, I could not have written this book without the heart-felt contributions of all my teenage patients. I hope that they can recognize their sharp, wry perceptions of themselves and their world in these pages.

Lastly, my eternal gratitude goes to my husband, Bob Siegler, who first met me when I was a teenager, and who has loved and supported me through all our adult years.

CONTENTS

Part II. The Five Faces of Adolescence

Contents

INTRODUCTION

"You don't understand," fourteen-year-old Molly screamed at her mother. "You never understand! All you care about is whether I'm nice to your friends and get good grades in school. I hate you!"

"Don't talk to your mother that way," her father shouted back. "Who do you think you are?"

"Nobody! I'm nobody to you. I wish I were dead and I wish you were dead, too!" Molly sobbed as she ran from the room, leaving her parents alone, stunned by her words. What had they done? Is it so wrong to want Molly to be polite and do well? How should they deal with their teenage daughter's intense anger and despair—ignore her? Discipline her? Comfort her? What's happening to Molly? Is her behavior hysterical? Manipulative? Truly suicidal? Does an outburst like this signal heavy weather, or is it just an ordinary adolescent storm?

I've written this book to help you find answers to these questions. As your child approaches the transforming changes of adolescence, your job as a parent will also be transformed. It's harder than ever to be a teenager in today's times and it's also harder than ever to become the *parent* of a teenager. You're trying to deal with problems that your parents never even imagined, at the same time that you're preoccupied with the intense economic pressures of today's economy, and left with much less time to supervise and support your kids.

There's a big difference between childhood and adolescence, too. When your children were small, their problems also seemed small. After all, how much mischief can young minds plan? How much damage can little hands do? But now, as your children cross the threshold into adolescence, the hazards your children face will significantly *increase*, while your ability to protect your children from these hazards will significantly *decrease*. After years of holding your children close, now you have to let them go.

Letting go is a difficult lesson for parents to learn, because it goes against so much of what our parental instincts have been telling us up to now (keep them safe; watch out for them; don't let them fall; don't let them fail). The lesson is even more difficult now, because the world is so different than when we were growing up—the streets are more violent; the drugs are more dangerous; the sex is much riskier. And complicating things even further, at the same time you're trying to find a way to help your adolescents learn how to manage, they're trying to find a way to manage without you!

When I wrote my first book, *What Should I Tell the Kids? A Parent's Guide to Real Problems in the Real World*, I was trying to help parents maintain what I called "the sanctuary of childhood" by creating "an emotional cushion of safety" for their young children in today's tough times. But as your children now approach adolescence, this sanctuary will inevitably be breached. Parents of adolescents often describe feeling as if they are crossing a border into uncharted territory, with no maps to guide them. This new book is my attempt to help you gain a firmer footing, as the ground beneath you shifts. The ideas I present here are based on my own experiences as an adolescent, my experiences as the mother of two adolescents, and particularly my experiences as the therapist of hundreds of adolescents over the past twenty-five years.

I hope that this book will enable you to understand the

twists and turns of adolescent development, and why this phase is so complicated and prolonged; I hope it will help you recognize your child's individual response to the demands of adolescence and develop some supportive parental strategies to address that response, and I hope it will help you make changes in yourself that will transform you from the *protective* parent of a child to the *effective* parent of a teenager.

Note: *In order to avoid the awkwardness of constantly using "he" and "she" and "him" and "her," I have alternated the sex of the adolescents that I discuss throughout these chapters.*

PART I

FORMATION AND TRANSFORMATION: THE ADOLESCENT JOURNEY

*T*his book is about adolescence, the developmental journey that transforms your son or daughter from a child to an adult. But your child actually began this journey a long time ago. Since your baby was born, both of you have been struggling together to negotiate a whole series of necessary separations. Your baby moved out of your arms as she began to walk; she moved out of your orbit as she began to go to school, and out of your protection as she began to act on her own initiative. These ongoing separations were, all along, helping to prepare you and your child for the most significant separation of all—that time when your child will be able to lead an autonomous life, no longer dependent on your care. But to accomplish this goal, your child must begin to diminish your importance and disregard your good advice. While this causes parents to feel (understandably) saddened, angry, and helpless, it actually serves a significant developmental purpose for your adolescent; it helps her to take her own risks and begin to manage her own affairs. As she matures, your adolescent forms new capacities to address developmental tasks in the present, at the same time that she transforms old solutions to developmental tasks in her past.

In the next five chapters, I'm going to explore how adolescence creates the conditions for this formation and transformation to take place. I will trace the enormous physical changes that alter your adolescent's sense of self; I will discuss the new psychological changes *that profoundly influence your adolescent's emotional life; I will explore* the impact of all these changes on your family life; *I will describe* the more perilous environment *in which today's adolescents mature; I will present what I call the* five basic fears, *which underlie and motivate a great deal of bewildering adolescent behavior; and I will conceptualize what I call the* five developmental tasks of adolescence—*tasks that all adolescents must solve successfully before they can safely cross over to their adult lives.*

In the first part of the book, I have also devoted a chapter to talking to your teens—helping you use what I call the four C's (compassion, communication, comprehension, and competence) to create and maintain a forthright, ongoing dialogue with your adolescent—a dialogue that I hope will enable you to keep track of each other's direction as you both embark on the adolescent journey.

CHAPTER 1

Adolescence: Old Struggles

What Is Adolescence?

Our memories of adolescence are fraught with feelings—passion and pain, abandon and anxiety, daring and dread. Remember the crush you had on your English teacher? The excitement of the crowded halls between classes? How important it was to sit with the right crowd at lunch? And all those forbidden firsts—the first smoke, the first drink, the first kiss? It's no wonder that so many stories take adolescence as their starting point or that so many cultures define the boundaries of adolescence with a special challenge to be met before we can cross over to the adult side—whether it's an Australian tribal "walkabout," a Los Angeles gang initiation, or an elementary school graduation in Massachusetts. What is adolescence? Why is it so memorable for all of us?

Adolescence is the name we give to the psychological space between childhood and adult life. Every society marks this time by separating the child in some way from his parent(s) and expecting him to take on new responsibilities. In many of the preindustrial societies throughout our world, adolescence takes a very short time (a few months, for instance). It is initiated by social recognition of the physical signs of puberty, and usually marked by a brief, dramatic rite of passage (ritual scarring, a test of strength or endurance, a drug-induced shift in consciousness). This is because in these societies, children are quickly needed to participate in adult work (food gathering, hunting, planting), and there is no time for a prolonged phase of psychological development. In these cultures, what I call "the sanctuary of childhood" often comes to a quick and decisive end by the time a child is eleven or twelve.

But in postindustrialized societies like ours, adolescence may take a very long time indeed, and be marked by a more subtle and extended passage. This is because our children need to accomplish so much before they can become self-sufficient adults. For instance, in our culture, fifteen to twenty years of education and/or apprenticeship may be required just to prepare a child to work. Acquiring this knowledge and skill takes a long time, whether you're a surgeon, a chef, a computer analyst, or an auto mechanic.

And it's not only preparing for work that requires years of training. Forming our own families (or choosing not to) takes us a long time, too. Ten to twenty years of social and sexual experience may be necessary before a child feels ready to choose a life partner. That's because societies like ours depend on romantic love as the principle of selection, and romantic love depends on opportunity and destiny—both notoriously unpredictable. We do not, on the whole, permit our parents to arrange our marriages, or enter into marital covenants based on the economic or social needs of our families (at least, not consciously!).

Because the adolescent journey has become so extensive and elaborate, we harbor a very large social group of the people we call adolescents, and consequently, this group has a profound and pervasive effect on the rest of us. Adolescents have created their own popular culture, and adolescent tastes and attitudes have deeply influenced our fashions, politics, literature, and music. The books we read, the TV programs we see, the clothes we wear, and the stores we frequent, often cater to an adolescent audience. (Teenagers, for example, are prime consumers of junk food and jeans, CD's and cigarettes.)

Some of this is for the best, since adolescents contribute energy and enthusiasm and idealism to our society. It is adolescents who join our sports teams, sing in our church choirs, serve in our armies, and organize against injustice. Evelyn, fifteen, is one of these adolescents. Deafened by an accident when she was eight years old, Evie has become an empowered student activist for the rights of the deaf. In addition to her political commitment, she also volunteers two afternoons a week, teaching American Sign Language to hearing-impaired preschoolers. Evelyn is living a life that embodies adolescent energy, adolescent enthusiasm, and adolescent idealism.

But some adolescent behavior displays a recklessness, impulsivity, and lack of judgment that endangers our society. It is adolescents, too, who begin to abuse drugs and alcohol, contribute to the rising statistics on suicide and unwanted pregnancies, and commit violent crimes. Hud, sixteen, is one of these adolescents. He has always gotten into trouble with authorities. But recently, Hud was expelled from his old school for smoking grass, and admitted to a new school for troubled teenagers. Angry and ashamed, Hud immediately provoked a fight with a much larger boy, and when this boy threw him up against a wall, Hud pulled a knife out and slashed him in the face. The cut required twenty-one stitches, but Hud can't understand why everyone blames him. After all, he states, "He was in my face, man. I had to take him out." Hud is living a life that embodies adolescent recklessness, impulsivity, and lack of judgment.

Parents have always worried about their children; it's part of their job. But as our children become adolescents, our worries loom larger, because while our sons and daughters are now capable of adult action, they still lack adult experience, adult perspective, and adult judgment. When a four-year-old throws a temper tantrum and screams, we are not threatened by his underlying rage, because we are aware of his physical limitations. As his parent, you can easily stand your ground, because if all else fails, you are still at least twice as big as your four-year-old. But when a fourteen-year-old screams and rages, the potential to threaten your life or his own is within his means. Now, standing your ground becomes a much more difficult parental proposition.

When a six-year-old doesn't want to eat for a few days, we assume that a slice of pizza and her favorite ice cream will set things back on track. But when a sixteen-year-old stops eating and becomes anorectic, we are no longer able to tempt her appetite with treats.

While the developmental tasks (control over one's anger or control over one's appetite) may be exactly the same for the young child and the teenager, *the potential harm of failing that task becomes much greater as we approach adolescence.* This is what makes adolescence such a challenging and alarming phase of development.

The Physical Changes of Puberty

Adolescence is the last phase before a child becomes fully grown and takes his place in the adult world. Many parents equate adolescence with the striking changes of *puberty*, but actually, these physical changes are usually the *midpoint* in a developmental process that was set in motion years before (as early as eight years old) and may continue until your child is well into his twenties or even thirties. We use the term "adolescence" to refer to the *psychological* alterations that take place during this phase of development, and we reserve the term "puberty" to describe the *physical* changes which accompany it.

By the time your child is nine or ten years old, pubertal changes may already have been set in motion within his body, even though outward signs of change (particularly the physical signs of sexual maturation) may not appear for several years. This is often a time of rapid and uneven growth; some youngsters grow as much as four or five inches a year; others gain ten or even twenty pounds. Hands and feet and noses seem to extend rapidly, and youngsters may outgrow their sneakers every other month. These rapid physical changes greatly contribute to the heightened awkwardness, sensitivity, and shame that many adolescents feel about their changing bodies, and these sensitive feelings may continue to plague them throughout these years.

For girls, the first signs of puberty are the slight swellings around the nipples of the breast that are often called "breast buds." Pubic hair and hair under the arms and on the legs appears next, and as a young girl grows, her height and weight increase. As fatty tissue defines her breasts, hips, and thighs, the girl's body takes its special female shape. Menstruation is the last step in this pubertal process. While the average age to achieve menarche is between twelve and thirteen years in our culture, girls can begin to menstruate as early as eight or nine years old or as late as fifteen or sixteen years old. As hormonal activity increases, sexual excitement produces lubrication of the vagina. These changes all signal your teenager's *physical* readiness to engage in sexual intercourse. (Her psychological readiness is another matter!)

For boys, testicle development is the first sign of puberty, as these body parts grow larger and more tender and descend between the boy's legs. As with girls, pubic hair now begins to show, and the boy begins to move into his growth spurt, where his height and weight increase. His male body begins to take shape—his shoulders broaden, his chest deepens, his penis begins to enlarge, and body hair appears on his face and chest. These hormonal changes are often signaled by a characteristic "break" in the boy's voice, a source of some embarrassment for male adolescents. As in the girl, the boy's body, too, begins to discharge new bodily fluids that signal his sexual maturity, and he becomes capable of the ejaculation of viable semen when he has an erection. Boys in our culture generally lag about two years behind girls, reaching puberty between fourteen and fifteen years. But again, the onset of puberty can be as early as eight or ten for a boy, or as late as sixteen or eighteen.

While boys are slower starters than girls (and preadolescent and early-adolescent girls frequently appear more mature than boys of the same age), boys quickly catch up and overtake girls in mid-adolescence. By fifteen years, the typical adolescent boy is heavier, taller, and has more muscle mass than the typical adolescent girl.

Those girls and boys who stand at the extreme ends of this continuum (very early onset or very delayed onset) are likely to be the most vulnerable to psychological conflicts about themselves and their bodies, since they will stand out sharply from their peers and will keenly feel this difference. While early developers may seem to attract the admiration and even envy of their friends (the eleven-year-old girl who's "built," the twelve-year-old boy who's "hung"), the boys and girls themselves are often totally unprepared to deal with the consequences of their physical transformation and its effect on those around them.

During early adolescence, then, your teenager must come to terms with enormous changes in her body image. Sometimes these changes may appear to be vehemently resisted ("No! I don't want to wear a stupid bra! I don't need it!"), while at other times the changes may seem to be avidly embraced ("Why can't I have a string bikini? Everyone wears them!"). To make matters even more difficult, breasts, pubic hair, pimples, a bigger nose, and body odor are not the only changes your adolescent has to deal with. Under new, hormonal influences, both boys and girls are becoming moodier, oversensitive, and overreactive. In addition, sleeping and/or eating habits may have changed, disrupting the rhythms of your family's life, and it may feel as if everything and everybody bothers your adolescent.

It's important for parents to realize how profoundly the *physiological* (hormonal) changes of adolescence contribute to the characteristic *psychological* changes—the elation and despair, excitement and enervation, restlessness and passivity, rage and calm, sweetness and cynicism. But sometimes we're not aware that these extremes of mood that I've been describing are also mirrored in extremes of thought as well.

Besides physical and emotional changes, your adolescent's brain is changing, too. He is beginning to think about himself and his world in a new, more abstract way, as changes in brain chemistry produce changes in brain behavior. This is what makes teenagers so responsive to poetry or politics, on the one hand, or so vulnerable to the fanaticism of cults or gangs, on the other. This is also why revolutionaries are often drawn from adolescent ranks. This is the time of life when extreme ideas are most easily and most ardently embraced. Often these ideas follow an experience of personal trauma, as we can see in the stories that follow.

Deion's twin brother (fourteen years old) was accidentally killed by a cop last year, when a stray bullet (meant for a drug dealer) ricocheted off a traffic sign and punctured his brother's lung. Deion cannot forgive or forget his brother's death. He has started to attend meetings of a militant sect that preaches that violent revolution is the only way African-American men will gain the power and respect they deserve. Deion has been raised in a Christian family and he's not sure he believes in violence, but he *is* attracted to the passionate commitment of the members of the sect, and he likes reading their literature about revolution. Deion's new intellectual abilities to think abstractly, coupled with the emotional devastation of his brother's death, have heightened his vulnerability to the extreme philosophical ideas of this group.

Deborah, sixteen, was raised in a Midwestern Jewish home. Her family has never been particularly religious, but after a group of local kids painted swastikas on the doors of homes owned by Jewish families in her suburban neighborhood, Deborah has begun to become more conscious of her Judaism. She has recently become interested in the philosophy of a Zionist group known for their militant position on the rights of Jews to defend themselves, and is interested in immigrating to Israel (which is the only place she maintains that she can feel "safe"). Deborah's new interests in her religious and cultural background, while initially stimulated by her anti-Semitic experience, draw upon her new intellectual capacities for abstract reasoning.

The Psychological Changes of Adolescence

Puberty sets in motion the biological maturity of the *body*. Adolescence sets in motion the psychological maturity of the *self*. Often these two processes are not simultaneous; one may be triggered far before the other, producing a lack of parallel development. We are used to thinking about physical growth as a steady progression ever upward and onward, but psychological growth does not have this linear inevitability. Psychological development is jagged and frequently erratic, with *regression* alternating with *progression* ("two steps forward, one step backward"). It is important to realize that while each phase of adolescent development creates new struggles and opens up new possibilities for psychic resolution, each phase also carries with it the old cumulative weight of your adolescent's previous childhood struggles and their outcomes. The entry into, and exit from, each earlier stage of development profoundly affects each subsequent stage. How your child enters adolescence, then, will have a lot to do with how he left childhood, and how he left childhood reflects the even earlier influences of his infancy.

Imagine you are building a block tower. Any imbalance, inept choice, or weakness created by earlier steps you have taken can bring the whole construction tumbling down when you go to add later blocks. This is the way development works, too. Early development sets down a foundation on which later development is added; any early fault creates later weaknesses in the entire structure. But don't despair! Even if the walls appear to come tumbling down (as often happens in adolescence), you and your child still have the opportunity during these years to build a better, stronger foundation that will support a more complicated and successful construction.

Because of the enormous changes we've discussed, there are bound to be lots of *discrepancies* (between physical and psychological maturity), *discontinuities* (between the kind of child you once had and the kind of adolescent he's become), and *inconsistencies* (between his behavior on one occasion or another) along the path of adolescent development. All of these produce the characteristic ups and downs of life with your adolescent.

Your teenager's new bodily maturity, for instance, along with the hormonal upsurge in sexual feelings, is often accompanied by a certain degree of awkwardness and tension between parents and teenagers. A twelve-year-old girl no longer feels comfortable sitting on her father's lap, and to cover her new bewildering discomfort, she squirms away from a hug, and says, "Ugh, Daddy, your beard scratches!" Or a thirteen-year-old boy who never objected to a kiss good night now avoids his mother's caresses. These are completely normal instances of young adolescents attempting to create a safe distance between themselves and their parents—a distance that permits them to begin to remove their sexual feelings from their family circle and place them more appropriately within their own generation.

While everything in adolescence may look and feel different, it's important to keep in mind that many adolescent conflicts are simply new developmental variations on old, familiar themes that you've been addressing since your child was born—helping him to separate from the family, strengthening his self-control, conquering his fears and anxieties, developing the ability to distinguish right from wrong, and consolidating his personality and character.

On the other hand, your child's developing physical and sexual maturity adds a powerful new chord in this old psychic arrangement. This is why adolescence seems so threatening—a three-year-old may tell you she's going to run away, but a thirteen-year-old can actually stay out all night. A six-year-old can break his toy, but a sixteen-year-old can put his fist through the living room window. And there's a big difference between an eight-year-old's crush on her gym teacher and an eighteen-year-old's real-life sexual affair with her college professor. The special separations of adolescence, then, take place in a brand-new context. Propelling these new separations forward are the physiological changes that accompany sexual maturation, and the psychological changes that are readying your child to live life without you.

Peter Blos, Ph.D., a psychoanalyst who has contributed a great deal to our understanding of the psychology of adolescence, has divided this important developmental timespan into five distinct but overlapping phases. It's a useful way to break down this process into more manageable chunks. The first phase (which largely goes unrecognized by parents) is *preadolescence* (nine to eleven). During this phase your young boy or girl is beginning to move away from the preoccupations of childhood and to prepare psychologically for the emotional and physiological changes that are about to come. This is often the time when boys and girls seem worlds apart from each other, and even appear to avoid each other's presence.

Early adolescence (twelve to fourteen), which is probably most familiar to us, is usually marked by the onset of puberty. This is when your adolescent's body changes, altering his role in the family and the world, and this is when he must reconcile his sense of himself as a child with his new-forming image as an adolescent. At this point, your early adolescent is still gazing back at his *past*, and his primary connection (though rapidly changing) is still with his family. As he begins to separate from the family, he moves toward his peers, who offer him new sources of emotional support. But these relationships are often still changeable, unstable, and insecure, so this can be a stressful time for your child.

By *mid-adolescence* (fifteen to sixteen), the bodily changes of puberty are firmly established, and parents have already begun to lose much of their power as caregivers and authorities. This parental diminishment permits your teenager to seek out intimate and supportive relations with his contemporaries. This may also be the time your adolescent begins to explore the exciting new sexual world that now lies within his grasp. The middle adolescent has moved past the claims of childhood ties, and lives for the *present*, concerned primarily with the pressures of his peers, who are his primary source of connection. This means that his judgment may be skewed, and his behavior unwise or even reckless.

By *late adolescence* (seventeen to nineteen), your teenager's identity (including his sexual identity) and character have become increasingly consolidated, and his personal values and goals have begun to evolve. Young adolescents are pre-occupied by possibilities. They dream of being a rock star or an astronaut, of playing professional basketball or finding a cure for AIDS. But by late adolescence, your son or daughter begins to realize that one can't just *be* something, one has to *become* something. Now your teenager's dreams of glory are transformed into the hard step-by-step work that produces the achievements of adult life. In late adolescence, the urgency about the present will be expanded to include some sense of the *future*. A late adolescent is capable of bringing more caution and more care to his life. Now he is ready to approach love and intimacy with a stranger who stands outside of his family circle and to make important choices. His maturity lends him better perspective.

And finally (having negotiated all of the earlier phases for better or for worse), your teenager becomes a *postadolescent* (twenty plus). By now, he has become knowledgeable about his own limits and realistic about his skills and chances. Using what he has learned in his adolescent years, he is capable of seeking his own satisfactions in love and in work, and competent enough to take on adult responsibilities. The expectations of these responsibilities will vary widely with his cultural, social, and economic background.

The specific course of your child's adolescent development, then, will be influenced by the timing of his physical maturation, by his infantile and childhood conflicts, by the nature of his personality and character, by the influence of his particular family history, and by the academic, cultural, social, and economic context in which he frames his experiences. And lastly (as with each of us in life), your adolescent's ability to negotiate the hurdles of these years also depends on fate—a mother's breast cancer when a girl is twelve, the parents' divorce when a boy is sixteen, a sister's prolonged hospitalization, a move to another town, a broken leg during basketball season, or the death of a best friend in a car accident—each event will define and shape your teenager's character. *Biology, psychology,* and *destiny* will all play an important part in charting the course of your child's adolescent journey.

The Five Developmental Tasks of Adolescence

In order to understand what it is about adolescence that makes parents tear out their hair, bite their nails, and lose their tempers, we need to understand fully the psychological purposes and functions of this important phase of development. Throughout these years, your adolescent is struggling to accomplish five significant (and, usually, sequential) tasks before he can move on as an adult in the world:

1. *Separating from old ties.*   Each and every adolescent must be capable of making his way in the world *without his parents.* To do this he must begin to see you as real people, with both strengths and weaknesses, and use his new perceptions to lessen your influence over him and develop his own sense of power. (This process of letting you step down from your childhood pedestal is as essential to your adolescent's growth as it is painful for you to experience.)

2. *Creating new attachments.*   As your adolescent separates from you and your power, an emotional space opens up that can make him feel sad and empty for a while. But this space is necessary to his growth, because it also leaves room for him to form peer attachments with members of his own generation. These attachments will go on to provide him with lasting love and companionship, way after you are gone. Without this capacity, *you* would remain the love of his life; no one else could ever compare to you, and your adolescent would never be able to become an autonomous adult, capable of creating his own life.

3. *Establishing a mature sexual identity and a mature sexual life.*   While your child has been experiencing romantic

and sexual feelings all throughout childhood (remember when he told you he wanted to marry you when he grew up?), it is not until adolescence that he begins to crystallize fully his sense of himself as a sexual being, and it is not until this phase of development that homosexual or heterosexual choices in love become fully defined. In adolescence, your teenager begins to pursue love for the first time, *outside the family circle*, and becomes capable, for the first time, of expressing this love through the uses of his mature body.

4. *Formulating new ideas and new ideals.* As your adolescent becomes more autonomous, he must also reexamine your parental standards. He has absorbed and internalized these standards throughout his childhood, and they form the core of his conscience and inform his values. But now he may challenge what he has learned from you, and new ideas derived from his peer and social affiliations may be used to develop his sense of what is worthwhile in the world.

5. *Consolidating character.* This overarching developmental task integrates aspects of the four previous tasks I've outlined. In order for your adolescent's character to become consolidated, he must have been able to separate from you, achieve some degree of confidence in himself as an independent agent in the world, develop his own ideas and ideals, and establish a loving, sexual life with a partner. When your adolescent has been able to achieve all of this, his own character will become more consolidated, and he will be able to function as a capable and productive adult.

As your adolescent is trying to accomplish all these tasks, you both are likely to be experiencing a lot of turmoil. As parents, you need time to adjust to the fact that your thirteen-year-old son is taller than his dad, or that your fifteen-year-old daughter is more voluptuous than her mom. You also need time to adjust to the fact that your son has a crush on his school nurse, or that your daughter's in love with the pizza delivery boy. Let's take a look at how each of these five important developmental tasks alters your sense of your life.

Separating from Old Ties

From the time of your baby's birth, *separation* has been a primary focus in his life, but now, as an adolescent, his separation from you takes on new strength and meaning. It's natural that you would have mixed feelings about this special separation. After all, as parents, you've spent over a decade fulfilling your job to cherish and protect your young—and now, you have to let go of them, releasing them into the world. This new developmental task leaves parents feeling saddened at the loss of childhood, nostalgic for days when they were so needed, anxious about whether their kids can manage without them, angry at being replaced by their child's peers, relieved that their child is growing up, and exhilarated at getting this far, safely.

Adolescents, too, have lots of mixed feelings about this new separation. They feel anxious about what they will encounter out in the world, worried about their own capabilities, nostalgic for the days when adults took care of their every need, happy to be growing up and participating in more of life, and excited by the opportunities that the world offers them.

As your child changes physically and psychologically, he is also changing the way he thinks about you. These alterations, too, have a history in his childhood. Mothers, in particular, undergo inevitable transformation, moving from the nurturant, protective figure of infancy to the powerful but ambivalent figure of toddlerhood, to the adored but relinquished mother of early childhood, to what often seems to us to be the hardest to bear, the repudiated mother of adolescence. Your infant desperately depended on you. He could not survive without a mother, and a great many of his behaviors were motivated by his need to keep his mother as close to him as

possible. Your teenager, on the other hand, see..
nate between a wish to have a mother and a wish to rid m..
self of a mother. It is a lifelong task for all of us to transform
these early and enduring ties to our parents. I once heard a
female comic describe the conclusion of her psychoanalysis.
"After five days a week for seven years, and one hundred fifty
thousand dollars, my analyst told me that my mother was the
most powerful person in my life. For Chrissake, I knew *that*
before I started!"

It's reassuring to realize that no matter how old you and
your children get, the psychological ties that bind you one to
the other will always be there. But this also means, of course,
that the conflicts that these old ties cause may always be there
as well. This is why holidays are often such a source of stress
in families. The old conflicts resurface when the family comes
together and everyone automatically assumes their old childhood roles. ("Mom, don't you think I know how to cook a
turkey? I'm thirty-seven years old. I've been making Thanks-
giving dinner for ten years!")

Creating New Attachments

It's important to remember that our children's romantic lives
begin in their childhood. They learn to love by being loved;
they learn to caress by being caressed, and they learn to commit to others by experiencing our commitment to them. But
by adolescence, both the adolescent girl and the adolescent
boy must now take all the attachment and admiration that
they felt for the objects of their first love and desire—their
parents—and shift these feelings to others who lie outside
their family circle. The significance of this shift cannot be
overemphasized. It is as difficult for them to accomplish this
as it is for you to accept!

It takes most children a long time to learn how to love,
and it can be very painful to watch them suffer the pangs of
young romance. But through these earliest experiences, your
adolescent will learn what he wants from a relationship, and

what he's prepared to give; he'll learn what sorts of people he gets along with and what sorts of people he can't bear, and he'll learn how to maintain his own sense of self, while still being able to stay connected to another. These are very complicated life lessons, but they will stand him in good stead when he eventually chooses a partner to share his life.

In early adolescence, your son or daughter may feel unsettled for a while, estranged from the familiar security of his childhood, but not yet joined to the new teenage world. Your eleven- to thirteen-year-old may alternate between an intense nostalgia for the years that lie behind him and an intense yearning for the years that lie ahead. This is why he sleeps a lot, or moons around the house, or appears melancholy and blue. Often, it is a "best friend" or "pal" who steps into this void, stabilizing the early adolescent's sense of insecurity, mitigating his estrangement with new companionship, and substituting for the parents' support and affection with his own.

A century ago, Freud recognized that adolescent same-sex friendships help us to move from our love for our families toward love for the stranger that we will eventually choose as a romantic partner. He saw these same-sex peer allegiances as a rehearsal for relationships with the opposite sex, and called them the adolescent's first attempts to "fumble toward heterosexuality." These friendships can be highly conflictual and filled with constant aggressive and competitive struggles, or they can seem almost like a love affair in which the friend is the idealized object of adoration.

"Crushes" on same sex friends, submission to bullies, memberships in gangs or clubs, all belong to this early adolescent yearning to fill the emotional void left by the diminished power of the parents. Often it is the most controlling, the most demanding, and the most exacting parents who are then shocked when their son or daughter forms an intense attachment to a friend who is equally controlling, demanding, and exacting.

Because the first loves of adolescence help a teenager renounce the ties that bind him to his parents, often these first alliances stand in sharp contrast to the familiarity of the family (a "good" girl may have a crush on the wildest boy in the class, or the son in a devoutly Catholic family may fall in love with a Muslim girl). That's because the more *foreign* this first love choice (someone with a different religion, race, or ethnic background), the easier it is for the adolescent to move away from his previous dependence on his parents. (After all, it's hard to kiss a girl who looks just like your mom.) It may not be until much later in adolescence that your child will be able to make a less alien and more integrated love choice (where aspects of his parents can be incorporated into his romantic choices). Because of this normal incestuous pull, late adolescents often have an easier time developing a love life when they live at some physical distance from their parents, such as in campus life. Living with roommates, setting up their own apartment, or joining the armed forces, can all help late adolescents feel free to develop new romantic attachments.

As we see our adolescents beginning to make these choices, we can often see the shadows of their childhood thoughts and feelings revealed just beneath the surface—a sort of "emotional pentimento." A young woman who was raised by two battling parents, for instance, can wind up compulsively fighting with all her boyfriends and driving them away. Or a young man who saw his mother cheat on his father may believe that all women are deceitful.

At fifteen, Marisa was one of the most popular girls in her sophomore class. Beautiful, sexy, and flirtatious, Marisa could have her pick of suitors, yet each time she "hooked up" with a boy, it turned out badly. While the boy was pursuing her, Marisa felt powerful and sought after, but once she had made her "conquest," she felt depleted and empty, and her interest quickly waned. It seemed as if all of Marisa's gratifications came from the *preamble* to love, and not love itself. She didn't even have any sexual feelings toward the boys she conquered. In fact, she was getting a reputation as a "cock tease" since she seldom followed through on any of her potential sexual promise.

Identifying with her divorced father, a notorious "womanizer" who had left the family when she was four years old, Marisa was trapped by her wishes to be more like her seductive father (a position she perceived as "strong") and less like her abandoned mother (a position that Marisa perceived as "weak"). Yet her own unfulfilled emotional needs had left her emotionally stuck in childhood, still wanting her father's love and compulsively enacting his abandonment of her by turning the tables on every boy she met. Despite her sophisticated sexual presentation of herself, Marisa was still a child, compulsively seeking affection and approval from men, and just as compulsively abandoning them. Unable to create a close, intimate, trusting relationship with one partner, Marisa's only self-esteem was accumulated through her constant seductive behavior.

At sixteen, James has never had a relationship with a girl, not even a friendship. He describes being unable to form or maintain a connection with anyone, because "opening up to someone will only get me hurt." Raised in a home in which his parents were cold and cruel to one another, but bound by their religious beliefs to stay together as a family, James described marriage as "sleeping with the enemy." A good student, a good athlete, and a good boy, last year James found himself feeling "cold, empty, and hopeless," and made a serious suicide attempt. Only when he realized how lonely and desperate he really felt underneath was he able to realize how frightened he has always been about trusting anyone. As James began to permit himself more access to his inner world in therapy, he has now felt more connected to others. He has begun to hang out with some of the guys on his varsity basketball team, and he's even gone to a few boy-girl parties after the games.

The difficulties for any of us in creating a successful love life cannot be overemphasized. Some teens are literally "lucky in love" and find their mates early, remaining loyal to them throughout their lives. But for most adolescents, choosing a partner will be a process of trial and error that can take years to accomplish. Even then, our high divorce rates (almost 50 percent) indicate that by the time they're adults, half of our sons and daughters will believe that they made the wrong romantic choices. Nevertheless, it is in adolescence, particularly late adolescence, that the ability to form these new emotional and physical attachments will be developed. This is when your teenager develops the all-important psychological capacity for emotional intimacy. Without this capacity he will never know true love, or be capable of deep and abiding relationships.

Establishing a Mature Sexual Identity and a Mature Sexual Life

It's a boy! It's a girl! There is no more powerful statement than the initial identification of a baby's sex. This identification (based entirely on the recognition of the child's *external* sexual characteristics) decisively cues us as to how that baby should be treated. The very way a mother and father hold, speak to, feed, diaper, hug, stroke, and play with a baby is immediately defined by whether that baby is a boy or a girl, and our reactions to the baby are equally dependent on what our particular society asks of boys and of girls.

While our children are still infants, we permit some of the distinctions between the sexes to remain blurred. We talk about "the baby," for instance, without continually defining it as a girl or a boy baby (it's often hard to tell, unless the baby is naked!), and babies are dressed (whether they are girls or boys) in pretty much the same way. As babies grow into children, the anatomical distinctions between them still do not necessarily separate them in our society. Boys and girls play on the same teams, read the same books, go to the same schools. Yet beneath the surface, strong social expectations are continuing to mold and shape your child's sexual identity. (Just think about how few boys are given dolls, and how few girls are given cars for their birthdays—even in these enlightened times—despite the fact that we obviously all want boys to become good fathers, and we certainly have no objections to girls driving cars!)

As our children approach preadolescence (nine to eleven) gender-based distinctions begin more sharply to separate the girls from the boys. (Girls stink! Boys are yucky! No girls allowed. No boys in this club.) This separation has a developmental purpose. It creates a safe psychological space that your children can occupy for a while before they must face the new and demanding *sexual* claims of adolescence.

As your children become teenagers, their sexuality will become a prominent defining feature of their lives. Now they will be expected to relate to one another in a whole new way, and the relationship between boys and girls will decisively alter. Sometimes, as girls and boys cross the boundary into adolescence, they seem to hang back or linger for a while, trying to diminish the physical differences that puberty brings. Both boys and girls may seem to be trying to obscure their new femininity or masculinity through dressing alike (boys with long hair and earrings, for example, or girls with army boots and shaved heads). This unisex look enables teenagers to continue to play with sexual ambiguity before crossing over to the sexual certainty that will be required of them in adult life.

By mid- to late adolescence (fifteen to nineteen years old), female and male have become boundaries that cannot be crossed without serious social consequences. Now your teenager begins to lay aside a great deal of the role-playing and experimentation that defined early adolescence, and begins to make decisive sexual choices. If your son or daughter is not yet able to make these choices, their peers begin to make them for them. ("He's definitely 'bi' "; "She's butch, look at the way she looks at you"; or "He walks like a queen.")

While sexual *gender*, of course, is a biological given at birth, sexual *identity* is a complex psychological process that takes place over many years. Heterosexuality, homosexuality, transsexuality, bisexuality (or even asexuality, for that matter) are childhood possibilities that become crystallized in adolescence with the emergence of sexual impulses and a mature body to pursue them. It is important to recognize that there is a lot we still do not understand about the development of sexual identity. Is homosexuality an inborn trait coded in your brain, your metabolism, or your genes? Is it learned through early experiences? Or the result of family dynamics? Is it a choice or a destiny? Further, there may be *no one answer* to these questions, but many, as we realize that a different weight needs to be given to different factors in different homosexual lives.

What we do know is that sexual identity (with all its presentations and preferences) is *formed* and *re-formed* throughout infancy and childhood, and then *transformed* in adolescence and adulthood. Until we have more specific scientific information, it probably makes the most sense to think of sexual identity as the outcome of a complicated sequence of biological, and psychological, events that is simply felt as *inevitable* by late adolescence in most, but not all cases.

Because the sexual self is not yet consolidated, teenagers are often particularly disturbed by anything sexual that appears out of the ordinary or "weird." Unusual sexual habits or choices may seem particularly frightening or disgusting to them, and feelings of bisexuality (which are quite normal in all of us) are often especially uncomfortable in adolescence. (This is why adolescents are often homophobic, making the fate of a homosexual teenager particularly painful.) While homosexuality (kept in the closet even by adults of the last generation) is much more openly acknowledged by adolescents today (particularly by urban teenagers, who may have access to a homosexual community that can support and encourage their identity), it is important to realize that most homosexual teenagers still lead emotionally isolated, even desperate lives among their peers. As your adolescent struggles to define a sexual self, it's important to let him/her know that it's normal to have loving and even fleeting erotic feelings for members of his/her own sex. These feelings do not necessarily mean that your adolescent is gay. It's also helpful to emphasize to your teenager that thinking, fantasizing, and daydreaming are not the same as doing. Many adolescents worry if they even have transient homoerotic or bisexual fantasies or thoughts.

With the onset of puberty, your early adolescent becomes capable of physically acting on his sexual urges and desires. His first sexual experiences, however, are still likely to be the exploration of his own body. *Masturbation* is a completely normal and useful step in the consolidation of healthy sexuality for both boys and girls. It continues to be useful through the adolescent years, in helping the adolescent to get used to the new surges of sexual feelings and responses that characterize this phase.

By mid- to late adolescence, in our society (except for social or religious communities in which sex is strictly regulated)—whether you approve or not—most teenagers (fifteen to nineteen) will begin (or are hoping to begin) some form of sexual experimentation. Early sexual activity is a fact of life among American teenagers. Almost one-third of all adolescents have had sex by the time they are fifteen, and over 80 percent have had sex by the time they are nineteen years old. *Experimentation with peers* will now become your teenager's primary source of knowledge and satisfaction, as your son or daughter learns about the ways in which a partner can enhance their experience of sexual excitement. These early sexual encounters enable your adolescent to experience how his/her body works, and permit him/her to both give and take pleasure.

In our society, both boys and girls often experience their new sexual capacity as a power they hold over each other. Despite the fact that we are fast approaching the twenty-first century, it is remarkable how this power is still used in stereotyped ways—boys are still encouraged to achieve a sense of *sexual mastery*, while girls are still encouraged to be *sexually vulnerable*. As one of my more perceptive female patients remarked, "How come boys see having sex as *gaining* something and girls always feel like they're *losing* something?" Even the current vogue among teenage boys to be the first one—the "virgin surgeon"—has old roots in ancient ceremonies of "deflowering" virgins, and continues to give credence to the value that many cultures (including our own) still place on the "purity" of maidens. As sharp and as hip as we've supposedly become, these old ideas still have a lot of currency among adolescents, sharply separating male and female adolescent attitudes toward sexuality, and conveying many confusing double messages. For instance, on the one hand, we want boys to value girls for more than their bodies; on the other, "getting laid" is encouraged and admired in boys. We condemn men for sexual harassment and coercive sex, but we also condemn women for "seductive behavior" and "leading men on." And of course, a woman who has a lot of sexual experience is still devalued (a "slut," a "tramp"), while a man with a lot of sexual experience continues to be admired, ("a stud," "the man").

In a holdover from childhood, both female and male adolescents have accepted the metaphor of the great American game, baseball, as the way to "score" one's sexual experiences. First base (kissing, French kissing), second base, (touching breasts or penis, "up your skirt" and "down your pants"), third base (oral sex, mutual masturbation), and finally, a home run (sexual intercourse). These sexual plays are all carefully charted among adolescents—"Did you get to home base yet?" "Did you let him do second?" "He says she went to third with him, but she says he's a liar."—and the vital statistics of all the players are known. As your adolescent matures physically and psychologically, he is likely to attempt the ultimate intimacies of *sexual intercourse,* the defining sexual experience of adulthood. At what point and with whom your adolescent decides to take any of the sexual steps I'm describing is related to the strength of his sexual impulses, his sexual confidence, his character, his family values, his own standards, and his opportunities.

While parents hope that their sons and daughters will delay sexual experimentation until they have found a partner to love and cherish, in fact, many teenage sexual experiences are not embedded in deep emotional feelings at all, but rather in a sense of sexual curiosity or challenge. Achievement ("I did it!") rather than attachment ("I love him") more often defines the experience, particularly if sexual experience per se is supported and expected by the teen's peers as a mark of manhood or womanhood (or, for that matter, simply adulthood).

It is important to understand that adolescents are rarely capable of a deep and abiding love and loyalty to each other when they first begin to form relationships. Today, teenage relationships tend to be serially monogamous. Teenagers get "hooked up" with or "go out" with only one partner until they "break up" (a process that can take a few days, a few weeks, or a few months, but rarely longer than that). The true integration of physical capacity with emotional depth, of sexuality with love, takes time and practice. (Of course, it is only fair to point out that many adults after years of marriage are not capable of this integration either!)

Formulating New Ideas and New Ideals

During adolescence, your teenager is trying to become a unique individual with his own ideas, values, and standards. But this process of self-definition can easily cause him to come in conflict with his family, and may produce many battles on the home front. As he strives to find his own place in the world, your adolescent may seek out another religion, repudiate your politics, express contempt for things you hold dear, or vigorously challenge you about virtually everything you believe. It's hard to remember that all of this aggravating, annoying, and angering behavior is part of your adolescent's developmental mandate to form his own ideals and consolidate his own conscience.

Claire, thirteen, has been raised by parents who are active in liberal causes and have tried to raise her to be a proud and independent woman. Recently Claire's class was asked to debate the pros and cons of abortion, and Claire was assigned a position on the debating team that spoke *against* freedom of choice. During her research, Claire discovered that she possessed a strong feeling for the rights of the unborn fetus, and that, despite her liberal upbringing, she felt horrified and repulsed by the idea of abortion. Now, months after the debate, her ideas have remained unaltered. Her parents are not amused by her position, and see it as a repudiation of everything they believe in. They wanted Claire to be independent, but not quite this independent, and they feel embarrassed whenever she expresses her ideas in front of their friends. Everyone in the family is tense and unhappy about this unexpected turn of events.

Sean, fourteen, raised in a Christian Fundamentalist family, was home-schooled until this year. A thoughtful, intense boy, he has always felt particularly close to his mother, the most devout member of his family and a believer in the literal truths of the Bible. She and Sean have had many interesting conversations about her belief in the creation and her distrust of evolution. Up until now, Sean had always admired and accepted his mother's ideas, but since he entered high school, he has begun to argue with his mother and question her religious beliefs. Sean's mother is devastated by his challenge and prays for his soul every day. She doesn't understand how Sean could turn his back on her.

Anne-Marie, sixteen, the younger daughter in a large, close, Ukrainian family, has fallen in love with the eighteen-year-old son of a Korean grocer. Kim is an only child with strong family loyalties. He is a premed student at a local college and also works in his father's store. Kim and Anne-Marie seem unlikely candidates for this kind of interethnic romance, since both of them are quite attached to their families, and their families clearly oppose their relationship. Yet even when forbidden, Anne-Marie and Kim disregard their parents' wishes, and often sneak out to meet each other.

In all of these stories, adolescents, beginning to form their own identity, have relinquished their attachment to ideas and ideals that their parents hold dearly, at some emotional cost to themselves and their families. Some of these youngsters will eventually repudiate these new ideas, allowing them to ally themselves once again with their parents' values. For them, their ideological rebellion is only a short detour. But for other adolescents, their new ideas and new ideals, even in the face of strong parental disapproval, will be maintained over time, and their ideological rebellion will lead them to follow an independent course.

Parents, too, will differ in how they approach these changing ideas and ideals. In some families, any deviation from the family's norm may be sharply criticized, while in others a great deal of freedom of choice will be accepted or even encouraged. Some families will tolerate and even support intellectual exploration and expansion, while others will strictly limit these impulses. Some families will close ranks against a rebel, while others will see rebellion as a useful tool, one that can strengthen a youngster's character. But all adolescents, whether they adhere closely to the path their parents have taken, or stride off in a new direction, will use these years to review and revise their beliefs, incorporating new ideas and new ideals, some of which will become a part of their own approach to the challenges of adult life.

Consolidating Character

Separating from you, creating new attachments, establishing a mature psychosexual identity and a mature psychosexual life, and developing one's own ideas and ideals are all necessary precursors to the overarching task of adolescence—the consolidation of character.

Of course, your adolescent does not start with a blank slate. He enters adolescence with some of the preliminary structures of character already in place. After all, building character has been one of your most important jobs while your children were still small—teaching them to listen, think, reason, act, and react with good judgment and good sense. Now that they are fast moving from childhood to adolescence, these lessons will mean more than ever before, because you will not be there to oversee their decisions.

Often parents worry because they're not so sure if their child's character can withstand the test of teenage life. The bold, assertive personality they admired when their child was ten may look like recklessness in adolescence; the shy, sensitive nature they observed in a six-year-old may now look too shaky. Parents have no way to tell how the qualities they observe in childhood will fare in this new adolescent territory. Will your eleven-year-old be imaginative or will she lose touch with reality? Is your fifteen-year-old high-strung or is she over the edge? Is your seventeen-year-old just moody or severely depressed? As parents, you must count on your child's character to see him through tough times (and the older your kids become, the tougher the times!). Crossing the street safely was a childhood lesson; in adolescence your teenagers must survive on the streets. In childhood, your kids learned how to make friends; in adolescence they must choose the right company. Now they not only need to refuse candy from strangers; they need to be able to turn down offers of drugs and alcohol. Parents count on character to carry their teenagers safely through the adolescent passage, and they hope that good character will also help to secure them a proper place in adult life. But why does all of this seem so worrisome? And why do all of the developmental tasks we've been discussing seem so difficult? In the next chapter, I'll be talking about today's times, the new problems adolescents must face, and why your job as a parent seems so much harder than when you were growing up.

CHAPTER 2

Adolescence: New Problems

Adolescence has been an age-old problem for all families in all cultures. Parents have always lamented the irresponsibility of adolescents—their recklessness, their aggression, their insensitivity, their moodiness, and their selfishness. Parents have always worried about the loves and losses of their teenagers, their successes and their failures, their joys and their sorrows. Family life with an adolescent has proven to be an endless source of material for authors through the centuries, from the Bible to TV sitcoms! Even the ancient Greeks complained about their adolescents, in much the same spirit that parents complain about today's adolescents. So why do parents seem more anxious, more overwhelmed, and more disheartened than their own parents felt, just a generation ago? There are several good reasons for our increased concerns.

Earlier Puberty

Our children are approaching puberty earlier than ever before, and the younger the child, the less emotionally prepared they are to deal with these physical changes.

No one is completely sure why our children are approaching adolescence earlier in their lives, but there seem to be several reasons. For one thing, puberty is triggered by height and weight, and our children are growing taller and heavier. These physical changes appear to be linked to nutrition as well as genetics. As kids in our culture become better nourished, they appear to be maturing faster. In addition, the additives in our foods (particularly the vitamin enrichment in our cereals and breads and the hormone-based feed given to our chickens and cows) may be triggering earlier maturity. Some scientists have also suggested that our brighter lights (which extend day far into the night) may be stimulating an earlier onset of puberty as well. This is because children's bodies are programmed to mature after exposure to a certain amount of light, and the more light exposure we accumulate, the more quickly we mature. Early puberty, however, is not so easy to accommodate, particularly when the child falls in the extreme end of the spectrum of normal physical development. Here's one young girl's experience:

Esther, a nine-and-a-half-year-old girl with large, soft breasts, attracted a great deal of overstimulating male attention in her fifth grade class. The girls gossiped about her, embarrassed by her blatant femaleness. The boys in her grade teased her, calling her "Breasty Esty," and, excited by her maturity, tried to touch her whenever they could. In addition, since Esther's body made her appear much older than her stated age, adults often related to her as if she were already a grown woman, and their sexual comments bewildered and humiliated her. On the street, grown men tried to catch her eye, and on the subway, men pressed up against her, trapping her against their genitals.

But reactions to Esther's new body were not confined to strangers. Within Esther's own family, there were disturbing responses as well. Her father, for example, no longer felt comfortable holding or hugging her, and her older brother teased her, calling her Dolly Parton. Esther's mother, concerned about Esther's early development, tried to restrain many of her ordinary physical activities (playing ball, in-line skating, biking, etc.). She didn't want Esther to move around too much because her breasts bounced and drew "unseemly attention" to her. Ironically, Esther's attempts to hide her breasts by slouching served to draw the attention of others to her body, as aunts and uncles, grandparents, and even gym teachers kept insisting that Esther "stand up straight."

When Esther first came to see me, she described herself as a "freak." She was deeply ashamed of her early development, chose all her clothes three or four sizes too big so she could hide her breasts within them, hunched her shoulders, and always wore her coat in my office. Her early development had also narrowed and constrained her sense of her own psychological identity, and eroded her sense of self-worth and esteem. (Esther saw herself only as "a great pair.") On the one hand, Esther had learned that her body gave her enormous power (look at all the attention she could attract from boys and men) but on the other, she felt confused because she had no idea what this power meant, or how to use it. Premature puberty had already deprived Esther of the emotional sanctuary that her childhood should have provided, and she needed therapy to provide her with some time and space to let her emotional development catch up with her physical development.

By the time Esther was twelve years old, she looked more like her female peers who were also developing breasts, and her sense of herself as a "freak" had diminished. By fourteen, she was beginning to take pride in her voluptuous figure, and she was developing an ability to manage her generous femininity.

Problems with earlier puberty are not confined to girls. Boys, too, can experience a great deal of confusion and conflict over their newly revealed sexuality and, deprived of sympathy by a culture that values "macho" behavior, may be even less able to deal with their own feelings and the responses of others. Here's how one boy experienced the early changes in his body:

Nick, who came to see me when he was almost eleven, described being plagued by strong sexual urges over which he had little emotional control. He felt continually embarrassed by his body's sensitivity to stimulation. ("Everything gives me a hard-on. I can't even sit on the subway without getting a boner.") His friends both envied and teased him. Since the boys swam nude at his single-sex parochial school, Nick was subjected to many sexual jokes, even from the swim coach. ("Hey, Nick, are you getting any yet?") Older girls, attracted to his maleness, seemed to expect things of him that he didn't know how to give. (His fifteen-year-old babysitter, for instance, tried to seduce him one evening as he came out of the shower.) Nick's early genital development had defined him as a sexual "stud" at a time in his life when he was still a young boy. For Nick, too, his newfound physical maturity had already sharply narrowed the focus of his sense of self and altered his worth in the world. He felt anxious and apprehensive a lot of the time, and had begun to spend a lot of his time alone struggling against his wishes to masturbate, which he knew was "wrong."

Nick's ability to discuss disturbing feelings in the privacy of his therapy enabled him to begin to integrate his bodily changes into a fuller sense of himself. Within a few years, as other boys began to mature and catch up with him, he no longer felt so alone and so upset by his early physical maturity. By fourteen, his developing interest in girls was helping Nick to feel "more normal," as he could now more naturally reciprocate their interest in him.

On the other extreme of the continuum, of course, delayed puberty can be just as disruptive and destructive to self-esteem. Girls who remain flat-chested or who do not begin to menstruate until they are fifteen or sixteen, and boys who are underdeveloped and do not get their growth spurt until sixteen or seventeen, often feel equally exposed to shame and inferiority in the face of the physical maturity of most of their peers. After all, it's hard to maintain a good sense of your female self, when that self displays no signs of femaleness. Similarly, it's hard to feel like a man without any visible signs of manhood.

Extended Adolescence

Our children are struggling with adolescent issues for a more extended period of time than ever before. Because of major changes in the world's economy, the need for increasingly specialized advanced education, and delayed marriage and childbearing, adult children may still be trying to address adolescent developmental tasks well into their twenties and thirties.

What we are now calling postadolescence has become a prolonged and indeterminate developmental phase in our society. It encompasses those years when adolescents have become physically and sexually mature, but have not yet achieved emotional or financial independence from their parents, found self-supporting work, or developed a sustained, intimate relationship. In today's times, many young men and women in their twenties and thirties are still struggling with these issues. They graduate from college, only to return to live at home, or they search through one relationship after another without finding a suitable partner, or, no matter how hard they try, they can't seem to find a job that gives them any satisfaction.

Some young men and women return to live with their families after the army or college, and are unable to leave home because they cannot earn enough income to support themselves in today's economy. And many of those who have been able to leave home, still lean on their parents for financial aid to supplement their incomes, buy a car, or take a vacation.

In addition, this may be the first generation of adolescents who cannot expect to do better economically or advance further socially than their parents, a depressing thought for us and for them. Downward mobility appears to be the model for the next century, and these generally negative financial expectations prolong the conflicts of the adolescent years and prevent many postadolescent children from achieving true independence from their parents. In this next story, we can see how a young man struggles with these issues:

Colin, twenty-nine, tall, dark, and handsome, lives with his mother and her boyfriend in Los Angeles. Since he was a child, Colin has always wanted to be an actor, but so far, despite his clear talent, and some small parts in several films, Colin has still not been able to make a living through his chosen work. When he first got out of college, Colin shared an apartment with three friends, all of whom were supporting themselves by taking what they referred to as "McJobs" (low-paying, routine jobs like working at McDonald's). This past summer, when two of his roommates moved out, Colin was not able to support his share of the rent, so he moved back home with his mom.

Colin puts all of the money he makes as a waiter into supporting his acting classes, head shots, and clothes to "look the part." Further, because of his acting commitments, he can take only jobs with limited, flexible hours that will permit him to audition and attend rehearsals and performances. Colin realizes that he is living at subsistence level, and that his lack of a decent income restrains his personal life as well as his social life, but he is reluctant to give up on himself or his dreams. As he approaches thirty, he finds himself increasingly anxious and confused. What will he do if he doesn't "make it"? What does "making it" mean? Getting a decent part in a film? What happens after that film is over? Colin describes feeling like a gambler who's trying to "break the bank" without any assurance that he'll have luck on his side. He wonders what else he can do if he has to give up his career as an actor.

Separation, divorce, or abandonment by spouses has compelled a large group of postadolescents (mainly women) to return home also. Pushed to the brink of poverty by their altered circumstances, these women often need to rely on their parents to keep their families together. That's Lorraine's struggle as she tries to recover from a devastating marriage.

Lorraine, a petite, slightly overweight thirty-two-year-old woman with a perky manner, is the mother of a little girl, five, and a boy, three. Married for six years to a man who turned out to be an abusive alcoholic, she has recently sued for divorce. In order to make sure that her husband can see the children only under supervised conditions, Lorraine had to borrow money from her family to fight him for sole custody in court. Although she has a good job as a computer analyst for a large financial firm, Lorraine has had to move with her children from her apartment in the city to her parents' home in the suburbs in order to "make ends meet." She has taken on a weekend job as well, working in a gift shop at the local mall, in order to save enough money to eventually move out of her parents' house.

Lorraine estimates that it will take her close to two years before she is able to live an independent life again. Meanwhile, she is grateful to have her mother around to care for her children, as she did not want to have to place them in a group day care setting or leave them with "strangers." Lorraine's troubles with her husband are not yet over, as she will have to go back to court in one year for a forensic reevaluation to see if her husband (who is now in AA) will be sufficiently recuperated to see the children unsupervised. She dreads the passage of time, and fears that the courts will be taken in by her husband's charm, as she was for so many years. Meanwhile, she is living in her parents' guest room, while her children share her childhood bedroom.

Increased Sexual Peril

Ordinary adolescent experiences of sexuality are taking place much earlier and in a much more perilous environment. There have been some significant changes in teenage sexual mores since our adolescent years. Social expectations have changed, as has the cultural climate in which teenage sexuality now emerges, and teenagers are willing (and likely) to become sexually active much earlier in their lives. A generation ago, the girls who weren't virgins in their senior year in high school were the subject of gossip. Today, the girls who are *still* virgins by their senior year in high school are likely to be the subject of gossip.

These alterations in sexual behavior fill parents with anxiety and dread because they are aware that sexuality today is so dangerous. While they know that the only completely safe protection from the present dangers of sexuality (which include genital warts, chlamydia, hepatitis, ureaplasma infection, gonorrhea, herpes simplex virus, syphilis, and, of course, AIDS) is *abstinence*, statistics indicate that there are almost three million cases of sexually transmitted diseases (STDs) among adolescents. These diseases have reached epidemic proportions in adolescent populations, doubling and tripling the rates of infection in the past twenty years. STDs affect both male and female fertility, predispose infected adolescents to several forms of cancer as adults, and, of course, in the case of AIDS, can cause death. The threat of AIDS shadows this generation of adolescents and their families. We are terrifyingly aware that our sons and daughters can die from having sex with the wrong person at the wrong time. But what about them? Are they frightened? What are teenagers thinking?

Despite the clear peril and the educational messages that emphasize practicing "safe sex," of the one million teenage pregnancies, *75 percent are the result of using no form of contraception at all.* Becoming pregnant as a young unmarried adolescent is a danger not only to an adolescent's physical health but also to her mental health. The rate of suicide attempts for pregnant adolescent girls rises sharply, demonstrating the hopelessness and helplessness these young girls feel as they face motherhood on their own. In addition, young adolescent girls are much more likely to experience difficulties associated with pregnancy and birth, placing their lives at greater risk than mature pregnant women. Why do teenage girls get pregnant? Let's take a look at Sherry's story:

Sherry, an overweight fifteen-year-old, who has been raised by her maternal aunt since she was eight years old, has been having sex with her boyfriend, Derrick, since she was thirteen. While she's been loyal to him, she's aware that he has had many different girlfriends besides her. "But," she says proudly, "he always come back home to me." Derrick is seventeen and will leave high school this year. He is planning to join the navy. But Sherry is only a sophomore, and she doesn't know what she will do when Derrick leaves school, because her whole life is focused on him. She is barely functioning in her classes.

When Sherry first had intercourse with Derrick, she had not yet begun her period, but last year, when she was fourteen, she began to menstruate. However, her periods have always been irregular and she and Derrick don't use any form of birth control, except withdrawal. Sherry reports that "sometimes he comes out, but sometimes he forgets." Over the last several months, Sherry's been putting on a lot of weight, but she didn't pay any attention to it because she's felt very hungry and she's been "pigging out" on junk food. She also noticed that she was occasionally nauseous, but she attributed this symptom as well to her "screwed-up eating."

When a friend in school told her she looked pregnant, Sherry "freaked out," and told her aunt. Their visit to the health clinic revealed that Sherry is, indeed, four months' pregnant. She could still have an abortion, but there are only a few places that do late-term abortions, and there is some risk involved in the procedure. Her aunt wants her to go through with it, but Sherry is frightened, and besides, she thinks she'd like to have the baby to keep her company while Derrick's in the navy. She hasn't yet told him about her pregnancy, and she's afraid of what he'll say or do. She hopes he'll be proud of the baby and not be angry.

We can see that Sherry's devotion to Derrick anchors her life even though his commitment to her seems tenuous at best. She probably also hopes that Derrick's child will tie him closer to her. But whether or not things work out with Derrick, Sherry wants the baby; she hopes it will fill some of the emptiness and loneliness she feels.

Carl, a husky, muscular eighteen-year-old, is a senior in high school and a "jock." A quarterback for his high school football team, Carl prides himself on being a "stud." He estimates that he has had intercourse with forty-two girls. His goal is to reach fifty sexual partners by the time he graduates. He feels he could accumulate more experience were it not for the fact that he has to pass all his courses and spend a lot of time at football practice. He asks every girl he's slept with to give him a lock of her pubic hair, and he refers to these memorabilia as his "scalps."

Last month, Carl began to notice lesions around his penis and genital area. At first he thought that they were just abrasions from being tackled, but then he realized that they weren't healing. When he was examined, the doctor told Carl that he'd contracted herpes, and that if he had intercourse with anyone during the active phase of the disease he could infect them with the virus as well. Carl has no idea from whom he caught herpes, nor does he have any idea how many girls he may already have infected. Despite all the sex education at school, he's never liked to use a condom ("It's like wearing a blanket"), so he's always depended on the girls' use of some form of birth control. He can't believe that there isn't a cure for herpes, and that he's going to have to deal with it for the rest of his life. Yet Carl's story is not at all unique. Thousands of young men share his heedlessness and obliviousness, as they turn to compulsive sexual conquests to confirm their masculinity.

In these changing times, more than ever, parents need to know the limits of their own power and their own protection. *Adolescents, particularly late adolescents, are most likely to choose to have sexual intercourse, whether you want them to or not.* It's important to let your kids know that you would like them to remain abstinent until they are old enough to manage the emotional and physical dangers of sexuality, but it's equally important for you to prepare them realistically to lead safe and responsible sexual lives, if they choose to become sexually active.

Widespread Substance Use and Abuse

The widespread use and abuse of drugs and alcohol have drastically changed the quality of life for our adolescents and exposed them and their families to more violence than ever before.

Sometimes we forget how pervasive the use of drugs is in our culture. Unless we realize how much we all *use* drugs in our daily lives, we can't begin to understand how easy it is to *abuse* drugs. Just one more beer—one more Valium—who's counting? It's the American way. Of course, this use (and abuse) is not confined to our country, nor even to modern times. Drug abuse has a long history in human affairs. All over the world people have cultivated and used drugs—to heighten feelings, to alter consciousness, to celebrate events. Working people have turned to drugs so they could endure, people of all classes have used drugs to deaden their pain; thousands of soldiers became drug addicts during the Vietnam war; and in the last century, women drank teas and tonics laced with opium derivatives.

Nor is drug use confined to adults of a society. Drugs are used to mark the adolescent rite of passage in many cultures. The thirteen-year-old in New Zealand who drinks a fermented beverage to enhance his rite of passage shares this ceremonial use of alcohol with the high school kid who chugalugs beer at his fraternity initiation. Today's teenager who's sniffing coke to feel high, or swallowing LSD to feel weird, or smoking pot to feel cool, is only a more recent example of a long and extensive human history of drug experimentation. If drugs are so much a part of our history and our present concerns only mimic the past, why should parents be so alarmed? What's the difference now?

First, *drug use in modern cultures is not confined to shared cultural or religious ceremonies.* Modern drug use is not able to be controlled by the *laws* of our society, let alone the *customs.*

This means that when it comes to drugs, every kid is on her own. She must decide what drugs she uses, when, and where. No adults are around to help her or to keep the use contained.

Second, *no culture has ever had the ability to produce the range and complexity of drugs that we have*—both legal and illegal— with so many varied and dangerous effects on the body and on the mind. The array of drugs available in our society is literally mind-boggling.

No longer is teenage rebellion confined to what experts call the "gateway" drugs—nicotine, alcohol, and marijuana. Now, a whole array of designer drugs, each potentially more dangerous than the next, is being offered to our kids at earlier and earlier ages. A generation ago an eleven-year-old was sneaking her first cigarette; now that smoke is likely to be marijuana. And where teenage substance abuse before meant consuming a six-pack, teenage alcoholism is now on the rise. Further, new studies are beginning to show that even "gateway" drugs have much more pernicious and enduring effects on the body and the brain than we had previously believed. So, not only can your teenager's physical and psychological health be *immediately* compromised, drug and alcohol use are also likely to cause long-term *permanent* damage as well.

Third, *the effects of many of these drugs are unpredictable and idiosyncratic.* That means that simple curiosity (which is normal for adolescents) can kill. Our kids can experiment with drugs and die! Fourth, *most drug use is illegal drug use,* and therefore its distribution is tied directly into violence and crime. This means that your adolescent is at risk by just *purchasing* illegal drugs, let alone using them. Last, but perhaps most important, *drugs interfere with psychological development.* At the very time in their lives when your kids need to be relying on themselves (their minds and their bodies) to grow and develop, they rely on drugs. This is what we mean when we say that drugs can be *psychologically addictive.* Even when withdrawal from the drug produces no physical symptoms, a teenager can still depend on cocaine or marijuana to become her "best self," and feel empty and inadequate without the drug's psychological backup. And beyond the use and abuse of drugs, the lure of easy profit and instant popularity attracts many teenagers to the sale of drugs. Here's how one young girl almost got caught in this web:

Lois, fourteen, attends a large suburban junior high school. It's a big change from the small local elementary school she used to attend, and in the beginning, things seemed overwhelming. But this year, Lois made friends with this "cool" girl, Vivian, who seemed really "fly," and who seemed to know everybody in the right crowd.

Vivian soon revealed that she smoked a lot of weed, but that her favorite drug experience was snorting Ritalin. She said it gave you a real kick. Lois was initially bewildered because she had never heard of the drug, but then, when Vivian told her that kids used Ritalin just to concentrate better—that they even got it from their pediatricians—she couldn't see how it would be bad for you.

When Lois snorted Ritalin with Vivian, she really liked the feeling that it seemed to give her, at least for a short time. Then, Vivian came up with a plan to get some Ritalin to sell. They would go to their grade adviser and complain that they were restless and had trouble concentrating. The grade adviser would send them to a psychiatrist, who would then recommend Ritalin, Vivian said. Once she got the prescription, they could sell it to other kids and make a lot of money. Lois was a little worried about the plan but she went along with it because she didn't want Vivian to think she was a "nerd." But things did not happen the way Vivian predicted because the grade adviser didn't send her to a psychiatrist. Instead, she called in Vivian's parents and advised them that Vivian needed to enter psychotherapy. Lois found herself remarkably relieved when the whole scheme fell apart.

Recent statistics on teen drug use have skyrocketed, heavily influenced by the current adolescent subculture in which drugs are romanticized. This sharp rise is not confined to any one drug (cocaine, marijuana, LSD, and heroin all showed major increases in adolescent use), nor is it confined to any one group (both girls and boys, white and black, older—seventeen plus—and younger—under twelve—adolescents have increased their use of drugs).

If you only have trouble with your children using "hard" drugs, but don't mind them smoking cigarettes, having a few beers, or passing a joint, then you should know that drug experts don't share your point of view. The preteenage and teenage use of alcohol, nicotine, and marijuana are seen as dangerous precursors to more serious abuse. And while many parents don't even consider alcohol a drug, it is in fact, *our most widely used and abused drug.* Almost five million of our teenagers have a drinking problem, and *alcohol-related accidents (most of them drunk driving) are a leading cause of death for teenagers and young adults.* The statistics for adult alcoholism are equally sobering (pun intended). Alcohol abuse is the fourth largest health problem in this country, right up there with heart disease and cancer (both of which have important links to the abuse of alcohol).

Cigarettes (another drug) have equally devastating effects on health. Smoking is a leading cause of death among adults, *most of whom started smoking as teenagers.* Currently, three million American teenagers smoke, consuming nearly one billion packs of cigarettes a year.

Nicotine, the active ingredient in tobacco, is as addictive as heroin (as anyone who has ever tried to stop smoking can tell you!). How many adults who are trying to stop smoking *now* fervently wish that they had never started smoking as teenagers?

Further, many kids don't even wait until they're teenagers to experiment with smoking. School-aged youngsters (ten to thirteen years old) are already at risk for nicotine addiction. Most children try cigarettes *before* they have reached eighth grade. By the time these kids are in high school, almost 20 percent of them have already become addicted smokers. Yet each and every cigarette pack carries a message that indicates that smoking is hazardous to your health. Why don't they pay attention?

Parents need to remember that young adolescents yearn

to become adults, and most youngsters get their first exposure to forbidden "adult pleasures" through teenage smoking and drinking. Many of them will never develop a taste for either; some will develop a dependence on one or both that will last their entire lives; and others will go on to deepen and broaden their experimentation to include an exposure and/or addiction to much more dangerous drugs—drugs that will damage both their psychological and physiological development. The earlier the addiction, the more likely that a child will have *later* psychological and physical problems, including early death. That's why you need to pay attention *now*.

But the use and abuse of drugs are not the only problems today's parents worry about. In addition, the violence bred by the distribution and sale of these drugs has drastically eroded the quality of life in our schools and communities. We can see evidence of what we fear all around us—the ever-present drug peddlers whispering in our school courtyards and parks, the proliferation of illegal handguns among juveniles, car-jackings, drive-by shootings, gang wars, and so on. Many adolescents, even in "good" neighborhoods, are constantly worried about being mugged, raped, assaulted, robbed, or killed. In "bad" neighborhoods, access to guns has made juvenile violence more deadly, and black teenagers, in particular, are six times more likely than white teenagers to become victims of homicide, a statistic we don't often keep in mind. Malcolm's story, which follows, is the story of many inner-city kids who are trying to live their lives.

Malcolm, seventeen, is the youngest of three children of a deeply religious single mother who has raised her children in the Muslim faith. Ms. Johnson has set down strict standards and expectations for her two sons and her daughter. Her eldest son, Jamal, who's twenty-one, has just joined the marines, and her daughter, Jasmine, who's eighteen and lives at home, is studying to be a nurse. Malcolm, her baby, is a "hacker," a computer wizard. But the Johnson family lives in a drug-infested neighborhood and Malcolm attends an inner-city high school. A teacher has already been attacked in Malcolm's school for interrupting a drug sale in the lunchroom.

Malcolm's brother has taught him how to be "streetwise," and he has tried to keep a low profile in his school, but recent newspaper publicity about his computer talents has brought him to the attention of powerful gang leaders, who want to use his computer skills to aid in their drug distribution plans. Malcolm is in constant terror that he will be coerced into some illegal activity. He would like to finish out school where he is, because he is eligible to receive a full scholarship from a big computer company that has a link with his school, but Malcolm is worried about his senior year. He feels vulnerable and wishes his older brother were still at home.

Malcolm is an example of a "good kid" caught in a web of fear. If he is able to avoid being swallowed up by the violence that surrounds him, he has a chance at a better life— a life that will permit him to reach his true potential. He has a dream, but first he must keep himself safe in order to pursue it.

Eroded Ethics

It's much harder for parents to teach the ethics, values, and standards we want our adolescents to hold, when all around them these same values are actively eroded by a changing culture. Parents talk with regret that the standards of good citizenship, of personal responsibility, and of self-control (old-fashioned virtues that enable us to raise children with a capacity for kindness, empathy, and consideration for others) seem to have eroded, but no one knows how or where to begin to shore up the values we want our adolescents to have.

The moral framework of childhood first begins to shake and tremble in early adolescence (twelve to fourteen). At this age your adolescent begins to replace, with a new structure of her own, the old parental pillars that supported her sense of right and wrong. Cut off from her previous reliance upon you to strengthen her in the world, youngsters of this age will

frequently seek out a powerful figure with whom to identify—an Olympic athlete, a sitcom star, favorite teacher or
coach. At this age, your adolescent is easily influenced by
others. That's why the widespread corruption of such figures
is so alarming. Not only does their downfall have an impact
on our society, it also has a very direct impact on your adolescent, because at this age boys and girls begin to turn away
from their families and reach out to the culture at large for
clues about how to live. The continuous display of corrupt
political figures, drugged-out rock stars who commit suicide,
and actors who are convicted on criminal charges leaves our
teens with fallen idols at a time when they are seeking to
admire adults outside the family circle, who can stand in the
place of the parents. When these figures are not available,
the adolescent is left with feelings of emptiness and cynicism,
like the youngster below, whose life fell apart when his idol
turned out to have feet of clay:

José, fourteen, was raised in a working-class neighborhood
in the city. The middle child of three, he has an older and
a younger sister. His father died of a heart attack when José
was eleven, leaving him in a family of three women. His
mother, Carmela, enrolled him in a sports program in a local
gym two years ago because she was worried that José never
seemed as aggressive as the other boys his age, and she
wanted to make sure he could protect himself on the streets.
He began boxing there, and attracted the interest of an older
man in the neighborhood named Torres, who is a well-
respected amateur boxing coach.

José developed a real attachment to Torres, and they often
spent time together on weekends, going to ball games and
hanging out. But recently Torres got into a bad fight in a
neighborhood bar. He picked up a bottle and attacked another man, slicing his arm and breaking two ribs. The police
were called, and Torres was arrested and arraigned on assault
charges. José is bewildered and devastated by what's happened. Torres had always insisted on self-discipline in his
training, and now José feels as if his whole relationship with
him has turned out to be a "stupid lie." He is also frightened

by the violence that erupted in a man he thought was calm and controlled. He's told his mother that he never wants to go back to the gym or to box again.

Economic Pressure

Today's parents are under tremendous economic pressure to survive and this pressure can compromise their job of raising their teenagers.

It has been typical for many years for both parents to work outside the home, but in recent years, many parents have been compelled to hold down *more* than one job, moonlighting to earn much-needed extra income. Over 60 percent of multiple job holders are married couples who are trying to provide a better life for their families. Many parents are so burdened and preoccupied by their job responsibilities that they have a hard time taking care of their teenagers. Many need to spend so many hours away from home that they have little time left to be parents. (In fact, the total time American children spend with their parents has decreased by almost 35 percent in the past thirty years.) This leaves today's adolescents with less parental supervision than ever before in a more dangerous world. Further, since most of our communities provide few opportunities for adolescents to gather together in safe surroundings, or to be supervised by other benevolent adults, adolescents increasingly are left to their own devices. Prematurely released from their parents' supervision, they may link up with outsiders who seem to offer them the security they lack—cults, gangs, political extremists, and so on.

In addition, because adults in our society are living longer than ever, many parents of adolescents are also caught in the middle—economically and emotionally strained by the responsibilities of taking care of adolescent children and aging parents at the very same time.

The stories that follow highlight how important it is for parents to remain both emotionally and physically in touch with their adolescent children during these vulnerable years.

The more hours parents spend outside the home, the less time they have to supervise their kids.

Nora is fifteen and her parents, Dotti and Ed Stratton, are both teachers. Dotti and Ed chose to make their careers in education in order to have time to build and enjoy their own family life. They anticipated being home early each afternoon and taking long vacations as a family over the summer, but things have not turned out the way they planned. Instead, shortly after Nora's tenth birthday, Ms. Stratton's widowed mother had a stroke. Dotti was determined to help her mother recuperate from her stroke and to ensure that she had the best rehabilitative care possible, but since the HMO that handled her mother's health care refused to cover these more extensive costs, Dotti decided to take on a second job, selling clothes at a local boutique, to help pay for her mother's medical expenses. Nora's father, Ed, began working a shift as a bus driver to supplement their income. This meant that both of Nora's parents were out of the house until late in the evening.

Nora's friends soon realized that she was on her own a lot, and her home became the local "free house" for her friends. At first, Nora enjoyed her new social status, but soon, as word got around, kids who weren't even from her school or her neighborhood began to crash her parties. They brought in beer and liquor and drugs and Nora was afraid to say anything.

One weekend two boys that Nora didn't even know held her down on her parents' bed and tried to rape her. One had his hand over her mouth so she wouldn't scream and the other was unzipping his fly when luckily some kids she knew barged in and interrupted them. Nora "freaked" and began screaming and crying. Her friends threatened the boys, made them leave, and calmed her down, but she remained terrified. Nora has resolved not to let anyone into her house ever again.

Renalda is sixteen and a half and has a fourteen-year-old sister, Lucinda. She is from a wealthy and educated Cuban family who now live in Florida. Her mother is a devoted physician with an extensive family practice among the poor. Her father died in Cuba.

Renalda deeply resents that her mother spends so much time with her patients and barely any time at all with her and her sister. When she talks about it to her mother, they get into heated arguments, with her mother insisting that Renalda "has no respect for her life's work." She accuses Renalda of being "a spoiled child of privilege" with nothing on her mind except her own needs and wishes.

Renalda's maternal grandparents were large landholders in Cuba before Castro came to power. They later fled, settling in Miami, where they are still involved in financing anti-Castro activities. Though her mother supports Castro, and has disdain for her parents' political views, describing the anti-Castro movement as "old ideas for old people," Renalda has hooked up with them and has been involved in some of their activities. She feels closer to this movement than she does to her mother, whom she feels has abandoned her and her sister.

Renalda wants to visit Cuba one day and see her ancestral home and land. She believes, with her grandparents, that Castro has destroyed Cuba, and feels ready and able to participate in terrorist acts against him. While Renalda keeps all her political activities completely secret from her mother, she insists her mother wouldn't notice anyway.

Alternative Family Forms

The high divorce rate in our country produces a large population of single parents and remarried, recombined families, putting new emotional pressures on family life. The fixed structures of the nuclear family of previous generations have been replaced by the more mutable dimensions of the alternative family that we see all around us—divorcing families, single-parent families, stepparent families, recombined families. *Change, complexity,* and *challenge* seem to be our watchwords, whereas *consistency, continuity,* and *comfort* were the watchwords of previous generations. While some of the changes in family structure have provided parents with more options for their own personal growth and development, not all parents face these changes willingly. Many feel betrayed or abandoned by a spouse and suffer acute anxiety and depression, which compromises their ability to function as *people* as well as *parents*. This further erodes the sense of safety and security their children need. While the story that follows may sound particularly complicated, problems like this are faced by more and more teenagers in our changing society:

Lydia was eleven when her parents divorced. Until she turned fourteen, she lived with her mother in her widowed grandmother's home in New Jersey. Her grandmother was her main caregiver, as her mother "fell apart" when her father walked out, and spent most of her days crying and lying in bed. She had little energy or patience for Lydia. Meanwhile, Lydia's father remarried and moved to San Francisco. He offered to take Lydia to live with him and his new wife, who had a thirteen-year-old daughter of her own, and Lydia wanted to go.

At first, things in her dad's family seemed idyllic, and Lydia was thrilled to see him more, to start high school, and to leave her depressed and depleted mother behind. But soon Lydia began to resent her new stepsister, who she felt had an "attitude." Lydia particularly felt excluded from the close, easygoing relationship between her stepsister and her stepmom, and she felt that her stepmother favored her own daughter over her. Initially, Lydia had thought it would be "cool" to have a younger sister, but she soon realized that there were many disadvantages. The two girls shared a room, whereas Lydia had always had her own room at home, and her sister was a better student, which made Lydia feel insecure. In addition, Lydia didn't see her dad as much as she had hoped. She resented the time her dad and stepmom spent with each other, and felt excluded from their romantic relationship.

By the time she was fifteen, Lydia decided to return to the East Coast to live with her mom, who seemed less depressed.

But by the following fall, her mom had begun a relationship with a man who was a construction engineer. He had recently been assigned to a project in South America, and Lydia's mom was thinking about joining him there. She wanted Lydia to come with her. After a lot of inner turmoil, Lydia decided to remain at her grandmother's home in New Jersey and finish up high school with her class. During her senior year, Lydia split her holidays between her father's San Francisco home and her mother's new home in Buenos Aires. She described feeling like "an orphan without a family." Next year, her mother's boyfriend will be returning to the United States to work on another construction project, this time in Oregon. Lydia is thinking about attending a West Coast college. She's hoping that will enable her to be nearer to both her parents.

Almost half the adolescents in our country divide their time between two parents—or are being raised by one overburdened parent whose emotional and financial and physical resources are often stretched beyond endurance. As parents try to deal with the increased psychological pressures of separation, abandonment, and divorce, and the increased financial pressures of endless court cases, new jobs, and difficult living conditions, they often have little time or patience for their adolescents. Unfortunately, the ongoing battle between the sexes has taken a great many psychological prisoners.

Adolescence, then, which is *ordinarily* a time of enormous physiological, psychological, and social changes, is now taking place in an *extraordinarily* perilous environment. Eating disorders, teenage pregnancy, drug abuse, alcoholism, smoking, suicide rates, sexually transmitted diseases, vehicular deaths, and violent crime are all rising at rates twice or even three times what they were a generation ago. Conversely, school performance, SAT scores, physical fitness, and emotional resilience seem to be dropping.

In addition, adolescents often repudiate our *comfort* (which they feel is infantilizing), turn away from our *consolation* (which they see as patronizing), and resist our efforts at *communication* (which they experience as scrutiny). Even the most solid parent-child connection can be expected to hit some rocky times as children struggle to leave the safe harbor of their family and push off into these uncharted waters. Parents are trying to provide the firm ground from which their teenagers can "look before they leap." This is no easy matter at any time, but in today's times, it's harder than ever.

How can we create a safe and secure environment for our adolescents, offer them a loving and nurturing atmosphere in which they can grow, and set down clear expectations for their performance? Adolescence requires rethinking and reworking some of our ideas about what it means to be a parent. You cannot go on treating your adolescent in the very same way that you treated your child. And the new adolescence I have been describing, with its special new stresses, requires new responses—responses that our own parents could never even have imagined. In this next chapter, I'm going to talk about the changes *you* will need to make as a parent to help you weather the storms of adolescence.

CHAPTER 3

Changes in Your Adolescent/ Changes in You

Identification/Disidentification

Becoming a parent is a new kind of growing up for adults. It requires new understanding, new capacities, and new responses. But where do parents learn these new skills? They aren't taught how to raise kids in college; it isn't tucked in somewhere between calculus and the War of 1812. Without formal education to break through and broaden our horizons, parents fall back on the only experience they have— *being the child of their own parents.* Even when they have few conscious memories of childhood, these early experiences of family life are so enduring that it is extremely difficult for any of us to evade or escape their influence. We know, for instance, that children who are physically beaten by their parents frequently grow up to abuse their own children, and that children of alcoholics frequently grow up to abuse alcohol. And, more positively, that children who are loved become capable of love, or that children raised with empathy are often empathic themselves.

But we can find ourselves influenced by our parents in more subtle ways as well. How many of us swore we would never, ever tell our kids "You do it now because I said so!" or insist, "You're my daughter and you'll do it my way!" or say, "If you don't like how things are done in this house, there's the door!" How many of us were sure we'd never, ever make a fuss about grades, or care whether our teenagers kept their rooms clean, or worry about their manners, or push them to become doctors, or tell them they couldn't date someone of a different race or religion?

In early childhood, children simply *imitate* the different characteristics of the people they love and admire. (Remember when your daughter dressed up in your high heels and lipstick, or when your son put shaving cream on his face and scraped it off with a butter knife?) But as children mature, they begin more fully to absorb aspects of your character; they digest your traits and capacities and make them part of themselves; they take powerful psychic impressions of you. We call this process *identification.*

Identification is one of the ways that you take in knowledge about your world and develop the skills you need to help manage your life. It is a complicated process that crosses both gender and generational lines. (A girl, for example, can identify with her father's ability to be confrontational, while a boy can identify with his mother's sense of humor.) Siblings as well as grandparents, aunts and uncles, teachers and friends can also be an important source of identification. All during childhood, and in adolescence, your son or daughter will continue to make new identifications that shape his personality and help consolidate his/her character. But our children not only identify with us in the *present*, they also absorb a psychic history of thoughts and feelings from the *past*— feelings that have been handed down from one generation to another. This is why a contemporary African-American teenager can still feel the burden of slavery, or how a Jewish-American teenager can still feel the horror of the Holocaust.

Equally important in his development is your teenager's ability to *disidentify* with aspects of his family—that is, to disavow disliked characteristics. A boy can swear he will never be as competitive as his older brother, for instance, while a girl can resolve that she will never be as inhibited as her sister. A son can hate his mother's pessimistic approach to life, while a daughter can despise her father's stinginess, and vow to be generous when she grows up. These disidentifications also play a significant role in shaping personality and consolidating character.

As your son or daughter becomes an adolescent, the old identifications and disidentifications of childhood are reviewed and revised. Fueling this revision are your adolescent's new cognitive capacities (his abstract reasoning powers and his higher levels of comprehension) as well as his increased emotional capacities to separate from you and define his own identity.

Both *identification* and *disidentification*, then, are ordinary outcomes of the parent-child connection. But it is important to understand that these processes may take place either *consciously* (in your teenager's awareness) or unconsciously (outside your teenager's awareness). In adolescence, as children become freed from their dependency on their parents, they become more critical of their parents' personalities and more conscious of their own ability to *emulate* or *reject* the choices you have made in your life. A teenage girl can decide she'll never let her figure go or forget to wear makeup (because her own mother got heavy and dowdy), or a teenage boy can decide he'll never smoke or ignore his health (because his father smoked three packs a day and got emphysema).

Generational Gaps

One of the most important things you need to do when you become a parent is to recognize the difference between *your* needs or desires and *your child's* needs or desires. All parents have trouble with this difference, because it's normal for us to want our kids to be like us. But sometimes they're only a bit like us—sometimes they don't seem to be like us at all— and that needs to be all right, too. As a parent you may forget that your teenager is a separate individual with his own thoughts and feelings, and that you need to leave room for his unique individuality to become established. Often, what you *think you're doing* for your adolescent and what you're *actually doing* may turn out to be two separate experiences. Here are some examples of parents who are not mindful of this gap:

What You Think You're Doing

DAD: "My father was a stickler for discipline. He was a tough guy to grow up with, but I admire him now, because eventually I learned standards that have lasted me all my life. Most kids today are soft and spoiled. I don't want my son to be a lazy slob, so I'm making sure he's learning high standards right from the beginning."

What You May Be Doing

TEENAGER: "I'd really like to please my dad and live up to his standards, but it's no use. My dad makes everything into a big deal, and he criticizes everything I do. No matter how hard I try, I'm never able to do things the way he wants. It's easier to just give up and not do anything at all."

What You Think You're Doing

MOM: "My mother never taught me how to dress. She was always too busy for me, and I had to take care of myself. All the girls used to make fun of my color combinations. I'm going to make sure my daughter is never embarrassed like I was. I'm going to choose her clothes myself, and make sure she always wears the right thing."

What You May Be Doing

TEENAGER: "Sometimes it feels like my mom cares more about what I *wear* than about *me*. She never lets me choose my clothes for myself. She thinks she knows everything, and I know nothing. And she's so picky about everything, too. She makes me feel stupid and ugly."

As you become the parents of an adolescent, it's useful to try to remember what it felt like to be an adolescent. A father who won't let his son learn how to use a drill unless he does it "exactly the right way" has no idea that his need for control could be eroding his son's confidence. But if he remembers how angry *he* was as a teenager at his own father's overly scrupulous standards, he can find a better way to introduce his son to the principles of carpentry. A mother, aware of how much she hated being compelled to practice piano, can permit her own daughter to take drum lessons instead—or no music lessons at all. She can decide to let her daughter spend her afternoons reading.

In all the years I have treated adolescents and their families, I have never seen a mother or a father who set out to ruin their children's lives. Even mothers and fathers who physically abuse their kids often believe they're "doing the right thing," or that they're punishing their kids "for their own good." The mother who picked out her daughter's clothes so that "everything will match" is acting out of love—not understanding that she is undermining her teenager's self-confidence and ability to make choices. The father who wanted his son to grow up with high standards is also acting out of love. He wants his son to have "the right stuff," and not to turn off or turn away from life's challenges. Most parents make all kinds of inevitable mistakes in the name of love.

Parents try to give their adolescents *what they never had*, so they insist that they play tennis (whether they want to or not). Parents try to give their adolescents *what they wish they had*, so they send them to competitive schools (without regard for their ability to cope with the pressure). And parents try to give their children *what they want for themselves*, so they press a daughter to become a lawyer or a son to go into the family business (without leaving room for their own choices).

The process can be further complicated by your adolescent's own temperament and character. Each baby, after all, comes into the world with a particular genetic inheritance that includes intellectual and emotional characteristics as well as physical ones (like blue eyes or red hair). These characteristics include things like intelligence, artistic or musical talents, physical restlessness, emotional sensitivity or resiliency, assertiveness and shyness, muscular agility, and so on. These traits will go on to play their part in your adolescent's eventual personality, creating the continuities of development we all recognize when we say things like "She was always a little dynamo—even as a baby she was into everything," or "He's always been musical; he used to hum along with the stereo in his crib."

Sometimes these characteristics are *accepted by us* and *acceptable to us*—we recognize and admire them. But sometimes these characteristics are *difficult to accept* or *unacceptable to us*—we may criticize or condemn them. Then, even our language will change as we describe our teenagers:

AN ACCEPTING PARENT:	AN UNACCEPTING PARENT:
"She's really got a mind of her own. It's remarkable that such a sweet-looking teenager has such a strong will. Nobody's going to push *her* around when she grows up!"	"She's impossible to manage. She's always been stubborn and difficult, and it's worse now that she's a teenager. I feel sorry for the man who marries her!"

It's clear to see that one mom will be able to help her teenage daughter to develop her strong will as a *positive* characteristic. She's created room for her daughter's character. But the other mom is critical and constantly geared up to do battle with her strong-willed daughter. She is distressed and disturbed by what she perceives (and defines) as a *negative* characeristic. She's creating the conditions for a self-fulfilling prophecy.

Independence/Dependence

Every adolescent needs to find a way to achieve a certain measure of independence. But it's important to realize that the nature of this measure will vary from family to family and culture to culture. Some adolescents may always live in the same house or block or community as their parents, and continue to maintain strong kinship ties to their families throughout their lives. Other adolescents will follow their dreams to other coasts and other countries, keeping their family connections only through fax and phone and E-mail. Your adolescent's eventual independence is hard-won, and getting there is bound to be a bit difficult for both of you.

But even though your adolescents are insisting on being themselves, they are still in conflict about their independence because it separates them from you. Many adolescents reveal their conflicts about dependence and independence through their daily struggles with self-care. This particular developmental struggle produces many of the parent-teen conflicts with which we are so familiar—the teen who won't wash or wear deodorant, the fights over the messy room or sloppy homework, the binge eating or the refusal to eat at all. Feeding, washing and organizing are functions that you once performed for your child, which your adolescent must now take over and perform for himself. Teens who are still struggling with dependence and independence sometimes refuse, in effect, to become their own good parents.

From the time Kevin was a little boy, his parents gave him

a bath every night before he went to bed. As he got older, he began to take showers in the morning like his father. But since he turned thirteen years old, Kevin wakes up at the last minute, races out of the door without breakfast, and doesn't take a shower for days on end. Both his parents are upset, because he's begun puberty, and he's beginning to get a strong body odor. Every once in a while (when they nag and nag), Kevin will emerge shiny and clean from a shower that seems to use up all the water in the house, but most of the time Kevin seems oblivious to all their entreaties about cleanliness, using deodorant, shampooing his hair, or even keeping his fingernails clean. His parents are completely bewildered by Kevin's lack of concern for his own bodily hygiene, and frustrated by Kevin's constant resistance to their efforts to get him to "clean up his act."

Kevin is deep in the midst of a struggle to take over from his parents the care of his own body. His need to have them still involved with him on a daily basis is reflected in his constant provocation of them through his slovenly habits and appearance. He is still torn between his old childhood identification with his parents and his new disidentification, in which he repudiates their care. He has not yet been able to integrate that aspect of parental caretaking that would enable him to keep himself neat and clean.

Coretta was a neat and tidy little girl who loved to help her mother fold laundry and organize her drawers. But now, at fourteen, she seems to have moved away from her childhood belief that "neatness counts." Her room usually looks like a tornado has hit it, her clothes and books lie in layers on the floor, and she is always trying to find her homework, her favorite pair of jeans, or the new CD she just bought. Each missing object generates tears and a tantrum, requiring her mother's help.

Coretta is in conflict with her old, neat self. One part of her wants to let go of her childhood connection to her mother and "let it all hang out," but another part of her panics at her newfound freedom, and still yearns for her mom to organize her life for her just as she used to organize her drawers.

Mourning Your Losses: Idealization/Deidealization

It's 7:30 in the evening, the family has assembled for dinner, and a surly stranger sits at your dinner table, picking at his food and ignoring your attempts at conversation. We realize that our children will change as they become adolescents, but we are often not prepared for the fact that they will change their thoughts and feelings about *us*. This process, called *deidealization*, is for parents one of the most painful parts of this phase. On a psychological level, your adolescents *are* trying to rid themselves of their need to have parents, so it is not surprising that you feel attacked and abandoned; you're picking up the right signals. Though this process of diminishing and dismissing one's parents is essential to your teenager's growth and development, it doesn't feel very good to you. Where you once got kisses and hugs, you now get sarcasm and dismissal. Where you were once admired and adored, you now get criticized and demeaned. Your young children saw you through rose-colored glasses, but now, as adolescents, this rosy glow begins to dissipate. Now, they see you "through a glass, darkly." A mother's smile that used to light up her child's world becomes "phony," a father's jokes that used to get childish giggles become "corny." Faced with a child who is fast becoming an unpredictable outsider, parents begin to become wary. They walk on eggs around their teens trying to avoid the inevitable blowups, or they give up and withdraw, trying to protect themselves from rejection, or they become angry and confrontational, criticizing and judging their teenagers at every turn. All of these parental feelings are understandable.

Parents also seem to become a constant source of embarrassment to adolescents. One of my teenagers refused to walk with me if I was carrying packages of any kind, because these packages clearly exposed me to the world as a callous, bourgeois consumer. Another son, observing what I considered routine hospitality toward his friends, asked me to "stop sucking up to them." For many years, it seemed to me that I could never get it right (whatever *it* was). I was either too warm or too critical, too interested or too detached, too cheerful or too anxious, too intrusive or too oblivious.

I envied my husband's calm, believing that he was handling these adolescent years with more temperance and wisdom, but unfortunately, he fared no better. If I was too involved, he was too detached, if I was too exuberant, he was too laid back, if my passionate discussions were scorned, so were his cool and controlled attempts at intervention.

And don't think that my expertise as a psychologist softened my sense of personal loss. I was certainly aware that it was normal for my adolescents to separate, and I knew that in this normal process, they would reject who I was, as well as who I had once been for them. But this knowledge didn't soothe the hurt I felt, as I saw myself discounted and devalued minute by minute, day by day. It's very difficult to be told (after you've been a major player in your child's life) that you have only a bit part. Nevertheless, it's essential to your adolescent's healthy development that you step back from the spotlight. Throughout the years of adolescence, your child is trying hard to make himself the *subject* of his own life as opposed to the *object* of his parents' life.

So, as your children begin to grow up, you have to face coming down to earth. In fact, it often seems that the higher you were (in your child's estimation), the harder your fall from grace during their adolescence. It is impossible for any of us to escape this process of deidealization without some sense of sadness and pain. We are, after all, mourning significant losses—your adolescent is experiencing the loss of his childhood and the shattering of the sanctuary of your love and protection. You are experiencing the loss of your role as a parent of a child, and the power, pleasure, and esteem this has always brought you.

To complicate matters even further, as you lose your glorious role as the all-powerful parent of childhood ("My mom is the best mom in the world"), your child *also* loses some of this reflected glory. Now without your power, your adolescent feels more inept, less capable, and more vulnerable than ever before. He must mobilize his resources to build a new solitary sense of self. That's why adolescents are so preoccupied with their sense of self, and why so many "self" words come easily to our minds when we think of adolescents—self-aggrandizing, self-inflating, self-destructive, self-demeaning, self-diminishing, self-deluding, selfish. It's no mean feat to find that middle ground where your adolescent has enough of the freedom he needs to begin to separate from you and widen his world, while you still remain steady and available, offering him love and support for his efforts.

So, as our adolescents are struggling to *decrease* their attachment to us and *decline* our help and support, we are often struggling against them, trying to *retain* our power and *restore* our place in their lives. It is hard for us to understand that the more intensely our children flout our authority, alter their feelings for us, or maintain their distance, the more intensely they may be struggling with their own underlying feelings of submission, affection, and attachment to us. Here's a mother who is trying to understand these complicated dynamics:

Ms. Erikson had always been extremely close to her son, Neil. The eldest of three children, Neil had stepped in as the "man around the house," when his father, a career lieutenant in the air force, was called up in the reserves. At the time, Neil was just ten years old, but Ms. Erikson described how she could really depend upon him and what a "little man" he was. He comforted her when she was depressed, helped her with household chores, and even pitched in to discipline his younger sisters and brothers. But now, at fifteen, Neil seems to find every excuse to be away from home, and he barely spends any time at all with his mom. And whenever Ms. Erikson tries to plan some special time when they can be together—lunch or the movies—Neil says, "Why don't you ask Dad?" Ms. Erikson feels sad and lonely without Neil's support, and she doesn't understand his recent coldness to her.

But we can see what Neil is trying to escape. Continuing to occupy his special place in his family would prevent him from growing up and growing away from his mother. Left without a husband for over a year, Ms. Erikson unwittingly encouraged her young son to take his father's place, and obliterated the generational boundaries between them in the process. But now, as Neil moves into the middle years of adolescence, he is trying to create more psychological and physical distance between himself and his mom, so that he can relinquish his needs for her and interrupt her needs for him. He is trying to extricate himself and encourage his mother to turn to his father. Because Neil was so close to his mother as a preadolescent, he has to exert even more energy now to separate from her and move on with his peers. His mother's sense of loss actually testifies to his developmental success.

Shattering the Sanctuary of Childhood

When your child was young, you prepared him to face his daily life through thousands of instructions, admonitions, and warnings: you made him look both ways before crossing; you encouraged him to believe that practice makes perfect; you told him that anything worth doing is worth doing well. You held your child's hand as he went to school, taught him what's good to eat, dressed him to face the weather, and intervened when things become too hard for him to handle on his own. You were busy being what I call "protective parents," creating "an emotional cushion" for your children and maintaining the "sanctuary of childhood."

But in adolescence, this sanctuary must eventually be shattered. No matter where you live, in the smallest rural town or in the largest inner city; no matter how you live, in a traditional "nuclear" family or in an "alternative" family; and no matter how well you live, with many financial resources or with few, your adolescent must begin to move out from under your influence and begin to take care of himself in the world. He will use the years of adolescence to wean himself away from his family, but it is up to you to make sure that the timing is right. A child who is too abruptly deprived of your guidance through circumstances over which he has no control (illness, divorce, death) is likely to feel prematurely disillusioned about his parents' power, and have a heightened sense of his own vulnerability in the world. That's because the *actual* separation and loss of the parent intensifies the normal adolescent experience of *symbolic* separation and loss, undermining his sense of safety and security. An adolescent who prematurely deprives himself of your parental guidance through precocious rebellion is also at developmental risk. By forcing a psychological separation from you, he can deprive himself of sufficient time to identify with your parental functions and to begin to be a good parent to himself. This can leave him feeling helpless and disillusioned at the very time that he most needs a sense of strength and optimism.

On the other hand, adolescents who remain overly dependent on their parents' guidance and are unable to separate from their influence are also at developmental risk. Adolescents who cling to the comforts of home, who ally themselves completely with your wishes and needs, and who turn away from the new challenges of this phase are delaying or even destroying their path toward adulthood. They essentially refuse to take their place in their own generation, and instead remain cosseted in a prolonged childhood. They are never truly able to feel powerful or competent on their own, but remain dependent on the parents' power. Separation then, from your care, your concern and your comfort, is essential to your adolescent's development, but the process must be timely and appropriate—neither too fast nor too slow, neither too much nor too little, neither too soon nor too late.

As the world changes, and as our adolescents change with it, we parents must walk a thin line between *overprotecting* them (compromising their ability to build the skills they will need) and *underprotecting* them (abandoning them to their own resources when their judgment is still fragile and undependable). It's an adolescent's job to push for freedom; it is the parents' job to insist on responsibility. It's their job to take risks; it's ours to counsel prudence. They may seek excitement, but we must press for their security. This is in the nature of things; this difference defines and determines the gap between the generations.

Without both sides fulfilling their normal roles, development can become dangerously skewed. Adolescents who are given too much responsibility, for example, can become overmature, "parentified children," who take care of their own parents. Those who feel unprotected in their families can become increasingly reckless, taking greater and greater risks, in order to compel their parents to care for them. Adolescents who feel ignored or abandoned can become depressed, retreating in despair from the ordinary challenges of their lives. Here are some adolescents who do not feel safe—their sanctuary has been prematurely shattered:

Rosa, a slender fourteen-year-old with a sweet smile, looked as if she was carrying the weight of the world on her shoulders. Her parents had separated when she was nine and Rosa lived with her hardworking mother, a lab technician who needed to take a higher-paying evening job to support the family, since her husband was a depressed Vietnam vet who was incapable of holding a job for very long. Rosa had primary responsibility both for her two younger sisters and for her father, toward whom she felt pity, "because my mom doesn't love him anymore." With her extensive obligations, Rosa had no time or energy left for any of the ordinary pleasures of adolescence. She didn't hang out, or date, or go to parties, or join teams, or sing in the chorus, or try out for a part in the sophomore play. Instead Rosa had become the "parentified" child, taking over the functions of an adult in her family. But she was paying a high price for her efforts. In the past month, Rosa's grades had fallen, she felt isolated from her friends, and she was listless and exhausted in school. Rosa's assumption of adult responsibilities had weighed her down and interfered with her ability to lead a normal adolescent life.

Chris, fifteen, was the last child in a family of four children, all one year apart. He lived in a good suburban neighborhood and went to the local high school. A restless boy and small for his age, Chris was often left on his own, or in the care of his quarreling older siblings, while both his parents worked long hours at their jobs. He had previously been suspended from school for swearing at a teacher and had already been disciplined for cutting classes. His exasperated parents had punished him by grounding him, but it was difficult for any punishment to be effective, because they often weren't around to enforce their restrictions. Chris continued to flounder, escalating his negative behavior until finally he was apprehended by the police for stealing a neighbor's car and taking it on a "joyride." By that time, his negative patterns of behavior had rigidified and his ability to gain positive satisfactions from his adolescent life had been severely diminished.

Stella was sixteen. Her parents had divorced the previous year when her father had "come out," revealing he was gay. Initially Stella had lived with her mom, but when her mom took a new job in which she needed to travel a lot, she shifted Stella's custody to her father. At first things seemed all right but soon, her father asked his long-term lover to live with them. Now Stella felt angry at her dad for loving someone else, and angry at her mom for "getting rid" of her. She felt as if she'd lost her connection to both her parents. Stella began to become increasingly depressed and had a harder and harder time "snapping out of it." In the mornings she just wanted to sleep and never wake up. She had read that the most painless way to die was to slit your wrists in a warm bath. Luckily, she panicked when she made the first tentative cut and saw the blood, and called 911. Shattering the sanctuary of Stella's family had almost cost her life.

Same or Separate?

When the security of childhood has been breached, but the new adolescent self is still unborn, there is a time (between the loss of the identification with you as an internal model and guide, and the replacement of you with his peers) when your adolescent can feel very much alone. This is when your son or daughter is most responsive to what I have called "the tyranny of the crowd"—the time of life when dressing the right way, saying the right things, seeing the right people—become all-consuming adolescent goals, dwarfing all other considerations in your son or daughter's life. To defy convention at this time of life, to be different, is to dare beyond reason. Only a fortunate few (those with the courage of their convictions) can afford such daring. Alas, I am sorry to report that I was not among those few.

I vividly remember that when I was just about fourteen years old, I desperately wanted a navy duffel coat with a Black Watch plaid lining (all the rage in those days) for my birthday. My mother, who had been a buyer for Macy's and had some flair for clothes, went out and bought me a duffel coat (on final sale), but there was one problem. The duffel coat she bought me was white wool with a bright red flannel lining. Even in my self-absorbed adolescent state, I could clearly recognize its beauty, but nothing in the world could persuade me to wear such a startlingly unique coat. The whole point of wanting the navy duffel coat was to look *exactly the same* as all of the other girls, not to stand out from the crowd in any way. This coat would set off alarms!

Of course, from my mother's point of view, I was special, and she wanted me to look special. What was wrong with that? But from my point of view, *being special meant being separate*, and it filled me with anxiety and dread. My mother found my reaction quite bewildering, and for a while she was very disappointed in me. She was also annoyed that she had spent "good money" for a coat that couldn't be returned, and that I now refused to wear to school.

My father, less patient than she with my adolescent peculiarities, was really angry. As the breadwinner in the family, he only saw that his hard-earned money was being wasted. He told me I was "spoiled rotten," and reminded me that I was not getting another coat this year and that I would have to "make do" with my old coat, since I refused to wear my new coat.

As loving as my parents were, they did not understand my adolescent conflicts, and so they made a number of unwitting mistakes. First, of course, in buying the coat *for* me, my mother was continuing to treat me as a child, despite the fact that I was now an adolescent. She needed to shop *with* me now, not *for* me. Her assumption that she could still choose my clothes revealed that she had not yet shifted parental gears; she was still operating as a *protective* parent of childhood, not an *effective* parent of adolescence.

Second, the idea of being special (an idea that all the children in our family had bred into their bones), while perhaps useful in my childhood, was actually a hindrance in my adolescence, as I tried to find a way to ally myself with my friends. My mother's wishes for me were antithetical to my developmental aims. I wanted to fit in, and to be the *same* as my friends. My mother, on the other hand, wanted me to shine, to be *different*. She still believed that she was my most important audience and that my performance was for her. She didn't realize that I was now being judged by a jury of my peers, whose expectations were quite different from hers.

And third, my father's condemnation of me as "spoiled rotten," while it reflected an accurate sense of things from his perspective, was not actually true. I had not gone out and bought the coat I now refused to wear; I had not asked for something that was beyond our means (I needed a new winter coat, anyway), and I had not been demanding of extra privileges. I had merely specified my tastes in my own clothing as if I were an *adult*, not a *child*.

Your Shifting Job Description

As your child approaches adolescence, we've discussed how you're going to have to let go of many of the structures and satisfactions that your old job (as the parents of young children) brought to you. Power, admiration, and respect were your precious rewards for the long hours, the sleepless nights, the dirty diapers, and the innumerable sacrifices that parents of young children must make. But as your children become adolescents, you will no longer be able to count on being loved or admired. In fact, as your children become adolescents, you won't even be able to count on being heard! But to make matters worse, your new job description (as the parent of an adolescent) isn't even consistent. In fact, it seems to shift from moment to moment. The reason this is happening is because your adolescent's thoughts and feelings and behavior are also shifting from moment to moment. One day, you're called upon to step in as a parent, the next, to step out. One day your daughter can't choose a dress without your counsel, while on another, your ideas about clothes are scorned. One day your son doesn't want your advice about his skin rash, while on another, he seems completely panicked about his pimples. It's hard to be the parent of a constantly changing child, and it's even harder to be the parent of a child who no longer knows if he wants a parent. This movement back and forth between obeying and disobeying, listening and not listening, loving and not loving, connecting and disconnecting will characterize a great many of your exchanges with your adolescent.

This is what makes your job, as the parents of adolescents, so difficult. Should you relate to the dependent part or the independent part of your adolescent? Shall you treat him as if he were sixteen years old or four years old? Can you accept him at face value or do you need to look underneath? Does he want to stand out or blend in? And while you know that many different kinds of development are taking place in your kids—emotional, physical, intellectual, social—it often seems as if there is no rhyme or reason to the pace or the pattern.

An intellectually accomplished twelve-year-old
painfully shy; a socially adept fourteen-year-c
be wetting her bed; a sixteen-year-old who's
can still be flunking school; and a sexually sophisticated
eighteen-year-old can still need to sleep with her stuffed ani-
mals.

Your adolescent's struggle with new, powerful aggressive
and sexual urges also requires that you change the way you
think and act. These urges were once safely contained by his
physical immaturity, but now your adolescent confronts his
impulses in a real world that permits and even encourages
action. This potential for action requires a reworking of your
old parental prohibitions. Before it was enough to "just
say no," and your child was likely to listen. In dire straits,
a "time-out," or "no dessert after dinner" would enforce your
will. But now, it's much more complicated. Too many limits
can produce defiance, evasion, or rebellion; on the other
hand, too few limits are not useful either, because unless your
adolescent has a clear sense of your expectations, he can feel
wild and ungoverned, as he struggles for self-control.

Remember that self-aware and self-controlled parents are
better able to teach their teenagers self-awareness and self-
control, as well. Teenagers in these families experience less
stress, score higher on achievement tests, have longer attention spans, and display fewer behavioral and physical symptoms, regardless of their parents' intelligence, social class,
ethnicity, or educational level. In other words, emotionally
effective and mature parents produce better adjusted children no matter who they are, where they're from, or how
much money they have.

But changing social realities have left many of today's parents feeling particularly uncertain and confused about when
and where to "lay down the law." How can you establish reasonable rules of behavior, while still permitting your kids to
shape their own lives? How can you insist upon your own
standards, while allowing your kids to develop their own judgment? How can you maintain specific expectations, without
compromising your adolescent's sense of himself?

Luckily, you bring some valuable *old* dimensions to your *new* job as the parent of a teenager: your enduring love, your capacity for empathy, your own understanding of what it felt like to be an adolescent, and last but not least, your capacity to maintain standards, and enforce discipline when it's needed. Don't be afraid to use these old skills. Without love, your teenager can never develop *self-esteem*; without understanding, he can never develop *self-confidence*; and without standards, limits, and discipline, your adolescent can never develop *self-control.* Building on childhood ties of affection and respect will help you to keep the lines of communication open with your adolescents, despite the fact that sometimes it may feel as if your teenagers have descended to a subterranean world that they alone inhabit and you can never penetrate. While adolescence is a time of enormous discontinuity in life, with heightened, intense reactions, a loss of balance or perspective, and rapid escalating mood shifts, remember that your teenagers are still children without an adult country. They have yet to choose their routes or to settle on their destination. This means that your influence can still be useful, if only you can find a way to get your message through.

Still Safe at Home Base

At one point when both our children were teenagers, my husband had the following science fiction fantasy: It's the year 2000. All twelve-year-olds are assigned a number in a national lottery and are randomly drafted into new families for the duration of their adolescent years, permitted to return home only when their adolescence is over.

While this fantasy reveals a parent's understandable wish to escape "teen trouble," it also reveals some interesting underlying psychological solutions to the realities of this phase of development. First, it highlights the importance of gaining some distance in the adolescent years. My husband fantasized *physical* distance (and indeed, boarding schools and camps were invented to give you this distance) but for most of us, the goal is *psychological* distance. How can we maintain some psychological distance so that we aren't always enmeshed in continuous conflict with our teens?

My husband's fantasy also offers parents an opportunity for *narcissistic disengagement* from their adolescents, another psychological solution to the struggles of this phase. Since you would be raising someone else's teen (and they yours), *your* narcissistic involvement in *their* teenager's accomplishments would be vastly diminished. Who cares if someone else's kid flunks his chemistry exam? Does it matter if another parent's child is musical or not?

And this fantasy solution holds out the possibility of a *fresh start.* Again, this is one of the most painful parts of living with an adolescent. Parents and kids aren't just dealing with their present problems, they're carrying over their old, ongoing childhood conflicts into adolescence. My husband's fantasy enabled him to dream about a new, uncontaminated relationship with someone else's twelve-year-old. The challenge for all of us, of course, is how to create these three important developmental opportunities—*psychological distance, narcissistic disengagement,* and *a fresh start*—while living with our adolescents.

As our world changes, our teenagers are changing with it, and that means that we, as their parents, must make important changes in the way we think and act as well. Many parents approach this phase in the life of the family with helplessness—as if nothing they do during these years will make a difference. *Nothing could be further from the truth.* Adolescents care very much what the adults in their life think about them. In fact, some of the conflicts and concerns may be a result of caring *too* much. No matter how blithe and blasé a facade your teenager presents to the world, underneath, he's still the baby you once held in your arms all night and nursed through that high fever. He just doesn't want to be reminded of it now.

CHAPTER 4

Talking with Your Adolescent

Changing Your Conversation

Even though it may feel at times as if you have completely lost touch with the child you once knew, you still have a powerful tool at your disposal to keep your connection going—good, plain talk. But this talk has to be geared to your adolescent's new place in life, or your message can't get through. That's what this chapter is all about—how to talk to your teenagers.

To create effective dialogue, you've got to be aware of the *form* as well as the *content* of your conversations. For instance, when you were the parent of a young child, your voice brightened and heightened when you needed to communicate with her. We're all familiar with this nursery voice—it lifts and lilts in order to dramatize what you're saying. But in adolescence this voice is bad news; it reminds your son or daughter of their baby days, evokes their past dependence on you, and erodes the new sense of equality (and even superiority) that they are anxious to create. ("Mom, stop talking to me like a baby!") Too much enthusiasm, too much intensity, too much indignation, too much anger, too much pressure—in fact, too much of anything is not likely to get the conversation going with a teenager.

After all, adolescents are having enough trouble dealing with their own extreme emotions. On a daily basis, their behavior alternates between heightened feelings on the one hand (hysteria over a broken date, panic about a test, excruciating embarrassment about saying the wrong thing) and the denial of feelings on the other (repudiated reactions, blithe indifference, cool disavowal, etc.). They need their parents to help them *modulate* their feelings, not *maximize* them. Your new role as the parent of an adolescent needs to be subtle and underplayed to be convincing and effective. Parents who lose their cool all the time lose their kids.

So, in this new phase of life, if you want to talk *to* your adolescent, not *at* her, and you want your adolescent to talk *to* you instead of talking *back* to you, you need to try and create a real dialogue. In a dialogue, two people respond to each other with respect; it's a back-and-forth, give-and-take interaction that allows both participants to feel they've had their say. More often than not when we talk to our adolescents we're actually talking *down* to them, closing off their response. A parental lecture is always one-sided, leaving your adolescent to suffer in silence, scream back, or slam doors!

Here's an example of such a lecture, where the parent winds up turning off her teenager, and talking only to herself:

MOM: "You've spent every single night this week glued to the TV. I haven't seen you do one stitch of homework! I'm sick and tired of your laziness. You're going to fail biology and every other course you have if you don't develop some good work habits."

SHARON: "Get off my back!"

Here's an example of the way a more respectful dialogue might go between a mother and daughter:

MOM: "You know, I was noticing that you don't seem to have much homework lately. Are you finishing it before you get home, or are you just lucky this weekend and your teacher is giving you a break? I've been a little worried about biology, because I know how upset you were with your last test score."

SHARON: "I did my math at lunch and Ms. Riley's been out sick this week, so the substitute teacher decided she wouldn't give us any homework over the weekend. Bio has been okay. I did better on the class quiz than I thought I would."

Using the Four C's to Connect

To avoid a monologue and to encourage a dialogue with your adolescent, you need to keep in mind what I call the four C's: compassion, communication, comprehension, and competence. Let's take a look at what each of these words can mean in your life, and how they can provide you with the key to successful conversations.

Compassion

Compassion (or empathy) is a powerful human capacity. It is different from pity, or sympathy. When you are compassionate you don't feel sorry for the other person; instead, you feel *for* them. You try to put yourself in their place, to stand in their shoes. But at the same time, compassion also helps you to maintain some psychological distance. By being compassionate, you are able to understand the person's plight, without being so drawn into it that you're suffering at the same level that they are. Think of it this way: If someone is drowning, and you want to save them, isn't it better to stand on the shore and throw them a lifeline, than to jump in the waves with them and take the chance that you will both be drowned? Empathy (or compassion) is an emotional lifeline.

Here are some examples of *compassionate* responses to typical situations in an adolescent's life:

> "Oh, no! What a bad break! Are you sure you lost all of your history paper in the computer?"
>
> "Boy, that fight with David sounds really harsh. You must be really bummed out about it."
>
> "I bet you feel nervous about the tryouts for chorus. I don't think I could do it, I can barely hold a tune!"
>
> "You have a right to be really angry about the stuff that was stolen from your locker."
>
> "I know you're feeling bad because you promised Lucy you'd go skating with her, but instead you went out with Matt, and she found out. It's so hard to handle these situations."

These are all responses in which the parent puts himself in his son or daughter's place, and tries to *connect*, rather than *criticize*.

Communication

If you start out compassionate (and that's not always easy!) your adolescent will usually be more willing to continue the conversation, setting the stage for the second "C"—real communication between the two of you. Through this communication you can now begin to understand your adolescent's distress. Watch for body language that indicates worry or fear—moodiness, tension, a "hangdog" slump that looks as if she's carrying the world on her shoulders. And trust your instincts. If you've been spending time with your kid and paying attention to her, and you feel something is not right, *go with your parental instinct, no matter what she says.* ("I know you said nothing's wrong, but when you start getting stomachaches, it's usually because you're worried.") Keeping the channel open between you and your teen requires a real commitment on your part. Many adolescents freeze up or try to hide when things go wrong in their lives. They feel ashamed, afraid, and anxious about needing help. They may think it makes them weak to tell you their problems, or they believe they're stupid because they haven't been able to solve things on their own. Adolescents often need a lot of encouragement to share their thoughts. Some openings that help "jump-start" a conversation include:

> "I was wondering if things got any better with . . ."
> "You know that idea we were talking about . . ."
> "Remember what you told me last week when . . ."
> "I've been thinking about your problem with . . ."

These openings all require some mutual commitment and conversational exploration. Always try to avoid inquiries with an adolescent that can be summarily dismissed, or answered only with yes or no, as your adolescent will take the opportunity to cut off further communication:

> Q: "How are things at school?"
> A: "Fine."
> Q: "Did you do your homework?"
> A: "Yes."
> Q: "Have you been drinking?"
> A: "No."

Good communication not only enriches your family life and increases mutuality and intimacy, it also enables you to enter your adolescent's inner world, and to find out what is truly troubling her. Communication also gives you an opportunity to offer significant information ("Yes, I have been cranky lately. I'm worried about my job.") and it gives you a chance to confirm important realities for your son or daughter. ("You're right, you're not so hot in French. Maybe we could get you a tutor before you feel really overwhelmed.")

Comprehension

Compassion and communication get things going between parents and kids. They set up the structures of the dialogue and keep it moving, but without comprehension, you have no clue about where to go with the dialogue, and no opportunity to address the real underlying problems your adolescent may be experiencing. Comprehension is the contribution *you* make as a parent to understanding the dimensions of your adolescent's struggle. It gives you a chance to share your perspective and your understanding with your adolescent. It's not enough just to be compassionate, and to open up lines of communication. To be a truly effective parent you have to also *understand the meanings* of what your adolescent is telling you. This means not taking things at face value; it means always trying to look for hidden messages that may lie beneath the surface; it means not being intimidated by these yet-to-be adults.

Here's an example of a parent who can't comprehend what his thirteen-year-old daughter is really trying to convey to him; he just doesn't get it.

DAD: "When are the auditions for the school play this year?"

DARCY: "I don't know, and who cares. The school play always sucks anyway!"

DAD: "I can't stand it when you use that awful language. If you can't speak properly to me don't bother speaking at all!"

DARCY: "Oh, forget it!"

Here's another response this parent could make that goes beneath his daughter's surface disdain and demonstrates more real comprehension of his daughter's psychological plight:

DAD: "When are the auditions for the school play this year?"

DARCY: "I don't know, and who cares. The school play sucks anyway!"

DAD: "Whoa! That sounds tough! A couple of weeks ago you really wanted to try out. Do you think you're turned off now because you're nervous about the auditions?"

DARCY: "I really tried last year, and the year before, too, and I never even got a bit part. What's the use?"

DAD: "You're right. I remember how disappointed you were, but you've worked hard on your acting, and I think you're more confident this year. Don't you think it's worth a shot? Try it. If you don't make it, then it's their loss."

This father refuses to take what his daughter says at face value. ("School plays suck!") Instead, he carefully listens for the underlying meaning of her response ("I'd rather not try than try and fail."). He also responds with compassion ("You're right. I remember how disappointed you were.") and draws on his comprehension to help her. ("You worked hard on your acting and I think you're more confident this year. Don't you think it's worth a shot?") But he throws in a little humor and a little loyalty to let his daughter know he's behind her, no matter what happens. ("If you don't make it, then it's their loss!")

Sometimes, once you've truly comprehended your adolescent's problem, you may need to *correct misinformation, modify distortions,* or even *absolve your adolescent of responsibility* in troubling events.

Here's a mother who gets an unexpected chance to do all three things. She is discussing with her eleven-year-old son his father's brief hospitalization that day for chest pains.

MOM: "I saw Daddy, and he's doing just fine. The doctors are taking good care of him."

TED: "It's all my fault. If we hadn't fought about my forgetting to clean up the yard, it never would have happened. I made him have a heart attack."

MOM: "Ted, what are you talking about? It's a good thing we got a chance to talk about this. People's hearts don't function well because they have heart *disease.* It's usually an inherited condition. Yeah, Daddy was angry at you and you at him, but you've had lots of these kinds of fights before and he hasn't had a heart attack. I understand you feel guilty about fighting with Dad, but that's another issue. You didn't cause his heart problems."

Competence

Ultimately, as parents, we want our adolescents to feel competent to deal with their own problems. We know that being a full-time parent is a time-limited job and that in order to help our kids, we've got to encourage them to think through a crisis on their own and show them how to develop effective strategies for real-life situations. This means using our skills to help our youngsters build emotional resources *now* that they can bank on *later* in their lives. When we help our adolescents to work out a resolution to a real problem in the real world, we also help them to grow, to become stronger, and to feel hopeful about their future. Hope is particularly important in today's times, when life's demands can seem so overwhelming.

To become effective parents, we need to try to use all four C's when we talk to our adolescents: *compassion, communication, comprehension,* and *competence.* Here's how they would all work together in a real dialogue:

"I know you feel dragged about not making the baseball team." (Compassion)

"It's really hard because you're a good fielder and you don't get a chance to show what you can do because your hitting isn't strong enough." (Communication)

"I think you've been really irritable and unhappy since the team tryouts because you feel upset you didn't make it." (Comprehension)

"You know, when I was in high school, I was rotten at sports. Finally, my father sent me to his best friend to be coached because this guy played pro baseball. Even though I was thin and small, I played much better the next year. Would you be willing to put in the time to improve your hitting and try out again?" (Competence)

In this dialogue, a father is able to understand his son's disappointment in himself without dismissing or diminishing his real feelings. (Who cares? Why are you so upset? Don't let it get to you!) By sharing his own adolescent experiences with defeat, he can also offer his son a model of competence and some hope for the future.

Here's another dialogue that effectively uses the four C's to reach a troubled adolescent:

"You seem sad today, even though it's your birthday." (Compassion)

"It looks like you're thinking about something that's making you unhappy. What's on your mind?" (Communication)

"I wouldn't blame you if you're upset because your dad didn't call you or send you a card. I used to get really upset with him when we were married, too, because he never remembered my birthday or even our anniversary. Let's face it, he's just a bit of a blockhead about things like that." (Comprehension)

"You know, maybe *you* could call *him*. We both know he has a tendency to forget things, even important things. Even though he and I divorced, he's not divorced from you. I know he loves you, even if he screws up sometimes." (Competence)

In this conversation, a mother offers her son a way of thinking about his father that preserves his sense of self by defining his father's personal limitations with compassion and comprehension, enabling her son to begin to feel more competent. This approach permits her son to interrupt his self-blame and to place blame where it belongs—with his thoughtless or self-absorbed father. But it also helps him to reach out to his father, rather than give up.

In this last dialogue, a father uses the four C's to help his daughter understand and manage a difficult friendship:

"I know you want Alicia as a friend but it's probably really hard to face her today after she stood you up yesterday." (Compassion)

"Alicia can be so inconsiderate sometimes. It's no wonder that you get really angry at her." (Communication)

"Maybe you're wondering if it's even worth it to have her as a friend." (Comprehension)

"It's important to recognize who Alicia is, because she may not be able to change, but you can. If you're going to stay friends with her, you can develop a thicker skin, so she doesn't upset you so much." (Competence)

Talking About Tough Topics

Many parents are intimidated by their teenagers. They are reluctant to engage in conversations that could become adversarial. But remember that the tougher the topic (sex, drugs, racism, suicide) the more your adolescent needs you to talk to. Otherwise he's likely to get all his information from his peers, the media, or the street.

It's particularly important to start talking to your preadolescent kids (nine- to eleven-year-olds). At this age risky behavior becomes linked to the forbidden pleasures of adult life. This is when it seems cool to be reckless and when the temptations and excitement of adolescence are just around the corner. Children of this age are already beginning to reject their parents' values, affection, and attention in favor of their peers, and *studies have shown that they are at the greatest risk for drug abuse.* Further, preadolescents who begin to smoke and drink at this early age remain at high risk for more sustained drug abuse later on.

Here's a mom engaging her ten-year-old in a conversation to lay the groundwork for his drug education.

MOM: "You know you're getting old enough for us to be talking about all the different drugs you're likely to hear about or see kids using."

JOEY: "I don't do any drugs, Mom."

MOM: "I know you don't yet, but soon kids will be asking you to drink or smoke marijuana, or maybe even to sniff cocaine or take pills. We want you to really understand that street drugs are not only illegal, they are very, very dangerous! They're not good for your body or for your mind. They can even be poison. Some kids die from bad drugs. We need to know we can trust you to make safe decisions for yourself."

But as your preteen becomes a teen, he may not always listen to what you've told him. When this happens, you'll need to find a way to remind him of your rules without driving him into greater rebellion, or further secrecy.

Here's a mom whose response to her son's behavior is so hysterical and disorganized that he's able to dismiss her observations and ignore her.

MOM: "What's that funny smell in here? That's not marijuana, is it? Oh, my God! I can't believe you'd do this to me [starts sobbing]. Do you realize that smoking marijuana is a criminal act? You could send us all to jail!"

STEVE: "C'mon, Mom, stop crying. I think you're getting really paranoid. I don't know what you're talking about. I had the windows open, so maybe the smell is outside, trees or something, whatever."

Here's another kind of dialogue that is likely to produce more honest results. By limiting her intervention to the issue at hand, this mom is likely to be more *effective.*

MOM: "Stevie, I want to talk to you about something. I've noticed that whenever you have Ali and Jared over, your room always smells like marijuana."

STEVE: "What are you talking about?"

MOM: "C'mon Steve, I'm not a jerk. Even though you open all the windows afterward, I can still smell it."

STEVE: "Ali and Jared were just sharing a joint. I didn't have any."

MOM: "I find that hard to believe, but that's not the issue here. Your father and I have made our position clear about drugs. We don't want you using them, and we forbid them in our home."

STEVE: "I know, I know."

MOM: "If you can't abide by our family's rules when your friends come over, we won't be able to permit you to have friends in our house."

STEVE: "Okay, I hear you!"

Sometimes teenagers pay more attention to you when you're not talking about *them.* Here's how you could jump-start a conversation about marijuana abuse with your adolescent by talking about his *friend,* rather than *him.*

Compassion: This father opens the conversation with an *empathic statement.*

"Nick's mom is really worried about Nicholas. He's been smoking grass a lot, and it's really ruining his life. He used to be a terrific basketball player and he was a very good math student, too, but now he can't concentrate or focus."

Communication: He offers his son more *information* about the event, and *confirms the hard realities* of drug abuse.

"Smoking grass makes you lose your interest and your energy. The more kids smoke it, the less they want to do anything else. Nick's been cutting classes in school, and not coming home at night on time. You know, a lot of kids think because you call it herb, it's natural, but since you smoke it like cigarettes, it causes lung cancer and heart disease, just like cigarettes."

Comprehension/Competence: He uses the conversation to expand his son's *understanding*, and lets his son know there's a *resolution* for this drug problem that offers some *hope for the future*.

"But it's hard to get Nick to listen to his parents because sometimes teenagers think they know everything. Nick's mom is going to try to take Nick to a rehabilitation center for kids who are addicted to drugs. She hopes they'll be able to help Nick to see what he's doing to himself."

If you're using the indirect approach, try to base your narratives on real-life stories about real people that your teenager knows—or if you can't do that, use public figures that he's heard about or seen on TV. That makes it easier for him to get the message. (There'll probably be no shortage of examples!)

Drug abuse isn't the only tough topic parents must address. Here's a dad trying to help his fourteen-year-old son deal directly with racism by leading with *compassion, commu-*

nicating with him, and offering him a chance to *comprehend* the situation and handle it *competently*, rather than resorting to rage or despair.

DAD: "Kareem, run down to the corner and get your mother some lemons."

KAREEM: "Forget it! No way I'm going into that asshole's store. From the moment I walk in there, he's on my butt."

DAD: "He's just an old man who doesn't like teenagers."

KAREEM: "Bullshit! He just thinks I'm a nigger, and all niggers steal. That's what he's thinking when I go in his fuckin' store."

DAD: "I know how you feel. When I was in medical school, I worked in a hospital that was in a really good neighborhood. While I was inside and had that white coat on and my tag that said Dr. Robinson, I felt safe, but the minute I walked outside, I knew that all anybody saw or cared about was my black face. I used to get hassled by the cops all the time."

KAREEM: "What'd you do?"

DAD: "Well, in the beginning I felt like punching their stupid faces, but then I realized that would just be giving them what they wanted, so I became supercalm, and superpolite. I got such a kick out of the look on their faces when they pulled my ID and saw that I was a doctor."

KAREEM: "You can't trust the man. They're all racists!"

DAD: "Just because some whites are ignorant and ugly, Kareem, doesn't mean you have to be. Let's both of us go to buy the lemons, and face that old man down."

Sex isn't an easy topic for parents to confront either. Here's a mom whose relationship with her sixteen-year-old daughter is good enough to encourage confidences. While this mother has her own point of view that she *communicates* to her daughter, she's also trying to let her daughter feel *competent* to make her own decisions.

LUISA: "Mama, you know that I'm the only girl in my class that hasn't had sex?"

MOTHER: "No. So this bothers you?"

LUISA: "Well, it makes me feel like maybe I'm a baby or something, like maybe I'm afraid."

MOTHER: "Are you afraid?"

LUISA: "Well, who wouldn't be with all the diseases there are, and I read an article in the newspaper that said that Latina women were more at risk."

MOTHER: "You're right to be scared of disease; it's a big problem today. But even if there wasn't AIDS, I would still hope you wouldn't sleep with anyone until you're married to him. I think you should love someone before you give yourself to him."

LUISA: "Oh, Mom, that's so old-fashioned!"

MOTHER: "I know, and I know times have changed, but it doesn't sound like you want to have sex with someone because you love him, it sounds like you feel pressured to compete with your friends. That's what worries me."

LUISA: "I don't need to compete with them. I can make up my own mind."

MOTHER: "I'm glad to hear that. I've raised you to think for yourself."

Missing the Boat/Catching It!

Very often dialogue with an adolescent gets distorted because you're only skating on the surface of the conversation and not reaching the depths. It's not unusual to feel like you're always "missing the boat" with your adolescent son or daughter, because very often their conscious communication hides less conscious thoughts and feelings, so what they say is *not* what they mean.

Here's an example of a dialogue between a parent and a teenager where the conversation goes nowhere and nothing goes well:

JONATHAN: "I'm sick. I don't want to go to school tomorrow. Anyway, I hate this school. My old one was better."

MOM: "You're not sick, you're just trying to get out of school. I'm tired of hearing your constant complaining. We've moved; you changed schools. Deal with it!" (*No compassion, no communication, no comprehension,* therefore *no competence* for parent or child.)

This parent is not making use of the four C's. As a result, she cannot comprehend her son's distress and she is not able to help him to competently manage his new life.

Here's another, more effective response to the same situation, where using the four C's leads to more of a sense of competence for everyone.

JONATHAN: "I'm sick. I don't want to go to school tomorrow. Anyway, I hate this school! My old one was better."

MOM: "I know it's been really hard to switch schools. But I don't want you to feel you have to get sick for me to understand how you feel. What do you hate about this school?" (*Compassion, comprehension*)

JONATHAN: "Yesterday, we got back our history test and I got a seventy-two, and I used to be good at history. The teacher's an idiot."

MOM: "I can see why you'd like to just stay home, but then you'd only fall behind more. You're right. Seventy-two isn't great, compared to how you used to do, but it's okay for this school because it's a much tougher curriculum than your last school. You just need time to catch up. Maybe you and I could look over the test and help you figure out your mistakes. What do you think?" (*Communication,* more *compassion,* leading to *competence.*)

Lying: A Different Form of Communication

Of course, conversations with your adolescent can falter and fail for many reasons, but one of the most common reasons conversations with adolescents go nowhere is that what they *say* is often not what they *mean.* In adolescence, your kids begin to lead an extensive internal life that they keep secret from you. Parents often have trouble recognizing that maintaining this secret life is an important normal developmental step for their son or daughter. Not only does it indicate that she is capable of independent thoughts and feelings, but it also signals that she's become capable of keeping these feelings to herself, an important aspect of self-control.

Now, your teenager is as likely to hide things from you (her sexual experiences, her failed chem test, the lipstick she stole) as you are to hide things from her (your disappointment about not getting a raise, your anger at your sister-in-law, your worries about the lump in your breast). This is, of course, a form of "lying," but you don't want to miss its meanings. After all, lying is an important form of communication, too, and like other behaviors, it can be seen to follow a developmental path, becoming more complex and sophisticated, as your son or daughter moves from childhood to adolescence.

The first lies of early childhood (three to six) are often simple *lies of denial* ("I didn't do it!"). Young children will often maintain their complete innocence even in the face of being caught red-handed. ("But I saw you break your sister's doll. I was right there when you twisted its head off.") This is because they are not even aware of the many ways in which they betray themselves—they are not self-conscious yet. They think they can eat chocolate and deny it, oblivious to the telltale stains on their mouths and fingers.

As children develop and become a bit more aware of the ways of the world, they frequently lie about things that they wish were so ("magical lies"), revealing their sense of their own limitations or their attempts to mask vulnerabilities. ("I can swim the whole ocean"; "My brother is so strong he can beat up your whole family.") An older child (seven to nine years old) is also becoming aware enough to avoid adult scrutiny. At this age, *lies of evasion* are quite common. I remember sending my two children in to wash their dirty hands before dinner, only to have them come to the table with filthy arms. ("You said wash your *hands*, Mom, you didn't say *arms*.")

But by early adolescence your child's mind becomes developed enough for real, convincing deceit. Mobilizing her ability to think abstractly, her judgment, her psychological awareness of others' motives and reactions, and using defenses like rationalization, sarcasm, righteous anger, and justifiable action, a teenager can create and maintain elaborate and convincing lies of all kinds. Many of the lies that adolescents tell are intended to protect the newly formed sense of self (*defensive lies*). These lies can be directed at anyone, but they often are offered as replies to parental questions for which there is no "good" answer. ("Did you study for the math test?" "Did you finish all the ice cream?" "Did you hit your sister?") In addition, these sorts of lies can help your adolescent protect her privacy and her secrets. ("Are you smoking?" "Do you have a crush on Colin?" "Did you buy the condoms I found in your room?") Lying to protect another is also common in adolescence, and testifies to the teenager's loyalties to her friends. (Q: "Who was at that party where everyone got drunk?" A: "I didn't know most of the kids." Q: "Who sold you that joint?" A: "I found it in the park in the grass." Q: "Is Janet a virgin?" A: "Mom, do you think my friends are sluts?") And, of course, *inflating lies* that promote an adolescent's status in her social community are also commonplace. ("My boyfriend sent me these gorgeous roses for Valentine's Day." "I got an A in French. What'd you get?" "I hooked up with Gary months ago; he really sweats me.")

Often adolescents lie when they feel that there is no room to tell the truth, or when the truth would be totally unacceptable to their parents. If you've noticed that your teen has been weaving a web of deceit, now's the time to take a careful look at your family life. Have your expectations of your adolescent been too high, and are her lies protecting her from your discovery of her failure to meet those expectations? (Altering or "losing" report cards or test grades fall into this category.) Are your rules and curfews too restrictive and out of "sync" with your teen's peer group? (Lies about lateness, unchaperoned parties, and concocted cover stories for forbidden activities fall into this category.) Is your teenager feeling insecure or desperate? (Stories of nonexistent boyfriends, cheating on tests, and plagiarizing another's work fall into this category of lying.)

And, finally, look at your own behavior, too. Parents bitterly complain that their teenagers betray their trust by lying to them. But adolescents just as frequently complain that their parents also lie and they accuse them of being "hypocrites" or "phonies." These accusations underscore your teenager's newfound sensitivity to moral issues and her newfound need to test her parents' truths. Unfortunately, many teenagers find these parental truths wanting.

Telephone Talk: An Adolescent's Lifeline

Though your teenager may find it hard to communicate with you (and vice versa), she usually has no trouble communicating with her friends. And a great deal of this communication takes place on the telephone. A mother who's just spent two hours waiting for her thirteen-year-old daughter to get off the phone can be exasperated. A father who needs to call his office and finds his son going over the day's basketball game with his buddies can be enraged. Teen telephone talk is often every parent's worst nightmare. The desperation with which teenagers need to contact each other at all hours of the day and night is both bewildering and angering. But to your adolescent, the telephone is her lifeline. To be off the line can mean that both literally and metaphorically she is "out of touch."

And in fact, an adolescent whose phone rarely rings is likely to be a lonely and disconnected adolescent. Popular teenagers often count their success by the number of calls (or beeps) they get in an hour. Every connection carries the message "I like you; I want you; I think about you; I need you." The telephone offers an adolescent constant reassurance that she is not alone or forgotten. As one of my teenage patients put it, "I'm not really me until I can talk to my friends. Then I know I'm there."

Unlike adults, who often see the telephone as an interruption or an intrusion in their lives, adolescents see the telephone as a way to plug into their lives and connect to the emotional, social, and intellectual nourishment they need.

Now, with the Internet (E-mail, America On-Line, etc.) available, the telephone is probably the least of your worries. Through computer technology, your teenager can make hundreds of connections over a weekend, talking, dating, and even having "cybersex" with others similarly inclined ("cybersluts" and "cyberstuds"). The lack of community control over these new sources of stimulation (many of them pornographic) has increased the need for parental discretion. Remember it's not a punishment to send your teenager to her room if she connects with fifteen sympathetic souls on "Teen Chat"!

Interestingly, both the telephone and the Internet can also function to help a teenager disconnect, by keeping others at a manageable distance. Telephone talk and computer chat can provide an early adolescent with a safe way to get relationships started with fewer expectations and dangers than face-to-face contact would produce. Both the telephone and the computer at this time in your teenager's life enable her to "reach out and touch someone" without its becoming a "hands-on" experience. It also enables her to delay and avoid encounters for which she is not yet prepared.

Good plain talk remains in adolescence, as it was in childhood, one of your most powerful tools as a parent—a tool that will help you recognize, acknowledge, and support your son or daughter. But to figure out what's going on, you need to know a bit more about your adolescent's inner world. That's where the five basic fears (the topic of the next chapter) will help you. These five basic fears acquire special meanings in adolescence; understanding them can give you the key to your teenager's troubles.

CHAPTER 5

The Five Basic Fears in Adolescence

An Ordinary Child's Life/ An Ordinary Adolescent's Life

Fear is essential to our lives. It reflects the power of our senses, our consciousness, our intelligence, and our imagination. Being afraid is also crucial to our survival, because it keeps us alert. Our fears tell us that what we are doing, or thinking about doing, could be dangerous. Fear teaches us to *think* before we *act*.

Young children are afraid of the world with good reason. No animal on earth is as helpless for as long a period of time as a human baby. It cannot walk; it cannot talk; it cannot feed itself. It is wholly dependent on the care of an interested and devoted adult for its survival, and remains more or less dependent on that adult for many years. Children's fears are shaped by children's lives. Being left in the care of strangers, seeing blood ooze out of a tiny cut, losing consciousness while falling asleep, seeing giant shadows moving in the dark are things that young children fear—and rightly so, since all of these warning signs could indicate a more serious danger. A young child cannot yet understand that Mommy will soon return, or that bleeding will stop, or that he will wake up alive and conscious in the morning, or that nothing fearful lurks in the dark. The child's mind is still developing, the child's body is small and vulnerable, and the child's imagination is easily stirred.

In addition, a young child has an undeveloped sense of time and space, of cause and effect, and of action and consequence. He does not understand how long two hours are, or how far away California is. He thinks that Daddy divorced Mommy because he wet the bed, or that the new baby got sick because he wished it would. Young children must be taught not to touch a flame, so they won't get burned, and that they cannot lean out of a window because they'll fall.

At first, young children see their parents as masters of their destiny. They believe that their parents can control all the events of their life, and this is reassuring. But quickly they learn otherwise. It frightens children to learn that accidents, disease, and death fall outside of their control and yours; it frightens parents, too. We must accept the fact that there will be many problems we cannot solve for our children. We can't stop a child's friend from getting leukemia; we can't keep a grandfather from dying; we can't stop a teacher from being mugged or a house from being burglarized or a plane from crashing. Some fears and anxieties we have may never go away, they just ebb and flow throughout our lives—like fears of illness and death. Some fears and anxieties help alert us to experiences that could be dangerous, like a fear of the dark or a fear of heights. And some fears and anxieties can even be helpful, like the anxiety that helps an actor prepare for a role, or a child prepare for a test.

Throughout the course of our lives, we may call our fears by many names: worry, nervousness, apprehension, anxiety, dread, horror, terror, panic. But I believe that five basic fears actually underlie many of our feelings: *fear of the unknown, fear of being alone, fear about the body, fear of the voice of conscience,* and *fear about the self.* Our capacity to feel these fears is a vital part of understanding ourselves and living in our world. In this respect, fear can be seen as a developmental accomplishment. Indeed, these five basic fears ordinarily appear in a developmental sequence, with fears of the unknown dominating infancy, fears of being alone and fears about the body emerging as the child begins to separate from the mother's orbit (two to five years), fears of the voice of conscience occurring as the child internalizes parental and social prohibitions (six to eight years), and fears about the self evolving as the personality of the child crystallizes and he moves on toward adolescence (nine plus).

Often teenagers appear to be afraid of things you can't understand, and *not* afraid of things you feel they should be cautious about. For instance, they no longer seem to be afraid of you (they dismiss or undermine your authority), they're rarely afraid of their teachers (they ignore assignments and blow off tests), and they don't even seem to be afraid of real-life experiences that are risky and terrifying (illegal drugs, drinking and driving, and sexuality that could result in disease or death).

In fact, sometimes it seems as if adolescents go out of their way to deny and defy all of the five basic fears I've described. Why doesn't your daughter's fear of the unknown, for instance, stop her from experimenting with LSD? If your adolescent son is afraid of being alone, and wants friends, why does he spend so much time isolated in his room? Why don't normal fears about her body stop your daughter from becoming bulimic and vomiting up her food, or your son from getting tattooed or piercing his lip? What's become of the voice of conscience that would have helped your teenager know it was wrong to steal your credit card? And why don't fears about the self and what others will think of them inhibit adolescents' self-destructive and antisocial behaviors?

Children's fears are visible. They balk at anything strange; they actively protest when we leave them; they cry when they get hurt; they easily betray their guilt and they openly express their worries about the way that other people perceive them. ("Mommy, Kenny said I was a butthead!") The thoughts and feelings of your adolescents are not so visible. In fact, teenagers spend a lot of time and energy hiding—protecting their inner world from adult scrutiny. But don't be misled. Teenagers may put up a good front, but appearances are particularly deceptive in adolescence. Adolescent fears are often deeply hidden or denied. This makes knowing your adolescent's true state of mind extremely difficult. Often teenagers appear heartless and insensitive to you, but actually, this is more likely their only defense against their fears, anxieties, and vulnerabilities.

If you were to have access to your adolescent's inner world, you'd see that this is in fact a time when the five basic fears that we traced in childhood continue to sharpen and intensify. After all, adolescence itself, with its tumultuous physical and psychological changes, is one great *unknown* challenge; your adolescent's desperate need to be a part of the right group testifies to his *fear of being alone*; *fears about the body* and *fears about the self* fuel your teen's absorption with "bad hair" days; and the constant adolescent preoccupation with bending or breaking rules and regulations (defying curfews, blowing off homework, drinking) attests to their need to explore the limits of their own *conscience* (even if they seem to be contemptuous of yours!). While the five basic fears are *formed* in childhood, they are *transformed* in adolescence, and continue to motivate your adolescent's attitudes and behavior.

But keep in mind that while all adolescents experience these fears, the ways in which they experience them are determined by their individual personalities and temperaments. Some teenagers seem to have heightened appetites for life. They take big bites of experience, and relish unexpected adventures. These teenagers embrace change and confront their fears. This makes them appear bold and even reckless. Other teens have small appetites. They chew their experiences slowly and swallow carefully. They remain wary and try to protect themselves. They may appear shy or even shrink from others. These teenagers resist change and are cautioned by their fears.

As a parent, you need to know what your particular adolescent can manage, and you need to remain alert to the signs that tell you when he's in over his head and needs your help. Young adolescents in particular (thirteen to fifteen) often have unexpressed yearnings for their parents to set limits on their risky behavior. It's a whole lot easier for them to blame *you* ("My dad's a real hard-ass about curfews" or "My mom will lock me in my room if she smells weed on my clothes") rather than face their peers and their own anxieties ("This party is getting too wild; I'm going home") or ("I'm afraid of smoking weed"). Let's take a closer look at some of the specific meanings of the five basic fears in adolescence.

Fears of the Unknown

Fears of the unknown are some of our deepest and most primitive fears. When we are young, we rely on the familiar in order to feel safe—familiar smells, familiar food, familiar voices. Anything unfamiliar—a stranger's voice, a new restaurant, a strange house—can fill a child with fear. But adolescence is filled with unfamiliar feelings, unfamiliar thoughts, and unfamiliar challenges. Facing and mastering all of these new experiences is very much a part of these years and contributes to the high degree of anxiety adolescents often feel.

Imagine if you woke up one morning and the body you had always known and depended on was transformed into something strange and disturbing. Your shoes don't fit; your nose and hands and feet are larger than you remembered them; your slim torso has developed fatty deposits. Hair has begun to grow in places where your skin had always been smooth, and your body even begins to smell different, not at all like your usual self. This would be bad enough, but beyond these bodily changes, there are changes in your mind as well. Some days you feel overwhelmingly sad, for no apparent reason, and then just as quickly elated. At times you feel sleepy and enervated or, alternately, you become nervy and restless. And on top of all that, your perceptions of other people seem to have undergone a strange shift as well. Your mom, who had always been your pal, seems annoying and even inane, while your dad, whom you used to respect, seems dull and ordinary. "Invasion of the Body Snatchers," right? No, just ordinary adolescence. Maybe it's no accident that many adolescents love science fiction films about aliens. Adolescents strongly identify with the idea of being possessed and occupied. Strange, alien ideas are, indeed, entering their minds without warning, and they often feel terribly alone and alien in a world that used to feel familiar.

Here's a family in the throes of dealing with the mysterious changes that adolescence has wrought in their daughter. She has confronted her fears of the unknown and is taking big bites of experience. Her parents are afraid of what lies ahead.

Kathleen sat in a chair far away from her parents, who shared the sofa in my office. Ms. Mahoney spoke first, tears beginning to fill her eyes even before the words came out. "I don't understand what's happening to Kathy," she said softly. "She used to be the sweetest, most responsible girl— a great big sister to her three younger brothers, a good student at school, a soloist in our church choir. But now, she's like a stranger, living in our house. She's barely civil, her grades are falling, and she won't join us in any family activities, including going to church. And what's worse is that she and her dad are always at each other's throats. They used to get along really well. They'd go fishing together, or we'd all go camping as a family. Now it's like living in a war zone. She's rude and he's angry or he's resentful and she's sullen. I know everyone says it's because she's fourteen and it's a difficult age, but I can't take it anymore."

Mr. Mahoney and Kathleen pointedly avoided looking at each other. He began to speak while Kathleen stared out the window. His voice was filled with anger. "Her mother is constantly making excuses for her, and trying to smooth things over, but the fact is, she's just an ungrateful little bitch. I worked hard to send her to a fancy school so she'd get a good education, and now, I wouldn't be surprised if they don't let her come back next year. All she's interested in are her friends, her clothes, her music, and herself. She doesn't give a damn about anyone else. She's breaking her mother's heart."

"Kathleen," I say, "I've heard from your mom, who sounds exhausted, and I've heard from your dad, who sounds pretty angry, but I really need to hear your side of the story. Do you think you could tell us how all of this feels for you?" "No one cares how I feel in this family," Kathleen replies. "I have feelings, too, you know." "I bet you do, and this is a good place to let your parents know about them." "They don't give a fuck about me," Kathleen replies. "Shut your filthy mouth," her father shouts. "You see what I mean?" Kathleen states. "You see how you can't even have an honest conversation with them? It's all for show. What will the neighbors think, if you raise your voice? What will Father O'Brien think, if you drop out of choir? What will your teachers think, if you flunk your finals? How will you get into a good college if you keep on with your bad behavior? Who would want to marry such a bad girl? It's all about them; it's not about me." Kathleen bit her lip to stop herself from crying.

"This is very important," I say. "Kathleen is letting you know that she doesn't really believe that you're worried about her and her life. She feels you're just worried about being embarrassed in front of your friends and your community. Kathleen, suppose your parents *were* really worried. How would they show that to you?" "They'd stop judging everything I do and see it from my side. My friends are bad, the music I like is bad, my taste in clothes is bad, using makeup is bad, getting my ears double-pierced is bad, dyeing my hair is bad, going to parties is bad. They're still treating me like a little goody-goody kid. I was a nerd then, and I'm not now. I'm so much happier. Why can't they understand that?" I say, "You want your parents to be able to recognize that you're not the little girl you used to be. You're something new. I can see you feel pretty mad at them, but sometimes, I bet you also feel pretty sad. It also sounds like you feel alone in your family. I think there are a whole lot of misunderstandings here that need to be worked out. One big misunderstanding is that now you're a teenager, and I'm not sure anyone has really come to terms with that."

While the Mahoneys may feel as if their beloved daughter has gone bewilderingly insane, what they're really facing are some of the normal changes of adolescence. Their daughter,

Kathleen, has a new task to master; she must begin to dismantle the dependence and attachment she felt for her parents, and prepare herself eventually to make her way in the world without them. To do this, she is trying to diminish their influence over her, at the same time that she begins to develop a new sense of self, a self no longer defined by what her parents expect of her. Her childhood self wanted to be "good," but her new adolescent self is trying to be "cool."

Understandably, Kathleen's parents are having a hard time keeping up with the changes in Kathleen. They're fighting her every step of the way—constantly offering their criticism (which is still powerful enough to upset their daughter) of her attitudes, her friends, and her life. The more they criticize, the harder Kathleen pulls away from them, and the harder she pulls away from them, the more they criticize. At this point in the vicious cycle that's set in motion, everyone feels bitter, hostile, and depleted by the constant struggle.

Yet things look a whole lot worse than they really are. Kathleen's grades have only dropped from honor roll to B's, she's still doing her homework, and she's not failing any of her subjects. Her friends, though no longer confined to her church community, are still pretty well-functioning kids—not the druggies or dropouts her parents fear—and Kathleen still cares about both of her parents—enough to speak up and tell them what she thinks. Kathleen and her parents have hit some rocky times, but they haven't crashed yet.

Fears of Being Alone

When you were a child, being left alone, without your parents' love and support, was one of your most vivid fears. Young children will do almost anything to try to stay near their parents, as if they somehow realize how vulnerable they really are without them. But adolescence is the time in your child's life when he must come to terms with living without you, so that he can eventually make a life apart from yours. As your adolescent loosens his ties to you, an emotional void opens up. Who will replace you? Who will want to be with him? Who will love and cherish him? Will he be rejected and (most frightening of all) *alone*? Before, his worst fear was to be left without *you*. Now his most painful fear is that he'll be left without any *friends*. That's why your adolescent's need for friends seems so desperate. This new fear dominates a great deal of your adolescent's emotional life, and taking steps to ward off this fear dominates much of your adolescent's social life. Sometimes you may get exasperated, as you witness your teen's repeated attempts to be accepted. The phone calls that last for hours, the Spanish notebook filled with notes to friends rather than notes about Spanish; the insistence on staying home on weekends to be with his friends instead of spending the weekends going on trips with the family. Your adolescent's experiences may also fill *you* with anxiety, as you remember your own attempts to join the right crowd; or fill you with dread, as you recall your own humiliating social experiences; or fill you with apprehension, as you worry about to what lengths your adolescent will go to secure his social standing. (Will he do crack to be cool? Is she having sex with boys so they'll like her?)

Remember that an adolescent's social life is no longer about "works and plays well with others," it's about his emotional survival. As he separates from you, he's left in psychological limbo; he must have a circle of friends (or even just one good friend) to help him make this all-important transition. Fears of being alone can dismantle his strength, erode his confidence, and undermine his sense of self. Nothing can devastate your son or daughter more quickly than rejection by their peers. *In adolescence, acceptance is all—aloneness equals anxiety.* Here's a family struggling to understand this second basic fear in their preadolescent daughter.

Amy, twelve, sat quietly on my rocking chair, her face hidden by her curtain of hair, her body stolid and still. Her slim, muscular mother sat across from her, restless and talkative, while Amy remained silent. "I'm at my wits' end," her mom exclaimed. "Amy has no friends, she refuses to join any clubs at school or participate in sports. All she does is eat junk food and roam around in her room. She's become a real loner. She listens to all this New Age music, and reads these weird books on astrology. She's gained fifteen pounds in six months and she was such an active kid—a tomboy like me, really. Her dad and I are divorced and he lives in another town, and coaches a soccer team. Amy used to love going to the games with him. Now she refuses. What's happened to her?"

"Your mom sounds pretty confused, Amy. It sounds like there have been some important changes in your life." Amy raises her eyes to look at me, but doesn't respond. "It sounds like you've made some new decisions about how you want to spend your time. Can you tell me a little about them?" "It's no big deal," Amy mumbles. "Why doesn't everyone leave me alone?" "I can see that I'm getting on your nerves with my questions, but I don't know you, and I'm really trying to figure it out. What about this friends thing? Has that been the way you've felt for a long time, or is hanging out alone something new?" Amy is silent, but her mother answers for her.

"Amy always had a best friend, Marcia, but this year, Marcia's father took a job in Seattle and the family moved, and since then Amy's been in a funk." "Oh, I see," I state. "There's nothing harder than having to separate from your best friend, and the year before you would have graduated together from eighth grade, too. What a tough break!" I say to Amy, who raises her head a bit higher now to meet my gaze. "When you've been best friends with someone for so many years, it must feel like no one could ever replace them." "No one can," Amy says with feeling. "Marcia and me were like sisters; we could even tell just what the other one was thinking without saying anything." "Were you born under the same sign?" I ask (remembering her interest in astrology books). "How did you know that?" Amy responds excitedly. "We were both Gemini, you see. We weren't only friends; we were really twins." Amy now perks up as she launches into a detailed description of her astrological sign and its effects on her friendship with Marcia, while her mother rolls her eyes and impatiently taps her feet.

Amy's mother doesn't understand that her daughter is actually in mourning for her lost friend, and like all mourners, she's depressed. She has lost interest in her environment; she's eating too much, she feels enervated and depleted, and most important, she feels totally alone. While her mother is sensitive enough to make the connection between Amy's retreat from her life and her best friend's move to Seattle, she is not aware of the particular contribution that the developmental tasks of early adolescence play in Amy's reactions, nor is she aware of the importance of the second basic fear. Amy's overeating, her physical inertia, her loss of interest in activities, and even the diminution of her attachment to her father all reflect her struggle to come to terms with the claims of adolescent development.

Just at the time when Amy would have used her connection to her friends to help her bridge the gap between her parents' world and the outside world, she's lost the one person on whom she depended. She feels stuck between childhood and adolescence—unwilling to go forward and unable to go back. She's already begun distancing herself from her parents (even her beloved father), but there's no one to replace them. From her mother's point of view, there are plenty of fish in the sea, but from Amy's point of view, only one of those fish will do, and it's already swum away. The more her mother diminishes the importance of her tie to Marcia, the more Amy will hold on to her grief; the more her mother urges her on to the future, the more Amy is likely to cling to her past. Amy's fear of being alone is fast becoming a self-fulfilling prophecy.

But once again, though Amy's development is stymied at this point, there are several signs that indicate that she has not entirely shut down. For one thing, in her interest in astrology we can see her attempt to continue to work out the meanings of the events that have happened to her, and to try to take charge of her fate. Her turning to junk food indicates that she is still trying to comfort herself rather than to punish herself, for example, by trying to eat. And indeed, Amy's profound reactions to her loss of Marcia confirm that she has a well-developed capacity for deep feeling, which she will eventually be able to offer to other friends in her life.

Amy is not yet ready to take her chances on new relationships. She needs to be permitted to mourn, and to begin to loosen her ties to her old friend. With better understanding of her behavior, her mom will be able to be less critical of and more empathic with Amy's plight, and with more empathy and encouragement, Amy is likely to begin to address her fears and reach out to the world around her to build a new network.

Fears About the Body

Even if your child has been able to negotiate the years of childhood relatively smoothly, as he nears adolescence the bodily transformations of puberty will inevitably heighten his anxieties, exposing him to a new level of fearfulness. ("Am I normal? Am I ugly? Why is my penis so small? Will I ever get taller?")

Adolescents react to the changes in their bodies with widely variable reactions. Some see the alterations of their bodies as a necessary nuisance; others view them as a visible betrayal of their previous selves. Some adolescents are proud and excited, welcoming these signs of change, while others view them with anxiety and dread, or even repulsion. Never before and never again will your body rule in quite the way it does in adolescence. This means that bodily fears will never be as heightened as they are now.

It is easy to observe how teenagers are tyrannized by their changing bodies—an unexpected zit, frizzy hair, freckles, glasses, the wrong nose, skinny arms, a fat butt—all can feel like a death sentence to a teenager, who believes that confidence and self-assurance depend on his appearance. Sadly, at the very time when your teen feels the least comfortable with his body, he depends on it the most. *In adolescence, how you look defines who you are.* This idea can be confirmed by just a cursory glance at the halls in any high school in our country. Even an out-of-touch adult doesn't need a scoreboard to separate the "nerds" from the "jocks," the "preppies" from the "druggies," the "skaters" from the "burnouts." Each group has its own look and style, as distinctive as a Chanel suit, tennis whites, or the uniforms of the New York Mets.

In their pursuit of the perfect body, teenage boys are willing to break their health with hormone shots, while adolescent girls are willing to vomit or starve themselves. Bodily self-denigration is typical of all teens. *It is virtually impossible ever to hear teenagers state that they are completely content with how they look.* A beautiful girl will complain about the way her hipbones protrude; a truly handsome boy will be obsessed by his shaggy eyebrows. Adolescents let us know about their bodily terrors all the time—in their exaggerated, irrational responses to what we feel are small, virtually undetectable changes in their appearance. We are often angered by their self-absorption, and worried by their loss of perspective. We find it exasperating that an ordinary pimple can keep a teenager miserable for days, or that a bad haircut can cause him to cut school. We need to hold on to our perspective to survive these years. A good sense of humor helps too—and a good memory! (Remember when you constantly chewed gum to make sure your breath wouldn't offend?)

Given this obsession with their bodies, it seems ironic that some adolescents seem to save very little of their energy for taking good care of themselves. Cleanliness is not always next to godliness with adolescents, nor does filling their bodies full of alcohol, nicotine, or drugs seem to faze them. Adolescents are capable of living with all sorts of inconsistencies— your daughter, who's a vegetarian, may smoke two packs of cigarettes a day. Your son, who's on the track team, may still drink a six-pack every weekend night. While adolescents are preoccupied with their bodies, their preoccupations are idiosyncratic and often irrational, obliterating crucial connections between their thoughts and their actions. (An adolescent may believe smoking nicotine is bad for the lungs but smoking marijuana is okay.)

Pubertal changes are not the only reasons that bodily fears are intensified in adolescence. Remember that the purpose of all these bodily changes is to enable your child to engage in mature genital sexuality. This means that fantasies and desires that were previously limited by your child's sexual immaturity can now be enacted and fulfilled. These fantasies about sexuality can be frightening, making an adolescent wish that he could retreat back to childhood, and not have to deal with the challenges and choices that lie ahead.

Anthony was a handsome fifteen-year-old boy whose features were blurred by excess weight. He was accompanied to my office by his mother and grandmother, both of whom fussed over him and touched him repeatedly. Anthony seemed content, and basked in their attentions. A bland, phlegmatic boy, he answered questions politely, but volunteered little.

Despite the fact that Anthony could easily be described as obese, his mother referred to him as slightly overweight, and indicated that she was only willing to bring him for help because their family doctor was worried about Anthony's high cholesterol levels. Since his father had died of a massive heart attack when he was only forty-seven years old, both women were preoccupied with Anthony's health. They lived in constant terror of his dying an early death and discussed their fears quite openly with each other in my office, as if Anthony weren't there.

Anthony himself seemed unusually serene. When asked about his life, he talked about visits and trips he had taken with his mother and grandmother, and his large extended family. He made many observations about his favorite restaurants, and offered his comparative criticism of meals he had consumed. Neither boyfriends nor girlfriends, nor school, sports, personal interests, or hobbies figured in his conversations.

Although Anthony was already in the middle of adolescence, he did not appear to have addressed, let alone mastered, any of the ordinary adolescent developmental tasks; he had not separated from his ties to his family; he did not appear to have formed any new attachments; his sexual identity seemed to be more babyish than boyish; he gave no evidence of forming any independent ideas or ideals (except in relation to food, where a critical voice was forming); and his character was not yet autonomously consolidated. Further, Anthony's lack of separation from his mother (and grandmother) was matched by their inability to let him go. Having lost a husband and son, respectively, they were both determined to keep Anthony close to home.

Anthony's obesity then served a dual purpose: It kept him locked in childhood, "spoon fed" by his mom and grandma, unable even to take "baby steps" away from them, and his "baby fat" enabled him to ward off the sexual challenges of adolescence. Unfortunately, Anthony's defensive retreat was successful, as indeed, an obese adolescent soon becomes an object of *pity* or *scorn* among his peers, rather than an object of *desire*. Anthony had great difficulty relating to boys his own age, whom he feared and envied, and he had virtually given up on the possibility that any girl his age would find him attractive.

Fears of the Voice of Conscience

Conscience must be taught by parents and learned by kids. In fact, your child's conscience is really an internalized version of your own voice. When this "voice" is properly embedded in the structure of your child's character, he will *not* do things that you would disapprove of—even in your absence. A firmly embedded conscience will enable your child to differentiate right from wrong, no matter who he's with or what he's doing.

But in adolescence, along with all the other changes we've been discussing, your son or daughter's conscience is also changing. In adolescence, your teen begins to live a life apart from your influence and your jurisdiction, and he begins to make his own mistakes and (you hope) to learn from them.

It's hard for parents to let their teenagers take risks, to fumble and fail, because the stakes in adolescence seem so high. Risk taking is scary for all of us, but risk-taking behavior in adolescence is particularly terrifying for parents. It's hard to stay calm and steady when your son comes home stoned, two hours late from a party, or your daughter tells you she had unprotected sex with a boy she met on a school trip to Washington. It's hard to trust the judgment of an adolescent who studies for his midterms the night before the exam, or one who hitchhikes home from the movies. And a teenager's poor decisions can have grave consequences. If that college application never gets filled out, your son can't go to college; if your daughter steals a jacket and gets caught, she's liable for prosecution; if he has unprotected sex, he can contract HIV; and if she uses "ecstasy," she can die. It's hard to let your teenager make the choice to listen to his conscience— or not.

Your fears are also intensified because in childhood, you were able to bolster and support your child's conscience by your *presence*, but now, you won't be there to help him make these decisions. In fact, you may not even know what moral dilemmas your adolescent faces from day to day. (Is it okay to drink, even though I'm underage? Is it all right to sneak into a club that doesn't admit minors? Is it a big deal to try coke? Should I have sex with someone I really, really like, or should I wait?)

In some teens, the voice of conscience continues to ring loud and clear; in others the voice of conscience becomes undependable and unpredictable; and for a few, the voice appears stilled and silent in the face of the varied temptations of adolescent life. These last are the adolescents we worry about the most.

The voice of conscience is regulated through an unpleasant but essential feeling we call *guilt*. Guilt has gotten a bad name in our free-wheeling, liberated society. But guilt is actually one of the most important of the civilizing emotions. It permits us to take into account the thoughts and feelings of others; it enables us to stop short of cruelty and aggression; it encourages us to sacrifice our own interests for another.

In adolescence, for a while, guilt gets reexamined and is sometimes even relinquished. Now an adolescent may feel defiant, or excited, or even triumphant about a misdeed, where he once felt worried or ashamed. Now your adolescent may no longer feel upset when he ignores his homework, or steals money from a friend's locker, or sells LSD. In adolescence, the voice of conscience is broadened to include different, and even contradicting, voices, voices that call him away from the path you've laid out for him.

Using his or her childhood conscience as a foundation, your son or daughter must now build a new, flexible structure that is more consistent with the standards and values of their peers. For some adolescents, this new structure will still greatly resemble the dimensions of the old structure. His friends will be chosen from among those girls and boys who enable him to continue to feel supported in his already established beliefs. But for others, adolescence will create opportunities for a revision or even a rebellion against parental standards and values, and this new moral structure will have a new shape, supported by a new set of peers.

There can be surprising reversals as our adolescents struggle to establish their own new sense of right or wrong. My neighbors, both extremely liberal attorneys with a passionate devotion to civil rights, were surprised when their adolescent son expressed his more conservative ideas about crime and punishment, including his belief in the death penalty. The owner of a neighborhood restaurant, a man of deeply conservative beliefs, was equally shocked when his teenage children veered sharply to the left, joining a political commune and devoting themselves to the voter registration of Caribbean minorities.

And then, to make things even more complicated, different children in the same family can come up with different solutions to their adolescent moral dilemma. This was the case in a family I knew where one daughter grew up to become a doctor who specialized in performing low-cost abortions, while her brother directed a pro-life political organization.

In adolescence, more than at any other time in life, your child's conscience is linked to his sense of peer allegiance. This is why adolescent boys make such good soldiers. Their sense of what's right and wrong can be easily submerged in the standards of the group. This is also why adolescents are so susceptible to cults and gangs. Again, their need to belong, to replace the power of their parents with the power of their peers, and their wish to believe in something—their country, their religion, their friends—leaves them susceptible to the agenda of others.

Jed, sixteen, had been referred to me because he had been expelled by his private school for writing graffiti all over the gym. He entered my office and slouched down in the chair, glaring. His jeans, high-top sneakers, and big shirt all proclaimed his interest in belonging to the right crowd. One sleeve was rolled up, displaying a tattoo of a snake that encircled his wrist. When I commented on it, he told me it was his own design, with some pride. The snake, he noted, was silent, but quick and deadly. I said that it sounded as if he, too, liked to lie low, without revealing his plans to anyone, but I was concerned about the fact that his plans hadn't gone so well this time. "What are you going to do now?" I asked. "I don't give a shit," Jed said. "I'd rather go to public school than to that faggot school anyway."

Jed's father was the manager of a large sporting goods store; his mother was a partner in a local gift shop. Both parents were practical and hardworking. Jed was the middle child of three sons. The mother spoke proudly of the eldest son. He had been a good student, was quiet and disciplined, and was now studying to be an engineer at a good college. The father spoke proudly of their youngest son, who was a good athlete and worked with him at the store, helping out. Neither spoke of Jed's strengths. Instead, they gave an account of his constant problems. Since he'd been about nine or ten, he was always in trouble, always pushing the limits, always breaking the rules. They didn't know how to handle his bad behavior. He was defiant in school, he cut corners with his homework, and he'd gotten a tattoo, expressly against their wishes. They had no idea what to do with him now that he was expelled. They were very troubled by his inability to know the difference between what's right and what's wrong. They felt that their family life had always emphasized the importance of fair play, of playing by the rules, and of good sportsmanship. The other two boys seemed inherently to abide by their moral standards, but Jed either couldn't or wouldn't. He had only two interests—his friends and graffiti. They were sick and tired of seeing his tag all over the neighborhood. You could always tell his work because it was elaborate and colorful.

Jed's parents (and Jed) are struggling, as he begins to revise the old dictates of his conscience, in light of his new teenage standards and expectations of himself. In Jed's new adolescent world, letting the world know who you are (through choosing the right tattoo, or spray-painting his "tag") is more important than leaving other people's property alone. Jed has adjusted his conscience accordingly.

One of the most painful parts of being the parent of an adolescent is that you can no longer protect your kids from the consequences of their own actions. In Jed's case, expulsion from his private school was a crisis. But a crisis is also an opportunity for change. This event compelled both Jed and his family to look at his life in a new way. They began to recognize that Jed's interests in graffiti might be put to some other less destructive uses. It opened up the possibility of sending Jed to a technical high school specializing in graphic and commercial art. In this school, surrounded by other kids who respected his artistic talents, Jed's sense of himself gradually improved, his need to engage in antisocial acts decreased, and his family began to make room for his individuality, and accept him in more positive ways.

Fears About the Self

While fears about the unknown, being alone, the body, and the voice of conscience all trouble your adolescent, the most pressing and powerful fear of all is his fear about his sense of self. This is because the major developmental task in adolescence is the consolidation of a sense of self (what the psychoanalyst Max Gitelson has called "character synthesis"). We are familiar through books and films with this idea of an adolescent who needs to "find himself." This is a particularly apt phrase because, in effect, your adolescent *has* lost a part of himself (his childhood sense of self) and he now needs to "find" a new part of himself (an adolescent part) to replace it. The self has accumulated in layers over all the years that your child has lived—and even before his birth, because the bottom layer is your child's genetic inheritance, his biological beginnings. We know that children inherit certain temperamental characteristics that they bring with them into the world. There are calm, placid babies; restless, sensitive babies; alert, active babies. As parents react and respond to their baby's temperament, they shape and are shaped by their baby's emerging personality. This, then, becomes the next layer of the self: the interactive experiences of parent and child. Your baby begins to perform for your approval and applause. He begins to display his characteristic behaviors in consistent ways and you can soon tell when your baby is "acting like himself" and when he's "not himself."

This loss of the old self is what turns a bold child into a shy adolescent, or a reasonable child into a stubborn adolescent, or a quiet child into a defiant adolescent. Of course, because of the physical changes of puberty, some of this new self will be a sexual self (with all of the excitement and anxiety that sex entails), but some of your adolescent's emergent sense of self will be about other equally important aspects of his identity. How he wishes to be perceived by others, what he likes to do with his time, what skills and talents he believes he has, what kind of a person he wants to be, and what he wants to do with his life are all adolescent challenges to be met and mastered.

During childhood and through adolescence, we encourage our children to taste from the extensive banquet we set out for them—piano lessons, Little League, soccer, basketball, cooking, orchestra, gymnastics—the menu seems unlimited. But by the end of adolescence, your teenager must begin to narrow these options, taking advantage of some and letting go of others. The more options, the more opportunities, the more chances your teenager has to find his life's work and his life's partner. The less options—by virtue of physical poverty or psychological poverty, by virtue of timing and temperament—the less likely it is that your adolescent will easily find his life's work or his life's partner. But since chance and destiny play such an important role in our lives, we can never predict the future. Some adolescents, with what appear to be very limited opportunities in life, will make sound and successful choices for the future, while others, who seemingly have the world at their feet, appear to throw their lives away. Adolescents with no money can be blessed with courage and conviction, while those with unlimited funds can be lazy and unmotivated. Happiness may be one child's lot, while success may be another's; adventure may call out to a third, while a fourth is blessed with security. But regardless of what happens, by the time your child leaves adolescence, whether he leaves it unwisely or well, he must choose an adult path. For better or for worse, he must consolidate a sense of self.

Seth is thirteen. His parents are frantic. Since he has been three years old, Seth has been training to take his place on the Olympic swimming team. Now, with hundreds of swimming trophies behind him, Seth wants to quit.

Kira, fourteen, was an A student her first year at her local high school, and has now begun to cut classes during the week, neglecting to complete her homework. Though she has an 11:00 p.m. curfew, she frequently stays out until 1:00 or 2:00 in the morning.

Rebecca, fifteen, raised in an observant Jewish family, has

run away, and is now living in an ashram run by a group of Indian mystics. She has changed her name to Jasmine, works in the garden raising the vegetables that the community eats, and refuses to return home.

Elaine, sixteen, was always good at science and planned to go on and become a pharmacist, but now she's discovered she's pregnant. She wants to leave high school, get her GED, marry her boyfriend, and become a full-time mom.

Marla, seventeen, never looks the same from one day to the next. One day she'll wear her hair down in braids and look like a Wisconsin farm girl. The next day she's in a miniskirt and a tight T-shirt. One week she's going to be a nurse; the next, she decides she should be a photographer.

Roberto, eighteen, was slated for a college scholarship to a prestigious technical institute. During his senior year, he got the lead in his high school musical, and now he wants to take a year off and try his hand at acting.

Andrew, nineteen, can take apart a car and put it back together again. He graduated from high school last June and joined his uncle's business as a mechanic, but now he wants to go to Germany as a drummer in a rock band.

All of these adolescents are struggling with their sense of self. Some are challenging the paths their parents have set for them, others are forging new trails in areas that they have never before explored, and a few are floundering, not knowing where to go or what to do next. These are ordinary adolescent stories. While these adolescents appear to have lost their way, many are actually in the process of "finding themselves," searching for that sense of self that we have been noting is so crucial to the resolution of adolescence. By adolescence, the self is anchored in a wide array of behaviors that characterize your teenager's way of being in the world. With the emergence of a continuous sense of self, *self-esteem* (good feelings about the self), *self-doubt* (uncertain feelings about the self), and *self-contempt* (bad feelings about the self) are all possible. Self-esteem regulation—the ability to keep up good feelings about yourself even when bad things are happening to you—now becomes a crucial developmental objective. When your teenager's good feelings are compromised—by striking out at a ball game, for example, or failing a spelling test, or fighting with his best friend—fears about the self get raised. "I'm such a loser," he may think; "Boy, am I dumb"; or "Nobody likes me."

As a parent, it's hard for you to stay still in the face of all this psychic activity. It's your natural impulse to want to rush in, repair all the damage you can see, and restore your teenager to what you feel is his rightful place in the sun. But this is the time to recognize that what *you* want for your youngster may not necessarily be what *he* wants for himself. I vividly recall a conversation with one of my teenagers during a more difficult time in his adolescence, when I told him that all I wanted was for him to be happy. "You see, Mom," he replied, "that's what I mean. What makes you so convinced that happiness is even a goal in my life? Maybe what I want for myself is more complicated than just being happy, and maybe I'm willing not to be happy to get it."

In adolescence, teenagers must begin to face their fears on their own: fears of the unknown, fears of being alone, fears about the body, fears of the voice of conscience, and last but not least, fears about the self. The five fears mark out the boundaries of what it means to be human. They define our perceptions, stimulate our senses, guide our judgments, and testify to our shared experience. By understanding these five basic fears and by using your understanding to create compassion for your teenagers' plight, you can offer them true support for their development, and help them to cross over safely to their adult life.

PART II

THE FIVE FACES
OF ADOLESCENCE

*U*ntil now, I've talked generally about adolescence, that ten- to twenty-year phase of development that transforms our children into adults. But no adolescent becomes an adult in a general way; each and every transformation is particular. Your adolescent calls upon his or her particular psychological resources to cope with the bodily disruptions of puberty, the social ties of friendship, the intellectual demands of high school, college, and the workplace, and the emotional claims of love and sexuality. And further, these resources are mobilized within a unique family setting that shapes the course of each adolescent's development and influences the outcome. No theoretical, textbook analysis will help you to understand your particular adolescent; you need to have some exposure to the kinds of problems that real-life teenagers and their parents face. That's why I've written the next part of this book.

In this section, I will explore the lives of five teenagers and focus on their individual responses to the challenges of adolescence. I have come to believe that there are several key responses that shape an adolescent's experience of these years. These key experiences are organized and expressed through feelings of anxiety, depression, rebellion, withdrawal, and overattachment. All of these are normal reactions to the special tensions of adolescence, and all adolescents experience some measure of these normal feelings. These feelings only become abnormal if they are too intense, or too prolonged, or if they interfere with your adolescent's ability to ultimately master the five developmental tasks I've already outlined (separating from old ties, creating new attachments, establishing a mature sexual identity and sexual life, formulating new ideas and ideals, and consolidating character).

It's normal for your teenage daughter to feel anxious about school, but abnormal if she refuses to attend classes. It's normal for your son to be mopey and moody, but abnormal if he can't get out of bed. It's normal for teenagers to fantasize, but abnormal if they ignore or obliterate the claims of the real world.

Some youngsters manage all these feelings well and seem to find a relatively smooth, straight path to follow during these years, with few obstacles along the way. For most, the path will twist and turn, creating some strain and confusion, until they arrive safely at their destination. But for a few, the path is so dense and tangled that they falter or fail, unable for a time to move forward or to make their way in the world. These are the stories I have chosen to tell; Elisa, thirteen, whose extreme anxieties precipitated an eating disorder; Frankie, fourteen, whose angry rebellion caused his expulsion from school; Jennifer, fifteen, whose deep depressive feelings made her try to commit suicide; Bethany, sixteen, whose emotional withdrawal resulted in a retreat from life; and Alex, seventeen, whose continued overattachment to his mother threatened his ability to become an adult.

I am also going to tell you about the lives of the parents of these teenagers, in order to highlight some of the special issues that affect today's families—how delayed childbearing, for example, can increase a teenager's anxieties about her older parents' mortality, or how an adversarial divorce proceeding can dangerously escalate a teenager's feelings of loss. I will try to explain the ways in which single motherhood, father absence, and adoption uniquely influence the course of adolescent development, and explore the effects of a parent's remarriage or a parent's alcoholism or a parent's death on a teenager's life.

Of course, not all of the issues I raise will be issues you are specifically addressing in your family, but nevertheless, I think you will find a great deal to think about. I hope that hearing how these particular teenagers and their parents fared will help you and your teenager become better traveling companions as you chart your path through adolescence.

CHAPTER 6

An Anxious Response to Adolescence

Why Are Adolescents Anxious?

The enormous changes that occur at the beginning of adolescence are bound to flood your son or daughter with some new anxieties, and mastering these anxieties remains one of the most important tasks of these years. Too much anxiety can compromise all areas of a teenager's functioning. It can inhibit her emotional life (by replacing enthusiasm with dread, and causing her to retreat from experience), her physical life (by flooding her body with the paralyzing symptoms of panic—sweaty palms, butterflies in her stomach, breathlessness, heart palpitations, etc.), her academic life (by eroding her ability to use her mind to function at school, causing her to "clam up" in class discussions or to "go blank" at tests). And, of course, overwhelming anxiety can dismantle a teenager's normal attempts to build a social life (by undermining her confidence and competence with her peers).

In early adolescence, some of your son's or daughter's most intense anxieties are stimulated by the bodily alterations of puberty. As parents, we can cushion the impact of these changes by admiring and affirming them ("You look beautiful"; "You're getting so strong") or call them into conflict by criticizing and condemning them ("Your bust is bigger than mine!" "You've got B.O."). At no point in life are bodily anxieties about appearance so heightened. To paraphrase Vince Lombardi, "Appearance isn't everything in adolescence; it's the only thing!" This is particularly true for female adolescents in our culture because of our emphasis on youthfulness, beauty, thinness, staying fit, and eating sparingly. At the same time that female adolescents begin to develop the normal fatty deposits on their breasts and hips that will define their new female bodies, girls in our culture often feel bad about themselves, and worry that they're becoming "fat."

It's hard to remember that thin was not always our cultural ideal. In fact, only a generation ago, in the fifties and well into the sixties, voluptuous images of women were greatly admired and held out as the quintessence of female beauty. In the 1950s, photos of Marilyn Monroe emphasized her swelling breasts, full hips, and tiny waist. She possessed *exaggerated* female characteristics, not *diminished* ones. In the 1960s, the image of an "earth mother" who was plump and powerful was still seen as eminently desirable. But increasingly, in the last decades, we seem to have moved away from *mature* femininity to *immature* femininity as an ideal. Current images of the female form in the media display a young, prepubescent female figure, thin, hollow-cheeked, barely breasted, slim-hipped, androgynous. Today, most teenage girls would describe Kate Moss as "gorgeous," and Marilyn Monroe as "gross."

Since social acceptance among her peers is essential to an adolescent, she must rely on her friends to help define her new sense of herself, sharpening her awareness of what's "in," or "cool," or "fly." The normal anxieties that every adolescent experiences about the bodily changes of puberty, coupled with this intense longing for acceptance and approval from one's peers (as well as one's parents), added to these new social pressures for thinness, can produce a lethal mix, making the search for physical perfection in a female adolescent desperate and relentless. When this happens, anorexia nervosa can take hold, an eating disorder characterized by severely restricted intake of food, which can produce a state of psychological and physical emergency. It's hard to relize that just a generation ago, anorexia nervosa and bulimia nervosa (a variant in which the teenager binges and vomits) were considered to be rare diseases. In today's times, teenagers talk about them in the same way they discuss their menstrual cramps, their moodiness, or their migraines. Something that used to be quite *extraordinary* in our society has now become quite *ordinary*.

Adolescent girls appear to be particularly vulnerable to eating disorders at both the beginning and the end of adolescence. In early adolescence (twelve to fourteen), the symptoms of anorexia are often linked to conflicts and anxieties about the changes of puberty, separating from the family, and struggling with the formation of a female identity. In late or postadolescence (seventeen to twenty plus), eating disorders often reflect developmental conflicts around the consolidation of character, the regulation of self-esteem and self-image, and the achievement of a mature sexual life. This is the story of how one young teenager struggled with her anxieties about leaving childhood, and how these anxieties predisposed her to developing an eating disorder.

Elisa: Born to Be Best

Elisa Scanlon, thirteen, is an only child. She lives with her parents in an upper-middle-class suburb and attends the local junior high school (one of the ten best public schools in the country). The principal of Elisa's school asked if I would see Elisa in consultation. In her initial phone call, she described how school personnel have seen a rapid decline in Elisa's functioning over the past year. A star student, gymnast, and musician in her elementary school, Elisa now seems tired and listless in class, and becomes nervy and hysterical over homework assignments and tests. She also observed that Elisa's weight has drastically altered in the past six months. And finally she mentioned that the school is concerned about

Elisa's obsessive and submissive attachment to an older girl, who appears to dominate her.

Charlie Scanlon, Elisa's father, is a handsome, fit, well-dressed, fifty-nine-year-old man who runs his own employment agency. He appears a bit detached, but seems cooperative and amiable. His wife, Mirabella, is fifty-two years old. A former runway model, who is now a partner in a corporate law firm, she is beautiful, trim, slender, and clearly "dressed for success," with oversized tinted glasses perched on top of her head. She appears tense and intense. Both parents are intelligent and articulate.

Elisa, a tall, very thin, pretty girl with long, dark hair, sat quietly between her parents on the sofa. Her enervation and passivity were in sharp contrast to her parents' vitality and strength. They extolled Elisa's virtues: She has always been a wonderful child; she has an IQ over 135; she is extremely musical; she has been a competitive gymnast since she was seven years old; she is an all-A student (except for biology where she got a B–, but she was taking it again in summer school); she was totally responsible; she kept her room neat and clean; she has never been rebellious or defiant. After at least ten minutes had gone by, I interrupted them. "I'm very happy to hear all about Elisa's strengths, which sound remarkable," I stated, "but, perhaps, first, I ought to hear about why Elisa is here, so I can see if I can help her." "It's nothing," her mother immediately replied. "The principal of the school she attends prides herself on being psychologically minded. She thinks Elisa is under too much pressure and needs to talk to someone, but we feel Elisa just needs to get back on track." Both parents look at Elisa. "What kind of pressure do you feel, Elisa?" I ask. Tears begin to roll down Elisa's cheeks. She raises her hands, with nails bitten to the quick and bloodstained cuticles, to her face. Her mother responds quickly before Elisa can answer. "Miss Barrow thinks she's been losing weight. But I don't know what the fuss is about. We're all thin. We take care of our bodies. All the studies say it's healthy to be thin. Elisa just takes after us." I look more closely at Elisa, who has encased her body in an oversized plaid shirt and baggy jeans. I can see that her wrists and arms and ankles are indeed quite slender and fragile looking.

"So"—I look at both of Elisa's parents—"There's nothing *you're* worried about; it's just the *school's* concerns that bring you to me." Mr. and Ms. Scanlon look at each other. Ms. Scanlon, again, speaks up. "Well, Elisa has always been an anxious, sensitive child. She's a worrier, and she's never been a good sleeper. It's just her temperament." She pauses and a worried frown appears. "Maybe it has gotten a bit out of hand lately, but it's not her fault. It's the company she keeps. She's come under the influence of this older girl in her school and she's on the telephone way past midnight. Elisa wants to do everything Caroline does and she listens to everything Caroline says. If Caroline looks at her the wrong way, Ellie's day is ruined. I've told her over and over again; she's too dependent on Caroline. She has all her eggs in one basket." Ms. Scanlon looks at Elisa, but Elisa looks away, twisting a lock of her hair around and around her finger. Her mother's frown deepens. "Maybe it would be a good idea for her to become more independent." "It sounds like that might be important," I reply. I ask Elisa's father what he thinks. "Ellie is a great girl." He turns to her. "We only want to do what's best for you, baby. You just need to calm down and eat more." He pats her hand and Elisa pats him back. I ask Elisa's parents to sit in the waiting room while I meet with Elisa.

"Are you always this quiet around your parents?" I ask Elisa. She looks up and nods. "It can be hard to be an only child," I state matter-of-factly. "Everyone expects a lot from you." Elisa looks at me and sighs heavily. "I can see that both of your parents are proud of all your accomplishments. Maybe it's difficult for them to admit that things aren't going so well for you right now. Maybe you don't want to disappoint them." Elisa begins to cry again. "You seem very unhappy," I state matter-of-factly. "I don't know what's the matter with me," Elisa sobs. "I feel like I'm dying or something. Maybe I have a brain tumor." "So when you begin to think about your life, you imagine the worst," I state. "Oh, yeah," Elisa answers. "I always think that I'm going to die or that both my parents will be killed in a plane crash or that one of those serial killers will pick our house and murder us. I can never get to sleep for hours." "With thoughts like those, who could get to sleep?" I state. Elisa gives me a small smile. "These are big worries. Are they also involved in some problem with eating, too? What about this weight thing? I'm not sure I get it." I continue, "Is Miss Barrow right? Have you lost a lot of weight?" "I don't know," Elisa replies. "How can I be too thin when I still look so gross? I hate my body." "What part of it do you hate?" I ask. "My boobs stick out, and my hips are gross." "It sounds like you don't like your female parts," I state. "Maybe you don't like all the new changes in your body, now that you're a teenager. Maybe it was easier to be a kid." Elisa is silent. I wait, but the silence begins to make her visibly anxious and she begins twisting her hair and nibbling at her cuticles.

"Tell me about Caroline," I say. "She sounds pretty important to you. Is she your best friend?" "Yes," Elisa responds sadly, "but I'm not her best friend. She has lots of girls who suck up to her." "What makes her so special?" I continue. "She's so beautiful," Elisa replies. "She looks just like a model." "So she's very thin, too," I reply. "It must be hard to have to share a best friend who's so popular." "My mom just doesn't understand." Elisa sighs. "I worry all the time that Caroline will blow me off." "It sounds like you have the feeling that you need *her* more than she needs *you*." "It's not a feeling," Elisa responds, sadly. "It's a fact. Without her, I'm nobody."

History of the Family

Mirabella Scanlon, the youngest daughter in a family of four smart boys, has always felt she gained a place in her family through being "the pretty little girl." Initially, she used these physical attributes to succeed as a model, but she turned away from her modeling career in her late thirties, entered law school, and began to build a new sense of her self based on the use of her intellectual attributes. Her rapid rise and promotion to partner in her male-dominated, competitive, corporate law firm gave her the feeling that, at long last, she could hold her own with her smart brothers. By choosing to have only one child, Ms. Scanlon felt she was relieving her daughter of the burden of competing with other siblings. Mirabella was bewildered by Elisa's current academic slump since she felt she had "given her a green light" to achieve— something she'd never had in her own childhood. Why wasn't Elisa taking advantage of her opportunities?

Mr. Scanlon, an only child himself, had lost his father in a car accident when he was only six years old. He was raised by his widowed mother and grandmother, who never mentioned his father again. Charlie became the total focus of all their attention and ambition, and he had felt obligated to succeed for their sake. Mr. Scanlon was proud of the fact that he was a "self-made man" who had let nothing stand in the way of his success—including marriage or family responsibilities. (That's why he delayed both until he was forty-five years old.) A man used to denying and dismissing his own feelings and "keeping up a good front," Mr. Scanlon was bewildered by Elisa's pervasive anxieties and confused by her eating disorder, which he characterized as "female troubles." At ease in the workplace among adults, Mr. Scanlon was much less comfortable with his role as the father of a teenage daughter. When Elisa was a child, he could indulge her and dress her up, showing her off at his office Christmas parties. Now, as Elisa becomes an adolescent, he felt threatened by her budding sexuality and bewildered by her "irrational unhappiness."

The Scanlons met in the library of Mirabella's law firm. Charlie was a client at Mirabella's firm (though not her client). He found himself immediately attracted to her. He admired her ambition, liked her boyish figure and good looks, and found her acerbic wit and sharp tongue appealing. On Mirabella's side, she described being physically attracted to

Charlie, and respectful of his financial success. In addition, his relaxed charm reminded her of her oldest brother, who had always been her favorite sibling. They began dating and married within three months. Neither one of them felt there was any purpose in "delaying signing the deal," as they put it. They both agreed that they wanted only one child. Since Mirabella was almost forty years old at the time, they began trying to have a baby right away. Elisa was born the following year, and was bottle-fed, as Mirabella did not want to have the full breasts she associated with nursing mothers and was anxious to return to her prepregnancy figure. She returned to work within three weeks of Elisa's birth, leaving the baby in the care of a full-time nanny from Ireland who had come to live with them. Both parents remember that Elisa was very attached to this nanny (named Aisling) and that it was only after she left their employ two and a half years later that Elisa began to have trouble sleeping. Other nannies came and went, but both parents noted that Elisa never let herself get so attached to any of them again.

Charlie and Mirabella described their marriage as "solid." They shared an interest in skiing and playing squash; they both liked to travel; they were both "workaholics." Charlie described Mirabella as "wearing the pants" in the family about domestic decisions, but he was entirely comfortable with letting her take charge, since it reminded him of his childhood. He explained that his mother and grandmother had always tried to anticipate his every need. Mirabella had worked with the architect and designer when they bought their home, scheduled all their social arrangements, and chose the restaurants where they ate dinner. Charlie decided where they would go on vacations, handled all the financial decisions, and ordered all the wines. They seldom disagreed about anything, and when they did, it was usually resolved without rancor. Both of them felt lucky to have found each other at a time in their lives when they had almost given up on finding a suitable partner.

Both parents were concerned about Elisa, but it was obvious that while they knew everything about her activities and accomplishments, they knew nothing about her inner world. They didn't know what made her sad, mad, or anxious. They didn't know what her worries were, or what hopes she had for herself. It was as if they accepted Elisa "at face value" and never looked beneath the facade of their high-strung, high-achieving girl. Most of their time with her was spent attending her numerous concerts, meets, matches, and so on, and they rarely "hung out" with Elisa around the house. In addition, as both parents kept late hours at work, they often returned home just before Elisa went to bed. As marital partners, Charlie and Mirabella were in complete attunement, but as parents were obviously out of sync with their daughter's developmental needs.

The Five Tasks of Adolescence

Elisa is an example of an anxious, sensitive child who has gone on to become an anxious, sensitive adolescent. Talented and accomplished, as she approaches the dramatic physical and psychological changes of adolescence, internal pressures are building up inside her that are already throwing her development off course. Reluctant to leave childhood and unprepared to face adolescence, Elisa is responding to the special demands of this phase with a great many anxieties, and she is unable to draw upon many emotional resources from her childhood to deal with them. These limitations are compromising her ability to master the five tasks of adolescence.

Despite her parents' substantial intellectual, social, and economic resources, a closer look at Elisa's history reveals that she had actually spent a relatively lonely and emotionally impoverished childhood, making it hard for her to *separate from parents*, from whom she still needed a great deal of emotional nourishment. Also, the Scanlons' large, beautiful house was set back on a private, wooded, dead-end suburban street. This may have increased its value as real estate, but its seclusion meant that there were few children for Elisa to play with in her neighborhood. Further, her extensive special activities (music lessons, gymnastic practice) took up most of her afternoons and weekends, so that she was unable to schedule play dates, or have sleepovers, or just roam around with kids her own age in an ordinary way. Because of this, as Elisa approached adolescence, she had little practice in *creating the new attachments* (both female and male) that are so central to the adolescent phase. She had never had a best friend or felt accepted by any crowd. In addition, Elisa had never played with a boy; she had never had a friendship with a boy, and she had certainly never had a "crush" on a boy. She was a long way from taking the first steps toward developing the normal boy-girl friendships that are a precursor to a *mature sexual life and a mature sexual identity.*

Further, while Elisa had been an extremely bright and accomplished student in elementary school, she was remarkably unreflective and naive for a girl of her intelligence, because she was so invested in "not knowing" so many things—not knowing about friends, not knowing about boys, not knowing about her anxieties, not knowing about her underlying conflicts with her parents. With such a lack of emotional and social development, how could Elisa possibly begin to *form new ideas and ideals* or to crystallize her identity and *consolidate her character*?

The Five Basic Fears

Elisa's current problems reveal how the five basic fears have come to dominate her life. First, her insomnia exposes her heightened *fears of the unknown*, a common symptom in anxious children. The anxieties that keep Elisa awake at night and fill her mind with fantasies of death and destruction display her abnormal reactions to the normal adolescent struggle for separation.

As we have seen, at the beginning of adolescence, most teenagers normally become somewhat disillusioned with their parents, and these disillusioned feelings enable them to accomplish the important developmental task of diminishing their parents' previous power over them. But Elisa, stuck in her role as the "perfect" only child of two high-achieving, older parents, was constantly fearful of hurting or disappointing or losing her parents. Unable to express directly to them her ordinary feelings of anger, her fantasies show an extreme version of her fears. Any separation from them is seen as catastrophic, and her guilt for her wishes to separate from them is revealed in her imagined self-punishments (a brain tumor), while her hostility toward them is captured in her fantasies of their death (a plane crash or murder). Anxious children are often overly dependent children who are angry and conflicted about the ties that continue to bind them to their parents. They project these conflicts onto the external world, which then seems to be filled with inexplicable and unexpected hazards.

The second fear (*of being alone*) is revealed in Elisa's overly intense relationship to her friend Caroline. As we saw in Chapter 1, same-sex relationships often serve as an important psychological bridge, helping a young adolescent to leave the family circle and cross over to the world of her peers. But as Elisa tries to separate from her parents, her fears drive her into creating an intense relationship with an older girl that actually repeats her previous childhood relationship to her mother. It's no accident that Caroline is older, beautiful, thin, and domineering—she's a new version of Elisa's own mother.

Of course, Elisa's *fears of her body* are the most prominent of her fears. They are so exaggerated that they have compelled her to develop an eating disorder. At the time that I saw Elisa she was already displaying the typical signs of anorexia nervosa, and rational eating habits had been displaced by odd, irrational eating habits. Elisa had become obsessed with thinness; she was constantly preoccupied with controlling her weight (through severely limiting her intake of food), and she continuously expressed to anyone who would listen her anxieties about gaining weight.

Elisa's daily diet, for instance, consisted of half a bagel with nothing on it for breakfast, an artificially sweetened yogurt for lunch, and salad greens without dressing for dinner, supplemented by constant cans of peach-flavored diet iced tea throughout the day. She had lost almost twenty pounds in the past six months and had already missed her period twice. In addition, even though Elisa was clearly underweight (five feet five inches, ninety-five pounds) at the time she saw me, she persisted in believing that she was "fat."

Elisa's thoughts about herself reveal that she is experiencing the normal female transformations to puberty with *disgust* rather than *delight*. In fact, she is trying in her own way to delay these normal transformations. She is trying to *regress* back to childhood instead of *progress* on to adolescence. And she is succeeding! Losing so much weight has already reduced the fatty deposits on her body that define her secondary sexual characteristics (breasts, hips, etc.) and interrupted the menstrual cycle that marks her womanhood. Elisa is actually preventing herself from growing up.

Elisa's inability to achieve in her school setting and her overreaction to stressful academic experiences (like assignments and exams) reflect her ongoing psychological struggle to maintain the perfection her parents expect of her, but it is important to note that her limited nutritional intake in and of itself may also have already produced important changes in metabolic and brain function. It is hard to pay attention when you're starving, and it is equally hard to have the energy necessary to work when your body is "running on empty."

Elisa's *fears of the voice of her overly harsh conscience* (the fourth basic fear) add to her difficulties as she struggles to keep control over her appetites, which seem so continuously threatening. Her bitten nails, too, reveal these struggles. Though this is a mild symptom (and one that is hard to break because it usually has a long history going back to early childhood), the self-mutilating aspects of this habit for Elisa are prominent (ripped skin and bloody cuticles), revealing the influence of a very punitive conscience. In addition to picking at their nails, some teenagers pick at their skin, while others pull out their eyebrows, eyelashes, or hair. Of course, there are more severe forms of self-mutilation than nail biting. Some teenagers compulsively slice at themselves with a razor or a knife, and are unable to stop until they draw blood. The current social fad for tattooing and body piercing can also become a compulsive, self-mutilative ritual, with teenagers piercing their tongues, navels, nipples, and genitals. Behind many of these behaviors is a relentlessly critical internalized voice ("You're worthless; you're no good; who could love you?"), which keeps urging the adolescent toward more and more elaborate self-punishments.

Finally, Elisa is consumed by many *fears about her self* that drain her of esteem and confidence. Her childhood sense of self-worth (based on her accomplishments) has already begun to dissolve, and Elisa can no longer take pleasure in many of her childhood interests. She isn't sure she wants to continue with the competitive gymnastic meets that occupied her weekends; she's worried about her continued capacity to be an A student, and she can't concentrate on practicing piano. Elisa has not been able to create a social life for herself either. She doesn't feel popular, she's worried that she won't fit in, and she isn't sure who she is or who she wants to be. She's anxious about the new sexual claims that lie ahead of her, and frightened of relationships with boys. Everything she's relied on to define herself in childhood no longer seems important or satisfying, and she's filled with self-doubts. Is she really smart? Do her parents love her for herself, or only her achievements? Will she ever be in the right crowd? Will she ever like her body?

We can see how Elisa's overanxious response to the five basic fears have caused her character to *fragment* instead of *crystallize*: her fears of the unknown adolescent challenges that lie ahead of her have caused her to suffer with insomnia; her fears of being alone have delayed her appropriate separation from her powerful parents; her fears about her body have caused her to seek ways to delay her growth; her fears of her overly harsh and perfectionistic voice of conscience are revealed in her eating disorder as well as other self-punitive behaviors. And, finally, she is riddled with fears about her newly emergent self, which have paralyzed her productivity and performance, and prevented her from moving on with her life.

The Parents' Part

There are some special dynamics in Elisa's family that have contributed to her heightened anxieties. For example, let's consider the simple fact that *Elisa is an only child*. Only children occupy a unique position in their family's life. On the one hand, they have the advantage of their parents' undivided attention; on the other, they have the disadvantage of bearing the brunt of all their parents' expectations—no sister or brother shares the family hopes or dilutes the family pressures. This is a heavy burden for any adolescent to bear, but particularly for an overanxious child like Elisa, who easily imagines the worst, is harshly perfectionistic, and lacks emotional resilience. While parental pressure to succeed can fill some children and adolescents with energy, determination, and confidence, enabling them to seek greater heights and reach greater goals, others, like Elisa, appear to break down, retreat from life's challenges, and become paralyzed by their fears of the future.

Elisa is also a child of older parents. Delayed childbearing has become a common phenomenon in our society. Not only are more American families having fewer children, they are having them later in their lives, particularly highly educated, upper-middle-class families, like Elisa's. A child born to older parents always struggles with some special anxieties. For instance, while all children worry about what will happen to them if their parents died, for most of them the death of a parent lies far in the future. But for Elisa, the death of her parents is not perceived as such a distant event. In fact, as a new generation of teenagers is raised by parents in their fifties and sixties, many of them will be compelled to face the death of a parent (or parents) before they become adults.

Exploration of Elisa's insomnia, for instance, revealed that she spent many hours lying in bed and worrying about what would happen to her if her parents died. At the time that I saw Elisa, her father was almost sixty years old. By the time she is ready to go to college, he will have reached retirement age. It is not so difficult to imagine that Elisa's anxious, anorectic attempts to delay her adolescence may contain an unconscious wish to remain a child forever. By not growing up, Elisa may believe she can "stop time" in her family. If she doesn't get any older, maybe her parents, too, won't grow any older.

Further, Elisa is having a hard time separating from her mother. Her friendship with Caroline is not really a new attachment, but rather one that mimics her attachment to her mother. In her therapy, Elisa continuously expressed a great many yearnings for Caroline's affection and approval, but it became increasingly clear that Caroline often excluded her, going off with older girls of her own age, and ignoring Elisa at large social gatherings. Interestingly, Elisa's earliest memories were of watching her mother dress up to go out to fancy business dinners, and in her sessions, she often described how excluded she felt from her mother's preoccupation with herself, her marriage, and her life. We came to understand that Elisa felt psychologically "starved" for her mother's love and attention. Perhaps deep down, she felt she didn't deserve to be properly fed. Maybe that was why she was "starving" herself physically now.

Her mother's own focus on her weight and physical appearance also played a major role in Elisa's anorexia. Ms. Scanlon's early career had depended on her being extremely thin. Indeed, she confessed that for about four years when she was a model, she herself had been bulimic, and unable to control her appetite. She remembered bingeing two or three times a day (eating an enormous amount of food in a short period of time) and then vomiting and/or using laxatives. In fact, because of the damage caused to the enamel on her teeth by her compulsive and continual vomiting,

Mirabella had been compelled to have all her teeth capped. Despite the fact that her weight was currently lower than normal, maintaining her thinness remained almost as relentless a preoccupation for Mirabella as it was for Elisa.

Mirabella's adult struggles underscore the fact that eating disorders are not confined to adolescents. In fact, there is hardly an American woman who believes that she is just the right weight. Most of us are always hoping to lose just a few more pounds and then we'll be perfect! Many anorectic adolescents are actually identifying with adults in their families (usually their mothers) who have continued throughout their lives to express similar worries and conflicts over their body image. It's pretty hard to convince an adolescent to eat well when her mother is constantly monitoring her weight, or fasts two days out of seven. It's also difficult for an adolescent to tolerate gaining weight when being thin is admired by your family and your peers. (Of course, on the opposite end of the spectrum, mothers who are obese—almost one-third of our population—are not providing their teenage daughters with a healthy model either. Obesity and compulsive eating are national diseases of epidemic proportions in our country, illustrating that rational eating habits based on the body's needs seem to be an elusive and difficult goal for most of us to achieve!)

Elisa's parents are both highly educated, and committed to raising Elisa with every advantage. Like many older parents, they have waited a long time to have a child, spending many years of their young adulthood pursuing their own ambitions and building their own careers. Accustomed to tallying up their own achievements as a way to feel worthwhile, Mr. and Ms. Scanlon have also done the same thing with Elisa. As a child, Elisa was pretty, slender, musical, physically agile, academically accomplished, compliant, dutiful, and responsible. But now, as Elisa approaches adolescence, everything seems to be falling apart. Instead of a confident, accomplished, and secure child, they are faced with an anxious, enervated, and anorectic adolescent. What went wrong?

In childhood, dependent on her parents' love and care,

Elisa was able to fulfill their every wish for her by becoming "the perfect daughter," but as she approached adolescence, and had to face the task of separating from them, Elisa began to feel frightened about her ability to face life on her own. Her previous reliance on her parents as her primary sources of admiration and affection had left her without any other sources of support. Her first attempts to form a new attachment (to her friend Caroline) turned out to be undependable, leaving Elisa feeling anxious, insecure, and lonely.

Though Elisa's parents loved her and tried to give her everything that they felt she could want, they were not able to help her truly develop a sense of a *competent* or *confident* self. They still saw Elisa as an extension of themselves, and since they were doing just fine, it was hard for them to notice that Elisa's emotional life was rapidly unraveling. Mirabella and Charlie had been used to fitting the care of Elisa into their busy, career-oriented lives, rather than adjusting their lives around Elisa's needs. A great many of the early warning signs of Elisa's psychological struggles simply escaped their attention.

What Needs to Change?

Both Mr. and Ms. Scanlon need to acknowledge Elisa's real-life struggles, instead of denying them. Their rationalizations of Elisa's thinness as "just like them," for example, prevents them from recognizing just how dangerous Elisa's irrational eating habits are, while their diminishment of her insomnia and current academic struggles gives them no power to help Elisa change her behavior.

In addition, *Elisa's mother, Mirabella, needs to consider that her own continued pursuit of thinness is giving Elisa the message that only thin is beautiful.* Our culture supports an entire industry of fat-free, light and diet food, spas and clinics, pills, products, and programs that focus entirely on dieting and losing weight as the answer to one's problems. Since it is virtually impossible to find a teenage girl who is satisfied with her body, many see anorexia as a way to stay slim rather than as a pathological life-threatening disease.

Both of Elisa's parents need to separate their own aspirations for Elisa from Elisa's aspirations for herself. It is natural for parents to hope that their children will be able to take advantage of opportunities that they may have been denied, but it is equally important to realize that your child may neither need nor desire these opportunities. (If you always wanted to play piano, maybe *you* should be the one taking lessons!) For an adolescent to succeed, she must feel that her success reflects her own desires, her own motivations, and her own efforts. Anything less is a setup for personal failure. Mr. and Ms. Scanlon must help Elisa to feel that she is following her own path, *not* a path laid down for her by them.

Charlie, Elisa's father, needs to make some special efforts. He is unaware of his lack of emotional investment in Elisa's growth, and through his nostalgia for Elisa's past (the time when she was "Daddy's little girl") he has been giving her the message, "Don't grow up and grow away from me." As long as Elisa continues to get this message, she cannot embark on her normal adolescent journey. *Mr. Scanlon's psychological presence is also very much needed at this time to dilute the intensity of Elisa's identification with her mother, and her mother's overidentification with her.*

Finally, Elisa herself must make the greatest changes on her own behalf. *She must begin to see her irrational relationship to eating as self-destructive,* alien to her true sense of self—something that needs to be discarded and disavowed, if she is to continue to develop in healthy ways. *Elisa must also begin to modify the harsh and relentless internalized voice of her conscience* that urges her on toward greater and greater physical perfection. *And she needs to find ways to manage her overwhelming anxieties*—to talk herself down from her own terrors. Once Elisa's weight stabilizes and she is out of physical danger, she will be able once again to take up the major psychological challenge of adolescence—the struggle to form an independent life apart from one's parents; a social life, an emotional life, an intellectual life, and a sexual life, among her peers.

All adolescents experience anxiety. It's a normal part of their lives. Some anxiety is even useful because it alerts them to prepare for what lies ahead, but too much anxiety is paralyzing, preventing them from facing the challenges they must meet. You can use the four C's I've described in Chapter 4 to help your teenager master her anxieties. Let's see how Elisa's parents might begin to talk with her.

Using the Four C's to Help a Teenager Like Elisa

Compassion: *Empathize with your teenager's feelings, don't ignore them.* Remember, what you won't acknowledge, you can't change. Instead of telling themselves, "She's just like us, there's nothing wrong with her wanting to be thin," Elisa's parents need to help her face the real facts: "You've been losing a lot of weight, honey, and Daddy and I are really concerned about you. Your worries about getting fat have gotten out of hand. We can't stand by and let that happen."

Communication: Even if your teen "doesn't want to talk about it," as a parent you've got to find ways to open up the lines of communication. *Express your thoughts and feelings clearly and don't be afraid to call upon other authorities if you need them.* Elisa's parents could tell her, "Dr. Morris told us that you have anorexia nervosa. She says that it's a very serious disease and that lots of girls your age get caught up wanting to be thin without realizing the dangerous consequences."

Comprehension: *Use your understanding of yourself and your contributions to the problem to build a dialogue that can help address the underlying issues.* For instance, Elisa's mom could say, "I've been thinking about all the years of your childhood that you watched me worry about my weight. Well, I'm beginning to see that I have a problem in this area, too, and maybe I've been giving you some really unhealthy messages. We've both got to start looking at this problem now, before it's too late."

Competence: *Encourage your teenager to come up with an action or solution to her problem that would strengthen her sense of mastery over her anxieties.* Elisa's mom might say, "Do you think you can figure out an eating plan that will work for you? I know it's important for you to stay thin, but I'm also going to insist that you stay healthy. If your weight stabilizes—even if it's at the low end of the charts, I won't be on your back about this—but you need to abide by the plan and get enough nourishment. If you can't do that, we're going to have to take other steps to make sure you're safe."

What Happened to Elisa and Her Parents?

While Elisa continued to maintain that she was still too fat, she did agree to a treatment plan that included weekly monitoring of her weight by her family doctor, weekly therapy sessions with her parents, and her own individual sessions twice a week. With this plan, no one in the family was able to fall back on denying the importance of Elisa's anorexia as a life-threatening symptom. She agreed to gain ten pounds, and maintain her weight around 105 pounds, if her parents agreed not to insist that she gain more than that. Within six months, Elisa's weight had stabilized, removing her from physical risk; however, her long-standing anxieties and their accompanying symptoms continued to compromise her social and intellectual functioning. Throughout that school year, Elisa continued to display heightened anxieties about her academic performance. Each special assignment kept her up night after night because she was never satisfied with her efforts, and each test filled her with crippling dread. Sometimes her anxieties became so great that she would have to stay home from school, while on other occasions, she would silently cry while taking her examinations.

At the end of the school year, in consultation with the school assessment team and the principal, Mr. and Ms. Scanlon decided to remove Elisa from her competitive public school, and place her in a smaller, more individualized progressive private school, where examinations were not given to the students. This move proved useful for two reasons. First, it alleviated the dread and terror that Elisa felt about taking examinations and being graded, and second, it separated her from her demeaning and destructive emotional reliance on Caroline, her first friend.

Meanwhile, Mr. and Ms. Scanlon agreed to modify their social agenda, and spend no more than two nights out during the week. This permitted the family to eat dinner together, which allowed them to keep close watch over Elisa's food intake, and also encouraged more real communication between Elisa and her parents, enabling them to get to know Elisa for who she was, not just for what she achieved.

In her new, smaller school, Elisa joined the chorus, where her musical abilities were permitted to flourish as part of a group, and she was not required to stand out as a piano soloist. Her school (which followed a learn-by-doing philosophy) also encouraged small group participation on special projects, which diluted Elisa's anxieties and fostered new friendships. Again, Elisa seemed to take comfort in being part of a group, neither set apart nor set above the rest of her classmates. No longer under the dominance of Caroline, Elisa began to be less timid and compliant.

In her ongoing psychotherapy, Elisa was able to begin to express her fears about her parents' death, and to realize too that she had actually felt emotionally "on her own" for a long time. She was able to understand that her fears were less about the future and more about the loneliness she felt in the past and in the present.

As she was able to see her parents more clearly and recognize their own compulsion to achieve, Elisa was able, for the first time, to feel anger at them for their expectations that she would always shine, reflecting their glory. But this recognition also permitted her to repudiate some of her own perfectionism, which decreased her anxieties about performance.

Interestingly, the first girlfriend she made in her new school was neither thin nor bossy, but a rather amiable, easygoing, plump thirteen-year-old, whose social development (like Elisa's) lagged a bit behind that of her peers. This undemanding friendship allowed Elisa to hover for a while at the edge of adolescence before taking a developmental plunge for which she was not yet ready.

Elisa never returned to competitive gymnastics, which is probably just as well considering the stress on her body that her anorexia had already produced. And for their part, Charlie and Mirabella were able to support Elisa's decision, concealing most of their disappointment. (Ms. Scanlon did try to suggest figure-skating instead, but Elisa firmly vetoed the idea.) As Elisa felt less external pressure from her parents' expectations and less internal pressure from her own expectations of herself, she became capable of producing high-level academic work at her new school. Eventually, she was also able to convert her preoccupation with being thin to a similar (but less destructive) preoccupation with eating seven different fruits and vegetables a day, and she made many attempts to persuade both of her parents of the importance of this nutritional regimen. Over the summer, Elisa gained another five pounds without panicking, and began to play piano once again.

One year later, Elisa was still thin but not anorectic, still anxious, but able to sleep at nights, and still immature, but developing a stronger sense of self. She reported that her head was no longer filled with "nasty thoughts," and that she no longer felt her body "ugly" (not great but not terrible, either). She had made a good start at the early adolescent task of separation from her parents, had been able to create new attachments, and was beginning to discuss her new ideas and ideals in her therapy, including her fears about sexuality. She had found her way back to her adolescent developmental path.

Warning Signs of Anorexia Nervosa

1. Restricted food intake
2. Rapid weight loss
3. Amenorrhea (absence of at least three consecutive menstrual cycles)
4. A pervasive, irrational fear of getting fat

Physical Consequences of Anorexia Nervosa

1. Cessation of menstruation
2. Decrease in bone minerality
3. Retardation of height
4. Diminishment of secondary sexual characteristics, including breast development
5. Prevention of normal hormonal activity (rapid mood swings)
6. Poor peripheral circulation (cold hands and feet)
7. Dizziness and weakness
8. Disruption of gastrointestinal functioning (nausea, constipation, etc.)
9. Compromising of immunological system (susceptibility to other diseases)
10. Organic changes in the brain (in severe cases memory, judgment, and perception can be affected)

CHAPTER 7

A Rebellious Response to Adolescence

Why Are Adolescents Rebellious?

Often it is difficult for parents to distinguish whether their adolescents are just being, well, adolescents, or whether their behavior reveals that they are really in trouble. How can a parent know what's "at-risk" behavior in adolescence? When does an adolescent step over the line? It can be hard to tell whether a twelve-year-old boy who breaks into an abandoned house is just up to mischief, or on his way to becoming a juvenile delinquent. It can be difficult to decide whether a fifteen-year-old who cuts school to tinker with the family car is simply a truant, or taking steps to shape his own vocational identity. In addition, just as we saw how our society gives teenage girls confused messages about how to be women, so, too, teenage boys receive a similar set of ambivalent signals about how to be men. On the one hand, we want them to be tender, on the other we admire them when they're tough.

For example, there is much more acceptance in our culture of girls who display signs of so-called *masculine* behavior (ambition, athletic ability, combativeness, assertion, competitiveness) than for boys who display signs of so-called *feminine* behavior (displaying one's feelings, admitting to fearfulness, sensitivity to art or music, lack of skill at sports, "soft-heartedness"). This preference for male characteristics in our culture can be clearly seen in childhood, where we look with admiration on the female who shows masculine characteristics, the "tomboy," whereas the male child who is effeminate, the "sissy-mary," is diminished and demeaned. We even use metaphors derived from the male body to define positive qualities of courage and conviction ("She has balls"), again demonstrating the inherent value we continue to place on masculinity, and our intolerance of its absence. On the other hand, as our boys become teenagers, we become increasingly critical and punitive about displays of aggression on their part. Now, aware of their new capacity for real action in the real world, and wary of the hormonal influence of testosterone on male adolescent behavior, we take a harder look at what traits we wish to support, in a population that often seems headed for trouble.

Unfortunately, statistics confirm our worst fears. Demographic trends indicate that between now and the year 2005, the number of male teenagers will increase by about 23 percent. This jump is particularly worrisome, because the rate of violent crime among teenagers has also rapidly increased over the last decades. Since the 1950s, each generation of teenagers has been more violent than the last, and they are engaging in violent acts at earlier ages. A recent report, prepared by the Council on Crime in America, noted that *"After all is said and done, the most serious criminals are males who begin committing crimes at a very early age, often before they reach puberty."* Since we know that the most aggressive and volatile group in our society is adolescent and postadolescent young men, deciding what is *normal* and what is *abnormal* behavior in adolescent boys becomes more important than ever—for therapists, for teachers, and for parents.

While it is true that the normal adolescent surge in testosterone increases male aggression, there are important changes in our society that also undermine a boy's ability to modulate and control his impulses:

1. The high incidence of abandonment, separation, and divorce leaves many adolescent boys without fathers at a time when the presence of male authority is essential to healthy development. The absence of a father's influence in family life is particularly widespread in poor families.

2. The rise in drug and alcohol abuse among adolescents exacerbates aggression, compromises judgment, and erodes self-control. The widespread sale of drugs to and by teenagers and the increasingly perilous defense of drug territories exposes adolescents to violence.

3. The decreasing male presence and authority in our schools and communities deprives male adolescents of responsible role models and leaves them more isolated and exposed to the temptations and dangers of the streets.

The way boys (and girls) are taught to handle aggression is influenced as well by ethnic, racial, class, and economic differences that are reflected in what we expect of our teenagers. For example, while sports activities and the accompanying requirements for "good sportsmanship" provide an acceptable outlet for many working, middle-class, and upper-class adolescents (an approved way to channel their aggressive impulses), the instability and chaos in the lives of poor adolescents often undermines their ability to participate in these kinds of structured programs, leaving them to their own devices. Even if these teenagers do find an outlet in sports, their anger often immediately converts the activity into an aggressive, "in-your-face" confrontation, devoid of the joy of the game.

This is why gang or "crew" membership gains its power among these teenagers. A gang can offer teenagers companionship in a life that would otherwise be spent alone in a tenement apartment. Gangs can seem to offer youngsters support and protection against the dangers of their existence—the violence, drugs, alcoholism, incest, fires, thefts, rape, and murder that are commonplace in our inner-city ghettos, and increasingly in our suburbs. Gangs are also often organized along racial or ethnic lines—Puerto Ricans, Dominicans, Chinese, and so on, so that acceptance into a gang can also inspire a sense of community and commitment to one's cultural comrades, and confirm a sense of ethnic solidarity. Particularly for teenagers who are not respected in their homes, in their schools, or in their neighborhoods, allegiance to a gang can provide the only sense of pride that they have ever experienced. The importance of this sense of pride cannot be overestimated.

Of course, while gangs like the Latin Kings, Zulu Nation, Crips, Bloods, and Netas, or racist groups like skinheads or neo-Nazis may offer impoverished teenagers the only family structure they've ever known, they don't give them something for nothing. In return for camaraderie, they expect complete commitment and total obedience to the gang's rules of conduct—and these rules are frequently brutal. Gangs may provide adolescents with a sense of family, but the family they're joining is usually extremely authoritarian and tyrannical. Infractions of the rules of the gang are promptly and often severely punished (usually with group physical discipline called a "beat-down," but sometimes with torture, mutilation, or death).

While we are familiar with the violence in alienated inner-city adolescents, in my experience, failing, alienated, and aggressive youngsters are not confined to any one ethnic, racial, or economic group. Adolescents I have treated from rich, suburban families have been as deeply deprived, self-destructive, or as violent as any of the adolescents I've treated from the inner city. I believe that the decisive factor is an *emotional* one, not an *economic* one. There are poor, stable, loving families, and rich, unstable, hating families. If an adolescent does not feel accepted by or acceptable to his family, if his school cannot offer him a chance to develop, and if his society does not find a place for him to become useful, then he is likely to become frustrated, isolated, and angry—and an angry adolescent is likely to choose to express his feelings in antisocial gestures and acts.

So, the bottom line is, there are more adolescents than ever before; they are likely to be angrier, earlier in their lives, and there are fewer people around whom they respect and who can help them control their tempers. As parents of today's adolescents, you've got to be able to help your kids channel the defiance and rebellion that are normal in this phase of life, in ways that don't undermine them or the society in which they live.

Let's take a look now at how one teenage boy tried to use a rebellious response to separate from his family and develop his own sense of identity, but how the course of his rebellion led him down a self-destructive path.

Frankie: Rebel with a Cause

Frankie is a tall, thin fourteen-year-old with an attitude. Everything about him reveals the stance he has taken toward the adult world—his dark eyes glance contemptuously at anyone who crosses his path, his junior high school record is riddled with disciplinary actions, and even now, he sits slumped down in my waiting room, his baseball cap placed sideways on his shaved head, his body encased in a "homeboy" uniform (baggy jeans, Timberland boots). Frankie is tense and wary at my approach. He lives in a large city and has been referred to me by his junior high school principal because he was discovered in the boiler room, having sex with a girl and smoking grass, one month before graduation. The girl ran up the stairs and escaped recognition, but Frankie was seen and caught. Even when Frankie was expelled from school, he refused to name the girl.

This is not Frankie's first brush with trouble. After a quiet start in his new junior high school, Frankie fell in with the toughest crowd, joined a "crew," barely passed his classes, and tangled with several teachers over his fresh mouth and challenging ways. He was suspended for two weeks last year when he and the gym teacher got into a shouting match, and he was suspended twice this year, for fights in the lunchroom with kids from a rival crew.

Review of Frankie's school records revealed that he was a smart kid (above average intelligence) with some learning problems (a moderate attention deficit disorder). He was particularly strong in math, spatial relations, and mechanical skills, but weaker in verbal abilities and abstract reasoning.

Frankie's mother, Angela Martino, is a worn-looking, pretty thirty-five-year-old woman, dressed in a dark suit with a demure white blouse. She looked up anxiously as I entered the room. Ms. Martino works as a receptionist and registrar in a private school outside her neighborhood, where Frankie had spent his elementary school years. Frankie is her only son, the child of a marriage that ended when Frankie was only a baby, with the discovery that her husband was having an extramarital affair.

Frankie's mom has been dating a thirty-eight-year-old man named Randy for the past three years, who has also been previously married and divorced, but has no children of his own. Their plans to marry have been delayed on many occasions, because Frankie has made no secret of his contempt for his mother's boyfriend. This issue has caused a great deal of tension in the household.

Frankie's father, John, was also present for this consultation. An attractive, well-built man who manages a neighborhood bar, he was dressed in jeans, loafers without socks, and a shirt open at the neck, displaying several gold chains. He looked younger than Frankie's mother, even though, at forty, he is five years older than she. He rose and introduced himself, stating that he was sure we would be able to quickly clear up this school problem; Frankie had just gotten himself involved in a little mischief; boys will be boys, etc., and he was sure that I'd be able to help them smooth this over with the school administrators and let Frankie graduate. Frankie appeared to pay no attention to his father's defense of him and his motives, but remained sullenly focused on the floor. We all moved into my office. His father put his hand on Frankie's shoulder, but Frankie shrugged it off.

Once inside, Frankie's mom began speaking in a soft, forlorn voice. "I don't know what happened to Frankie," she explained. "I used to be worried about him because he was such a quiet little boy; I mean, he kept everything inside. But since he started at this school, it's like he's simmering all the time, ready to explode. He was never hotheaded like he is now." "I'm the one with the temper," John stated. "Angela never raises her voice." He continued sarcastically, "She's always been a saint—Saint Angela." Ms. Martino flinched, as if her ex-husband had hit her. Frankie raised his head and stared at his father. "Shut your mouth, asshole," he said flatly. His mother quickly intervened. "Frankie, he's your father. Don't talk to him like that. Show some respect." "I don't play that shit!" Frankie shouted. "He don't have respect for us, we don't need to respect him." His father replied, "You've got a big mouth for a fuck-up." The room went quiet and Frankie clenched his fists.

"Whoa! Is this the way you two generally talk to each other?" I asked. "I don't talk to him," Frankie answered. "He's never around." "So I guess you're resentful that your dad only shows up when you're in trouble." "Hey," Mr. Martino says, "I'm here, right, and this isn't my idea of a good time, kiddo." "Yeah," Frankie sneers, "we all know your idea of a good time." Angela starts crying. I state, "I can see there's a lot of history in your family that hasn't been settled yet. But since the school has asked me to make a recommendation about Frankie's future, I'll need to take some time today to talk to him. Then we can continue." I ask both parents to wait outside for a while.

Once his parents left, Frankie lit up a cigarette (without asking, of course) and met my gaze. "What's the deal, Frankie?" I ask. He responds, "It's that bastard, Rosenberg. He's all up my grill. He saw me running up the stairs and put the school guard onto me." "Yeah, but how come you took the chance and how come you got caught? You've probably been having sex and smoking weed all year. Why get caught one month before graduation?" "It's whack!" Frankie mumbles. I reply, "Maybe there's more to it than that. Maybe getting into trouble *is* the only way you get your parents to come together." "Bullshit!" Frankie shouts. "Don't work that shrink bullshit on me." "Okay, I'll shut up," I say, "but think about it. You said your dad is never around, but now he is. Meanwhile, you're not going to be able to graduate from this school, and we have to figure out what to do about next year." "Fuck that," Frankie says. "I don't need to go to school." "Yes, you do," I reply, "and your school is offering you a chance to repeat the year if you're willing to come in and talk to me." "If I come, will I graduate?" Frankie immediately asks. "Not this year," I answer, "but maybe next, if you can stay out of trouble. I looked over your test results, and you're smart enough to handle school. But something else is going on. If you agree to come to see me every week, I think you have a shot at graduating. Think it over." "What's the point?" Frankie asks. "You'll just go bitching to my parents." "I wouldn't do that, and I couldn't do that," I reply. "What you tell me is completely confidential. That's our bargain. It's even against the law for me to break it. The only way I would tell your parents about anything you said is if you were going to do something that would hurt you or somebody else. Even then, I'd tell you first, and try to get you to tell them yourself." Frankie looks disinterested. "This sucks! I'm gonna bounce," Frankie replies. "That's your call," I answer, "but I'm going to save this time for you tomorrow," I state. "I'm going to talk to each of your parents now," I remind Frankie, "but I won't tell them anything we said." "We didn't say nothing," Frankie states flatly as he walks out, flicking his cigarette on the floor.

History of the Family

Angela described her romance with John, Frankie's father, the youngest son in a large Italian family. Angela and John both grew up in the same community, and both of them attended single-sex neighborhood parochial schools. Angela was pleased and flattered when John began to pay attention to her. She was eighteen and he was twenty-three. She felt he was handsome and sexy.

Angela was the only child of a widowed mother. Raised by her mother and her maternal grandmother, who lived with them, Angela was attracted to John's pleasure-seeking and somewhat reckless attitudes, which were so different from her own overprotective upbringing, with its constant emphasis on caution and safety. She remembers John as "a breath of fresh air," and states that they had "lots of laughs" until she got pregnant and had Frankie. Then everything seemed to change. She expected that then John would grow up and help her to raise Frankie. But instead, he just went on living his old, fun-loving life.

Even worse, after he got the job managing the bar, he began to drink heavily, to gamble, and to snort cocaine. His work kept him out until two or three in the morning, and Angela felt terribly alone. She begged him to stop using drugs and drinking, but John only made fun of her fears. She began to spend more and more time with her mother and grandmother at her childhood home, where she felt safer and less lonely. After a while, she and Frankie began staying overnight on the weekends, when John worked particularly late hours.

One Sunday, when Angela returned to her apartment to find some clean clothes for Frankie, she discovered her husband in bed with an old classmate of hers from Catholic school. She never lived with him again. She moved in with her mother permanently, filed for divorce, and got uncontested custody of Frankie. From that time to this, she explained, she has only been able to count on John for money. Otherwise, she explained, he still lives the life of a teenager. He does whatever he wants and goes wherever he wants and sees whomever he wants. She laughed bitterly. "He should be in this office instead of Frankie. He's a classic case of arrested development."

Angela described her relationship with her current boyfriend, Randy, as very different from her relationship with John. "Randy is a man, not a teenager. He's been through some hard times, so he knows what life is really like. His mother was really crazy and had to be put into an institution when he was only fourteen years old, so he and his dad raised his two younger sisters, and they did a good job, too—one's a nurse, and the other's married to a really nice guy. I know he'd be the right kind of father for Frankie, if Frankie would only let him, but Frankie hates the idea of someone else in my life. Last year, when Randy gave me this beautiful bottle of perfume for my birthday, Frankie threw it out the window."

Angela went on, "But it's not all Frankie. Randy doesn't have much patience with him. At Frankie's age, Randy was working after school every day and making dinner for his sisters, while his dad drove a truck. He thinks Frankie is just lazy. The only reason they haven't come to blows is that Randy is a big guy; he used to play football in high school, so Frankie tries to stay out of his way. I don't know what to do," Angela continued. "I think Frankie is basically a good kid, but he's so angry—at me, at his dad, at his school, at the world. He has no respect for anything or anybody except the kids in his crew, and I know they're a bad influence on him. They steal, they sell drugs, and I don't know what else. Maybe I could send Frankie to parochial high school—John would help me out—but I don't think Frankie would go, and I don't know how to make him. Randy thinks we should send him away to a boarding school and get him out of the city, but we'd have to force him to go and then suppose he ran away?"

"What about Frankie's drug problems?" I ask. "He was caught smoking marijuana. Is that all he's into?" "I've found some black pills in his room," Angela replied, "and a few months ago, I found a mirror on the floor. I'm not stupid. I know you cut lines of coke on mirrors. I mean, I grew up in a neighborhood where lots of guys did drugs, but I don't know how deeply Frankie is involved. I can't get any support at all from his father on this. He thinks I'm just uptight. He thinks that every teenage boy does drugs, and that it's no big deal. I wouldn't be surprised if he's even offered Frankie drugs on the rare occasions when he picks him up for a weekend. You'll have to ask him."

After Angela had left, I interviewed John. The youngest child and only son in a large Italian family of six children, he described a childhood in which he was petted and adored by all the women in his family. His story of his marriage resembled his ex-wife's in virtually every detail, except in his evaluation of his own role and responsibility. In his eyes, "Angela was a sweet kid, full of fun. We had a lot of good times together, until she got pregnant. Then her ma and her grandma took over, as if I didn't exist. They were always fussing over Angela, as if she was carrying the Christ child. I was just in the way. If I wanted to take Angela out dancing, her mama would tell me it wasn't good to jiggle the baby. If I wanted to go for a drive, she'd be afraid we'd get into an accident and Angela could lose the baby. All I heard about day in and day out was the baby. I felt I had no room to breathe. Angie began spending all her time at her mother's house, so I began to hang out with my friends—you know, the friends I'd had before I got married. Whenever I came home I felt like I was married to three women, not just Angie. Sure, I drank a little too much, and I did some coke and I screwed women, but I mean that's no big deal in my neighborhood. You don't get married and die, do you? But then she caught me screwing one of her friends, so she divorced me. I didn't think she'd go that far, but what the hell, it's probably for the best. I don't think I'm the domestic type anyway."

Frankie's dad listened to my summary of the dangers that Frankie faced right now if he dropped out of school, hung out with his crew, continued to do drugs, and remained as angry as he now felt. But it was clear that his take on Frankie's life was quite different from mine. For one thing, he didn't particularly value whether or not Frankie was able to succeed in school. "School is for morons," he stated. "I never learned anything I needed in school. What he really needs is to go to work." "What kind of work could he do?" I asked. "I could set him up with some of my friends," John replied. "My friend Vinnie runs a garage and we're tight. He'll give my kid a job." "Does Frankie like cars?" "Who the hell cares what he likes?" John replied. "If he won't go to school, he'll have to work. I've done all right for myself." "But you have a job that you've learned over the years. Frankie doesn't know how to make a living yet." "Then he'd better find out fast," John replied. "That's what I'm afraid of," I reply. "It's easy for Frankie to decide that the best and quickest way to make money is to deal drugs. How would you feel about that?" "He's just a punk," John replied. "He couldn't hold his own." "It's the punks that get killed," I reply, "not the big shots."

The Five Tasks of Adolescence

Frankie is a young man whose life has taken a sharply different turn in adolescence. In childhood, protected by the maternal world of his mother and grandmother, and academically sheltered by the private school he attended, Frankie was described as a quiet, shy little boy, loving and responsive. But, with the hormonal changes of puberty, and the psychological demands on him to become a man in his neighborhood, Frankie clearly feels pressured to separate himself sharply from the women in his household, and to disidentify with their values. But what kind of man? And how do men behave?

Unwittingly, Frankie has begun to identify with his absent but powerful father. Consciously, he hates his father for leaving him and despises his womanizing ("I know your idea of a good time"), but unconsciously he's still yearning for his presence in his life and is trying to prove he's as much a man as his father is. Like his father, too, Frankie has begun to feel constricted by domestic life, and is seeking out thrills and excitement—repudiating his earlier childhood acceptance of his mother's ideals, and taking on some of his father's good-time values, without even realizing it.

Frankie may also have turned so sharply away from his

mother in adolescence because of the intensity of his earlier childhood attachment to her. After all, he was the only man in her life until she met Randy. Frankie is not only *protective* toward his mother; he is also very *possessive* of her, and deeply resentful of another man's claims upon her. His growing sense of his own sexuality has made the situation with Randy (who is clearly his mother's lover and sleeps in her bed) too hot to handle. By creating new attachments to his crew, spending time with them out on the streets, Frankie doesn't have to face the idea of his mother and Randy at home together, but unfortunately these new attachments put Frankie at some risk.

But there are other important factors at play here, apart from the family dynamics. Frankie's learning disabilities have only recently been diagnosed. When he was younger, Frankie's mild attentional problems didn't interfere with his ability to focus and study in his small supportive private school, but now, exposed to a great deal of noise and stimulation as he changes from class to class in his large boisterous public junior high school, Frankie has had to struggle to concentrate and he's having a hard time doing his work. As his learning problems began to increase, Frankie may have turned to marijuana to medicate himself, and take the edge off his academic anxieties. This has produced a vicious cycle: academic pressures make Frankie smoke grass; smoking grass interferes with his ability to concentrate and do his work; not doing his work makes his teachers angry and critical; criticism makes him anxious and angry, and increases his wish to smoke grass to modulate his bad feelings about himself.

Frankie was trying, in his own way, to accomplish the five tasks of adolescence. Through his more aggressive behavior, he was actually attempting to *separate* himself from his "saintly" mother. (He is unable to separate adequately from his father, of course, because he has never had an adequate attachment to him.) He has been able to *create close new attachments with his peers*, but unfortunately he seems to be traveling in "bad company." He has become sexually active at an early age, and has definitely begun to *develop a sexual identity and to participate in a sexual life,* but how mature a life is it? Interestingly, Frankie has also *formed some new ideals of his own* (for example, his sense of loyalty to his crew and refusal to betray his girlfriend). And Frankie has begun to *consolidate a sense of his own character,* though in accomplishing this, he has had to obliterate a large part of his childhood identity.

The Five Basic Fears

Frankie's life can be split into two distinct and discontinuous phases—the good little boy (until he was eleven years old) and the big, bad teenager since then. One of the factors contributing to this alteration in his character was his transfer from one school to another. A change in schools or neighborhoods is difficult in early adolescence, and this change heightened the first basic fear for Frankie, *fear of the unknown.* Frankie entered junior high school without any of the resources that he needed to make his way among this more streetwise population of kids. Additionally, separated from his old school, his old neighborhood, his old friends, and his old family relationships (his mother had just begun her new relationship with Randy), Frankie truly felt on his own to cope with all these enormous changes, and *his fears of being alone* were intensified by these circumstances.

In addition, Frankie's *fears about his body* were stimulated, too, as he moved into this new, tougher environment. Many of the older boys in his junior high school carried knives, or belonged to gangs or crews. They admired and respected a physical strength and prowess that Frankie was afraid he didn't have. To turn to his mother and grandmother with his fears would be humiliating. And on the one occasion when Frankie tried to talk to his father about his worries for his physical safety, his father began to box with him, taunting him by weaving and bobbing and encouraging Frankie to hit him. When Frankie turned away, his father said, "C'mon, get 'em up, pussy."

We can see how Frankie's new identity as a "bad boy"

helped him to deal with all three of the fears we've described. Joining a crew ensured him of companionship so he wouldn't be alone, affiliating with older boys who were "in the know," alleviated his fears of the unknown, and becoming tough, like his companions, helped him to feel that he could take better care of his body.

But what about *the voice of his conscience*? Does Frankie know what's right and what's wrong? Does he care? Is he well on his way to becoming a juvenile delinquent? Here, Frankie's *failure* to lead his rebellious life without getting caught is a good sign, because it reveals that Frankie is still in conflict about his delinquency, and he may unconsciously be asking for help. Frankie has not lost his wish to do well in school ("Will I graduate?"), he has not relinquished his affection for his mother ("Shut up, asshole!"), and he has not engaged in the more violent and aggressive acts of some of the members of his crew (thefts, muggings, and assaults). These conflicts keep alive the part of Frankie that still wants to be the "good kid." The voice of his conscience is still speaking to him, even if it's not reaching him.

Finally, Frankie is still struggling with the fifth basic fear, *fears about the self.* He is uncertain what identity he wants to assume or who he wants to be. At this point, it is not at all clear whether Frankie will continue along his rebellious route or whether he will be capable of carving out another path that offers him more success and more satisfaction in his life.

How have Frankie's parents contributed to his rebellious response to the claims of adolescent development, and how have their own struggles undermined Frankie's efforts to consolidate his character in healthier ways?

The Parents' Part

Angela, Frankie's mother, clearly preferred Frankie's old identity as her shy, quiet, good little boy. She has been so afraid that Frankie was going to turn out "just like his father," throughout his childhood, that any sign of "bad behavior" became an occasion for a lecture about the dangers of his father's life. Without realizing it, by constantly bringing John up, Angela was keeping Frankie's father very much alive in Frankie's mind. She was producing the very experience she was most afraid of—*Frankie was being encouraged to identify with his devalued, absent father.*

Angela was afraid that she kept Frankie too close to her when he was little, but she explained that she felt she had no choice because John was "too rough" with Frankie, and she had to protect him. She didn't know how to feel about Frankie's sweetness when he was little, and she was aware that she'd given him a lot of mixed messages. On the one hand, *she'd been afraid he might grow up to be effeminate* (because he was so close to her and her mother and because John felt he was a "sissy" when he was young), so she tried to encourage him to be tougher. On the other hand, as Frankie began to show more aggressive signs of assertion, she felt unable to deal with him. *She had trouble setting limits when Frankie began to cut classes and do drugs, and was unable to discipline or punish him when he refused to listen to her.* Angela described feeling helpless to limit Frankie's behavior as she had felt trying to limit John's behavior, when they were married. Perhaps it is no accident that Frankie, her son, was also "caught screwing a woman."

Further, *Angela was unable to shift from being the mother of a young boy to being the mother of a young man.* Angela found Frankie's new adolescent maleness (his new hard body, his simmering sexuality) both frightening and disorienting. She felt herself wanting to pull away from him, and even described avoiding hugging and touching him. She was unaware that her behavior was perceived as emotional abandonment by Frankie. Preoccupied with her new relationship with Randy at the very time that Frankie went into a new, tough junior high school, Angela ignored her initial worries ("I had a lot of doubts about Frankie in that school") because she didn't have the interest or energy to seek out an alternative ("I didn't want to have to deal with it, so I hoped for the best").

Angela also felt very guilty about how attracted and attached she was to Randy. She realized that there were many times when she wished she *could* have sent Frankie away to boarding school, so she and Randy could begin a life together, but she just couldn't get herself to do it. Randy was also putting a lot of pressure on her because he wanted to marry and have a family, but Angela was afraid that Frankie would feel left out and rejected if she had a baby. *She felt constantly torn between what she felt were Randy's needs and what she felt were Frankie's needs.* She felt that she'd failed both of them. Angela realized that Frankie needed the influence of a man, but she hoped that it could be Randy and not John (who she felt provided a bad model for Frankie with his drugs and his women).

Frankie's father has been unable to provide much ongoing emotional support for his son's growth. Raised to feel special and "entitled," John grew up to be a self-centered man with poor frustration tolerance, little sense of responsibility, and a quick temper. John was no more prepared for the challenges of raising an adolescent boy than he had been for the responsibilities of being a new husband and father. As the pampered youngest son in a large family, John was used to getting by on his charm, and letting others take care of the work. His job as the manager of a neighborhood bar (supplemented by his successful gambling activities) kept him in enough money to maintain his status in his neighborhood and to bring him the satisfactions that he valued.

Further, John has a completely different set of expectations for Frankie than Angela does. For Angela, responsibility, schoolwork, morality, and love are all-important values. For John, excitement, fun, money, and sex are all-important aspects of life. A "man's man," John's pleasures involve drinking with the guys, going to fancy restaurants with "foxy" women, and driving his speedboat, his pride and joy. John wanted a son he could pal around with, someone who could be "one of the boys." He was as bewildered by Frankie's shaved head, crew activities, and "homeboy" attitudes in adolescence as he was by his quiet, shy, sensitive demeanor in childhood. Ironically, only recently had John begun to admire Frankie's "guts," to respect him for "not ratting on the girl," and to feel a sort of pride in his sexuality. ("I told him, women will always get you in trouble.")

What Needs to Change?

Frankie is trying to accomplish development tasks of adolescence, but he is torn between both of his parents, unable to fulfill either one's expectations of him. *He feels caught between the choice of being his mother's gentle, good little boy and his father's tough, bad little boy.* In his adolescent attempts to separate out from his mother and to become a man, Frankie feels drawn to *disidentify* with her and to *identify* more with his dad. But this only offers him a choice between two extremes. *Frankie needs to find his own developmental middle ground between his two parents.*

He also needs another arena (besides his crew membership) where he can feel confident and competent. His mild learning problems, combined with his underlying emotional struggles, have interfered with his ability to perform and produce in school. In addition, the shift from his protected private school to a more stimulating public school has made it much harder for him to focus and concentrate, so that school has become an experience of failure. Further, Frankie's friends offer him no peer support for any academic effort he might try to make. In fact, doing well in school would interfere with his wish to be perceived as "cool."

Repeating ninth grade would not be a viable solution for Frankie. It will only humiliate him and make him feel more rebellious. Further, staying at the same school will intensify his attachments to the members of his crew (many of whom will also be repeating ninth grade). Frankie needs to change schools. Parochial school may provide him with more of the support and structure he needs, or an alternative high school (aviation, industrial arts, etc.) could help him to translate some of his potential into real skills. Frankie would not and could not survive in a boarding school at this time. He would probably see this decision as a total abandonment by his mother and it would intensify his sense of bitterness and isolation, increasing his rebellious response rather than reducing it.

Frankie also needs to gain a better understanding of his father's limitations and his stepfather's strengths. Some father-son sessions may help Frankie to confront his father about his hurt and anger at his abandonment. Some Randy-Frankie sessions may also help both of them understand each other's expectations, and to realize what could be gained by their reconciliation. Randy's clear disapproval of Frankie leaves him no room to redeem himself, and Frankie's profound envy of Randy and jealousy of his mother leave him no room to like or admire Randy. This prevents Frankie from being able to accept any of the real-life advantages that Randy could offer him.

Angela needs to stop comparing Frankie to John, so that each and every move he makes becomes just another confirmation of the fact that he's "just like his father." Her fears have created a self-fulfilling prophecy, leaving Frankie no room to be himself, and she has unwittingly interfered with Frankie's ability to consolidate a male identity that conceivably could combine some of his father's enthusiasm and assertion with his mother's sense of love and responsibility. *Both parents' continued hostilities toward each other, of course, continue to make it very difficult for Frankie to concentrate on his own life.*

Finally, Frankie is not yet a drug addict, but he is a drug abuser, and if therapy alone is not able to help him control his smoking dope, then he may need to join a drug rehabilitation program for adolescents, before he can really break the cycle of drug dependency. To do this, *his parents will need to take his drug abuse seriously (without either diminishing or exaggerating its effects) and support Frankie's efforts to "get clean."* They need to open up an honest dialogue with Frankie that addresses his real problems. This will be difficult for both of them, since Angela is unable to confront Frankie with his drug abuse, while John, himself a drug user, sees nothing wrong in Frankie's drug habits.

Often, when teenagers abuse drugs it is because they feel

Warning Signs of Adolescent Antisocial Tendencies

1. Has a high degree of irritability and aggression and often gets into fights
2. Acts impulsively without thinking through the consequences of his/her actions
3. Takes unnecessary or unacceptable risks that disregard the safety of himself/herself as well as the safety of others
4. Displays consistently irresponsible behavior at home, in school, etc.
5. Often lies, cheats, or steals
6. Is defiant and rebellious about rules and regulations
7. Shows a lack of remorse and is indifferent to the feelings of others

---

Warning Signs of Adolescent Drug Use/Abuse

1. Unusual and rapid shifts in mood
2. Sleepiness and a tendency to "nod off," or alternatively, hyperalertness, agitation, and restlessness (accompanied by dilated pupils)
3. Alterations in appetite (the "marijuana munchies" or the complete lack of interest in food that accompanies cocaine or amphetamine use)
4. Disinterest in normal activities and an inability to maintain motivation, focus, or concentration
5. The telltale smell of marijuana in the house, or a sudden interest in burning incense in his/her room
6. Signs of paraphernalia in drawers or closets (cigarette papers, water pipes, mirrors, straws, razors, syringes, etc.)
7. Inexplicable disappearance of money and/or easily missed household items (radios, watches, jewelry, etc.)
8. Inexplicable appearance of unusual amounts of money or unusual and expensive purchases (new clothes, gear, equipment that clearly isn't within your teen's budget)

they do not have the strength to cope with pain of any kind—disappointment, frustration, anger, fear, insecurity, despair, sadness, rage. So when they feel any of these emotions, they look for a way to *obliterate* the feelings, rather than to *master* them. This is what happened to Frankie. For years, his pain has gone unacknowledged and unaddressed, feeding his anger and rebellion. Adding drugs has produced a more volatile and unpredictable outcome.

Using the Four C's to Help a Teenager Like Frankie

Compassion: Try to see your adolescent's delinquent behavior as a "cry for help," and *use compassion to get underneath the "macho" facade that your rebellious adolescent has created* to defend himself against more vulnerable (and unacceptable) thoughts and feelings. "I know that you're really angry at us and at life for some good reasons. But we don't want you to think you need to get into trouble in order to get us to pay attention. We need to try harder to understand what you're dealing with."

Communication: *Don't let your adolescent's intense anger intimidate you, and don't match it with your own anger.* Instead, talk forthrightly about the problems he's facing and your understanding of them. "I think that things really got bad for you when you had to switch schools. I didn't realize how big a change it would be, but now I can see that you had to make your way in a really tough environment, all on your own. You must feel strong about surviving, but I'm worried that you've also paid a high price for your success. The crew you hang with is into drugs and violence. We can't stand by and let your life go down the drain."

Comprehension: *Try to help your adolescent see some of the underlying pressures that have been troubling him, without humiliating him or dismantling his sense of self.* Share your understanding of his plight. "I know that you were doing really well in elementary school, and once you're smart, you're always smart, but I think it would be easier to do well in a small class that's quiet, so you can really focus. I think you've given up on doing well in this school, but you still need an education to get into college, or get a good job. It's time for us to make some changes."

Competence: Frankie's parents need to pull together and help Frankie *make a plan that offers him some hope for the future.* They also need to offer him other arenas to feel successful outside of school, so that he can begin to feel in better control of his life. "Your dad was thinking that you might like to work at his friend Vinnie's garage this summer, or, if that doesn't appeal to you, we can help you find another job, but we're going to insist that you separate from your crew, and that you stop smoking grass for the next two months. If you can't do that on your own, we're going to take you to a drug rehabilitation program to get help. You need help, and so do we. We're also thinking about some new alternate high schools for September. It's up to you if you want to go to one of these, or you want to go to your dad's old parochial school, but no matter what, you're not going back to your old school or your old friends."

What Happened to Frankie and His Parents?

Frankie's conflicts have already compromised his functioning in three important areas of his life. His social life, defined by membership in a crew, was leading him into progressively more serious antisocial acts. His undetected and unremediated learning problems were leading him into more widespread academic failure, and his family life was too conflicted to provide him with the kind of emotional support he needed. In addition, Frankie's chronic use of marijuana was draining his energy and affecting his judgment.

Because Frankie had moved beyond smoking grass to some experimentation with cocaine and amphetamines, I encouraged Frankie's mother to enroll him in a summer drug re-habilitation program for teenagers in her community *before* he came into therapy in the fall. I hoped that this program would help Frankie separate from his crew, and also give his mother and Randy some ongoing therapeutic support to pre-pare themselves for Frankie's return.

At the residential program, living with other kids his age struggling with more severe drug addiction as well as drug abuse, Frankie began to get a better perspective on himself and his life. All jobs at the rehab center were performed by the kids themselves, and Frankie was initially assigned to food preparation. Much to his surprise, he discovered that he liked working in the kitchen, and that he received a lot of com-pliments on those days when he was responsible for planning and executing the menus.

Meanwhile, the rehab center also brought Frankie, his mom, and Randy together to see whether their conflicts could be cooled down. On one weekend pass, Frankie was able to go fishing with his dad, bring some bluefish home for his mom and Randy, and then prepare dinner for them. Randy, in particular, with his strong sense of domestic re-sponsibility, was impressed with Frankie's skills, and more im-portant, was able to tell him so, which diminished some of the tension between them.

In the fall, Frankie made the choice to enroll in a food-arts program in a special high school out of his neighbor-hood. Travel time, and a part-time job at an Italian restaurant owned by one of his father's friends (instead of Vinnie's ga-rage) kept Frankie very busy and out of touch with his old crew. His ongoing relationship with his girlfriend (the same girl he had refused to name) filled up whatever time was left over.

Frankie began once-a-week therapy, but refused to go for special tutoring to address his learning problems. ("I'm not retarded.") Luckily, the more practical focus in his new school took some academic pressure off him. Still, Frankie had to work really hard in subjects like English and social studies, where the work was more verbal and conceptual. His high grades in food arts, however, were helping him feel good about himself in a new way. He also made the decision that he wanted his therapy for himself and refused to invite anyone else in his family to his sessions, stating, "It's just you and me; that's the way I want it."

At Christmastime, Frankie's mom finally made the decision to marry Randy and a date was set for the following May. Even though Frankie had several angry, tense weeks, his relationship with Randy actually improved once he realized that his mother's decision was final.

As Frankie's new identity emerged and consolidated, he also felt more comfortable spending time with his dad, usually on his boat, or at his bar. John even began to talk to Frankie about "fronting the money" for him to open up his own restaurant (reminding Frankie to be sure to have a bar because the real money is made on drinks, not on food, in the restaurant business). Frankie was wary about his father's plans, telling me, "He's a big talker," but he felt good about the offer, nevertheless. Randy also proved to be an unexpected ally in Frankie's future plans to become a chef. He respected Frankie's efforts and appreciated the hard physical work and long hours that food preparation required.

Frankie's biggest psychological challenge was internal. How could he let go of his anger and bitterness toward his father for abandoning him so many years ago? How could he relinquish his childhood attachment to his mother with less violence? Through his therapy (punctuated by many missed sessions at first), Frankie was able to begin to see all of the adults around him—his mother, Randy, and his father—as people with their own problems, and to modify the *premature disillusionment* he experienced with his father and the *prolonged idealization* he experienced with his mother.

Frankie's girlfriend (whom Frankie brought with him to several of his sessions) was also able to contribute to Frankie's maturation. The child of divorced parents who constantly fought about money, she was very motivated to be self-supporting and freed from her family. She encouraged Frankie to believe that he could have a good future if he worked hard, and she obviously admired and respected him, which offered him a great deal of emotional support.

Within a year, as he approached mid-adolescence, Frankie was relatively clean and sober (he still got drunk sometimes at parties), he had maintained his close relationship with his supportive girlfriend, and he had developed a new and satisfying aspect of his identity (his interest in food preparation). Interestingly, Frankie linked this new interest with his old memories of the times he spent in his grandmother's kitchen, helping her prepare dinner for their family. "That's when I felt good, you know," Frankie explained. "Everything smelled nice and I felt like nothing bad could happen to me." Through his adolescent cooking skills, Frankie was able to integrate the positive aspects of a favorite childhood activity with the possibility of respected adult work. At this point in his life, Frankie seemed more thoughtful, more controlled, and much more able to manage the developmental demands that faced him as a mid-adolescent, without resorting to the rebellious, antisocial stance that initially defined his entry into adolescence.

CHAPTER 8

A Depressive Response to Adolescence

Why Are Adolescents Depressed?

Just as we saw how both anxiety and rebellion can be heightened by the changes of puberty, so, too, depressive thoughts and feelings reach a peak during the adolescent years, spurred by powerful hormonal influences, which disrupt and destabilize your adolescent's mood, producing the extreme highs and lows that are characteristic of teenagers. These mood swings can cause an adolescent to lose her perspective (and sometimes her life) over a disappointing relationship, a failed midterm, or even a fight with her parents. Phrases like "What's the use?" "Who cares, anyway?" or "What's the point of living?" commonly punctuate a great deal of teenage conversation, revealing the underlying depressive pull in an adolescent's life.

But in addition to the pressures of a changing physiology, your adolescent has begun to cope with new psychological pressures as well that increase her vulnerability to depressive feelings. Grief and mourning, after all, are natural reactions to the losses that she must now sustain—the loss of her childhood, the loss of her previous dependency on her parents, and the loss of a familiar sense of herself. These necessary losses are a part of each and every adolescent's experience, and by mid-adolescence, the depressive feelings that accompany this normal developmental disengagement from family, friends, and (often) school, must be integrated into your teenager's newly forming identity.

We are familiar with these sad, blue, melancholy, gloomy, brooding, and disconsolate adolescents. We see them lying on their beds, staring into space, crying for no reason, and sleeping on the weekends. While both boys and girls experience these underlying depressive feelings, there are important differences in the way they express their feelings. Our society encourages girls to *have* feelings and *show* feelings. Indeed, feelings themselves are often perceived as "feminine." But boys are encouraged (still!) to *hold back* and *hide* feelings, or at the least, to keep them under good control. In a movie in which Robin Williams plays the more "manly" half of a gay couple, he rehearses his partner's responses to sports in order to teach him how to "act more like a man." Williams asks, "How'd you feel about the Dolphins game?" to which his more "feminine" partner replies, "Oh, I don't know. Hurt? Betrayed? Abandoned?" What's funny about this exchange, of course, is that we all assume that "real men" wouldn't have such deep feelings, or if they did, they certainly wouldn't reveal them in this blatant manner.

If, in addition to the normal potential for *symbolic* losses in adolescence, real-life circumstances create a situation of *actual* loss, an adolescent's depressive reactions are bound to become intensified. For example, if an adolescent must move from one neighborhood to another, one city to another, or one country to another, the accompanying feelings of *displacement* are likely to increase her sense of loss. Or if, as an adolescent *psychologically* disengages from her parents, she must also sustain an actual *physical* disengagement from them through abandonment, separation, divorce, or death, an adolescent's intensified feelings of loss may precipitate an actual clinical depression.

It's important to realize that adolescents may express these depressive feelings in ways that are hard for parents to recognize. Preadolescents and early adolescents (nine to fourteen), for instance, can reveal a bewildering array of behaviors that often *mask* an underlying depression. Complaints of boredom, for example, or difficulties concentrating, fears of being alone, restlessness and agitation, drug and alcohol abuse, and accident proneness may all be what are called "depressive equivalents." These symptoms are easily misunderstood by adults, and are even commonly misdiagnosed by professionals.

Adolescents tend to split along gender lines in their depressive symptoms, too. Promiscuity in teenage girls, for instance, can be an attempt to distract themselves from deep feelings of depression. Getting pregnant can be a female adolescent's attempt to "fill" the emptiness, sadness, and loneliness that some girls feel at this stage in their development. (Addressing this underlying depression may be our best chance to lower statistics on teenage pregnancy.)

Anger, violence, high levels of irritability, sullenness, and feelings of alienation, on the other hand, may mask the depression of teenage boys. Many juvenile delinquents (as we saw in the story of Frankie) use the excitement and danger of antisocial acts to counteract empty, helpless, and hopeless feelings about themselves.

In both sexes, psychosomatic symptoms (headaches, backaches, stomachaches), intense preoccupations with the body, and fatigue syndromes may also be associated with depressive conflicts. Many depressed teenagers also have particular difficulty focusing or concentrating on their schoolwork. This, of course, results in poor grades and eventual academic failure, which then only increases the teenager's feelings of worthlessness and depression, resulting in a particularly common adolescent vicious cycle.

By mid- to late adolescence (fifteen to nineteen), teenagers begin to express depressive feelings in ways that more closely resemble adult responses. The older adolescent may experience all of the characteristic symptoms of adult clinical depression, including feelings of guilt and unworthiness, dramatically lowered self-esteem, eating and sleeping disturbances, lack of hope for the future, and the complete loss of

perspective on life. This latter feeling is particularly dangerous as it permits the emergence of suicidal ideas and acts.
Clear expressions of the wish to die, accompanied by an actual plan
for self-destruction, puts an adolescent at immediate suicidal risk
(the secret accumulation of sleeping pills, a hidden razor, the
selection of a building that has easy roof access, etc.).

In our culture, young white males between the ages of fifteen and twenty-one are at an extremely high statistical risk
for suicide. (Young black males are more at risk for homicide.) While girls in this age group *attempt* suicide more frequently than boys, they tend to choose less violent means,
so that boys are more likely to *accomplish* their acts of self-
destruction. This high rate of suicide in adolescence is linked
to the heightened sense of psychological instability I have
been describing: the sense of loss resulting from the separation from the parent(s) as the teenager seeks independence,
the emotional volatility associated with the hormonal changes
of puberty, the lack of control over impulses linked with the
emerging adolescent potential for action, a sense of immor-
tality and a limited sense of the finality of death, and the lack
of a cohesive sense of self.

Some sense of disorientation and depression is bound to
be a *normal* part of the adolescent condition, but when depressive feelings have persisted for an extended amount of
time, when they continue to increase and intensify, and when
they have blocked out any other kind of feelings, they have
become *abnormal.* (This is the case as well with anxiety and
with rebellious anger.) *The intensity, the pervasiveness, and the*
persistence of feelings over time testifies to their pathological potential.
In this next story, I'm going to talk about the effects of a
depressive response to adolescence on the life of a young
woman and her family. I hope that by telling you her story,
you will learn a great deal about how a depressed teenager
feels, and how she can be helped with these feelings.

Jennifer: Beating the Blues

Jennifer was fifteen years old and her parents were in the middle of a bitter and prolonged divorce proceeding, when she tried to kill herself by swallowing twelve Valiums that she had taken from her mother's medicine chest. Her mother was out at a movie with a friend that evening, and Jenny was rescued only because her ten-year-old brother, David, came into her room to borrow a CD, and found her unconscious. When he couldn't wake her up, he called 911, and Jenny was taken to the hospital, where they pumped out her stomach. She was kept for observation for forty-eight hours, and released in the care of her parents with a recommendation for immediate and intensive psychotherapy.

In my office, Jennifer's parents gazed warily at each other over her head. Ellen Berenson, Jennifer's mother, sat alone in a rocking chair, while Jennifer and her father sat together on the sofa. Her mother, a plump, attractive, angry woman with a strong sense of aggrievement, began. "This never would have happened if my husband cared more about his family than he cares about himself." "Oh, for God's sake, Ellen, can't you ever let up," Jennifer's father, Alan Berenson, a tall, heavyset man with curly black hair, shouted. "We're not here about us or the divorce; we're here about Jenny. You can't focus on her for one minute without taking the martyr's role. It's Jenny that tried to kill herself." His eyes teared, and Jenny reached over and hugged him. "Jenny's been unhappy for a long time," he continued, "way before I ever made the decision to leave my marriage." Alan sighed heavily and looked at his daughter, who now stared out of my window. "Jenny's still just a kid," her father explained. "I don't believe she really wants to die, but I think this is all too much for her. And since I left the house, things have gotten much worse."

Ms. Berenson broke in. "Now who's the martyr! I suppose Jenny's unhappiness is all my fault." "You know you've always taken out your anger on Jen," Alan shouted. He turned to me again. "She can't control herself. She's always resented the relationship I have with Jenny—even when Jen was little, she called her 'Daddy's little precious' in this nasty way. She felt we were too close. That's one of the reasons we can't settle our divorce. I won't give up custody of Jenny or Davie, and she's fighting me tooth and nail."

While Alan spoke, Ellen looked darkly at both him and Jenny, impatiently tapping her foot. "You seem really angry at Alan and at Jenny," I commented. "What are you thinking about?" Ellen answered, "I know this is serious, but I also know Jennifer did it for the attention. She's always been sulky and discontented. God knows, I've tried to help her, but she just shuts herself up in her room and she doesn't want to do anything or go anywhere. It's not my fault if she doesn't want to make friends or do better in school. It's not my fault if she eats junk food and gets fat. It's not my fault if she won't shower or use deodorant or shampoo her hair. She just refuses to make an effort. Everything is too much for her, and then I get blamed."

Jennifer suddenly stood up and shouted at her mother, "Shut up, shut up, can't you ever shut up! I hate you!" Tears streaming from her eyes, she pleaded with me, "I want to live with my father. Please! I've never gotten along with her, and now it's just worse. All she does is talk shit about him and tell me how much I remind her of him. She's fine with David; he's always been her favorite, but she hates me."

"Don't be ridiculous," Ellen replied, shaken by Jenny's outburst. "Of course I don't hate you! You're my daughter and I love you." "Yeah, yeah," Jennifer stated bitterly. "You wish I were dead!" "That's a very important idea," I stated, "that we all need to pay attention to, because Jenny *has* just tried to kill herself with your pills, Ms. Berenson. Maybe that's important. Maybe somewhere deep down Jenny really is afraid you don't want her around." "Oh my God." Ellen started crying. "How could you believe that, Jenny, how could you?" Jennifer and her father were quiet. Ellen composed herself. After a few minutes, she turned to me. "You see how her father has her brainwashed," she stated.

"I can see," I replied, "that the same thing is happening

right here, right now, that must have happened at home, all the time. This conversation has become about each of you and your anger at each other, and who's to blame for everything, but not about Jennifer. It's important for you to realize that Jennifer has made a very serious suicide attempt that could easily have killed her. If she was willing to go that far, and take that risk, she's got to be feeling desperate. We've got to get some real answers here that help us understand why Jenny believed that her life wasn't worth living. While the divorce is probably making everything worse, it sounds like these problems have been around for a long time. I'm going to ask you both to wait outside, while I give Jennifer a chance to talk to me."

Jennifer, a chunky teenager with beautiful blue eyes and black curls like her father, looked forlorn and overwhelmed. "I can see," I said, "how hard it must be for you to have to deal with the tension between your parents, and how angry you are at your mother. I guess it just all built up and got to be too much to handle." "It's no different now than it's ever been," Jenny stated, flatly. "So this has been going on for so long, it feels like there's no use trying anymore." Jennifer started crying. "I want to live with my father, I want to live my father," she repeated with more feeling. "Have you told that to both of your parents?" I asked. "I talk about it all the time," Jen said, "but the minute I raise it, my mom starts to scream and yell about how selfish and ungrateful I am, that she's given me a good home all these years, and that I'm just like my father, walking out on all responsibility. I hate her!"

"So then, what happens? You feel guilty and bad about yourself, so you back off?" "I guess so," Jenny replied, "I don't know what I feel. I just want out. There's this weight in my chest and I can't push it off. I'm not strong enough. I want to die." "You can't lift the weight alone," I said. "You need some help. But don't you think killing yourself is too high a price for you to pay? We've got to figure out a better way to get your mother to listen, a way that doesn't hurt *you*." "I'll kill myself if I can't live with my dad," Jennifer shouted. "I hear you," I replied. "You feel trapped. On the one hand, you hate your mom, but somehow you still feel guilty about her, and on the other hand, it sounds like you want to live with your dad, but you must be angry with him, too, for walking out and leaving you with your mom."

"And don't forget *her*," Jenny said vehemently. "Who?" I asked. "His girlfriend or paramour, or whatever they call it." "What's she like?" I inquired. "She's nice to me on the outside, but I know she's a phony," Jennifer replied. "She wants him all to herself; she doesn't want me around." "Uh-oh." I shook my head. "So we've also got the old stepmother problem here. I need to know more about all of this so we can figure out a way to help you. Let's start with your depression. I need to know a lot about your bad feelings. Do you ever remember feeling better than you do right now?" Jenny thought for a few moments. "I was pretty happy when I was very little, and we were all together." "What was life like then?" I asked. "I remember doing a lot of stuff with my dad," Jenny replied. "We always did things together. I remember he pulled me on a sled in the winter; in the summer, he taught me to swim. But then things changed." "How old were you when they changed?" "Five or six years old, I guess. I think I was in kindergarten." "Wasn't that when your brother was born?" I asked. Jennifer thought for a moment. "Yeah, but it wasn't his fault or anything, he was just a baby. It just got different. Mom was busy with him 'cause he was sick, Dad was at work a lot. I didn't see them as much, and when I did see them they weren't in a good mood, so I couldn't be in a good mood." "So we have a kind of *before* and *after* thing here," I stated. "Before you were five or six when things were pretty good, and after that when things started to feel bad. This is interesting, this change. We've got to have time to understand this together. Let's set up an appointment for tomorrow."

History of the Family

Jennifer's parents, Alan and Ellen Berenson, had been college sweethearts who met at a fraternity party at the large state university they both attended. Both of them felt they had been shy and awkward as adolescents, and they felt relieved to find each other and be rescued from the dating game. They married the week after graduation, but delayed having children for five years, while they worked to build up their shared business, a small advertising agency. Ellen remembered enjoying working alongside of Alan as a copywriter, while he took care of the artistic end of things. She felt they were real partners. But after she became pregnant with Jennifer, she made the decision to devote herself completely to family life. (Ellen's mother had owned a gift shop, and she remembered how much she hated when her mom worked late and she was left in the care of her older sister, whom she described as "cold and mean.")

Ellen didn't want to raise a baby in the city, so they moved out to the suburbs, bought a house, and Alan began commuting. But suburban life was not what Ellen had hoped it would be. She didn't find any close friends in her community, she missed the convenience of city life, and she felt increasingly "out of it," separated from her partnership with Alan. Ellen had just decided to return to work as a copywriter, when she found herself pregnant again. She had an uncomfortable pregnancy because she gained more than forty-five pounds, and in addition, David was three weeks late and labor had to be induced. When he was finally born, it was a difficult breech birth, and Ellen felt depleted and depressed for months afterwards. Then, for the first few years of his life, David was very ill with allergies and began to have frequent asthma attacks, particularly during the night. Ellen began sleeping in David's room so she could care for him, and she became quite close to and overprotective of him. She had great difficulty separating from him, even to go to the movies with her husband for a few hours. Meanwhile, Jennifer was increasingly compelled to turn to her father for emotional support, as her mother seemed absorbed with her brother.

After David's birth, coincidentally, Alan's business began to grow rapidly, and he spent more and more hours at the office trying to manage his new responsibilities. Things rapidly worsened between the couple, as each of them grew increasingly bitter about the other's preoccupations. Alan felt that Ellen was completely focused on the baby, and ignored both him and Jenny. Ellen felt that Alan was completely focused on the business, and ignored her, lavishing all his emotional attention on Jenny.

Three years ago (when Jenny was twelve), Alan began an affair with one of the graphic designers that his firm employed. She was a divorcee with a three-year-old girl. They fell in love, and a year later, Alan left home, moving in with Dorrie and her daughter, Rachel. He filed for divorce at that time (Jenny was thirteen), but the proceedings have dragged out for more than two years. Ellen has remained hurt and bitter. She is resolved to continue the court battle to ensure that Alan will have only limited access to the children. She feels that this is his "fit punishment," because she's "devoted her life" to them, while he's "devoted his life to his business and his affair."

Alan, on the other hand, feels that even if he hasn't been a good husband, he has always been a good and responsible father, and that his wife's position is self-serving and vindictive. He refuses to relinquish sole custody to his wife. He feels she overprotects David, spoiling him, and underprotects Jenny, exposing her to continual hurt and rejection. The court case continues, with no end in sight.

Both parents agreed that Jenny was a spunky, relatively cheerful little girl who had always been particularly attached to her father. It wasn't until her brother was born that she appeared to lose her liveliness and become more subdued. First, they attributed her moodiness to normal sibling rivalry, but, they both insisted, Jennifer never expressed any envy of the baby. Instead, she seemed to take to the role of the "big sister" right away, taking on a lot of responsibilities for David. David reciprocated by adoring his big sister and following her around wherever she went. They noted that it was only in the last three years that Davie began to turn away from his total reliance on Jennifer. Now, he wants to hang out with his boyfriends and do "boy things." Alan felt that this change in Jenny and Davie's relationship was a good thing for both children, but Ellen thought that Jenny felt rejected by David—adding, perceptively, "In the last three years, both of the men in her life have deserted her! No wonder she's depressed."

While Alan seemed very shaken by Jennifer's attempted suicide, Ellen was convinced that Jenny didn't mean to die. I pointed out to both parents that even when an adolescent doesn't intend to die, many of them do, "by accident." In fact, this could easily have happened to Jenny, if David hadn't discovered her. Both parents readily agreed to a treatment plan for Jenny. She would come to see me twice a week and we would also meet as a family once a week in the beginning to discuss important issues in Jenny's life, like where she should live right now.

The Five Tasks of Adolescence

Jennifer is an example of a child who has been struggling all along with some unaddressed depressive feelings, most clearly in regard to the birth of her younger brother (one of the ordinary sadnesses of life for an older child) but also, more significantly, with an ongoing unsatisfying attachment to her mother. She tried to master her sense of loss and sadness and reconnect to her mother through identifying with her (taking on the maternal role of the "big sister" at her brother's birth). While this is a useful defense (because it encourages maturity), it also deprived Jennifer of an opportunity to express any of her angry and hurt feelings about David's birth. (Good sisters don't have bad feelings!)

Unable to get the emotional support she had hoped for from her depressed and overwhelmed mom, Jenny increasingly turned to her father for comfort. But as "Daddy's girl," Jennifer soon became entangled in Alan and Ellen's marital hostilities. The birth of her brother heightened the psychological split in her family. Now her father openly defended Jennifer's interests, while her mother protected her baby brother.

In the years between five and twelve, Jennifer was able to derive some self-esteem from her close relationship to her brother, but by the time David was seven years old, he was separating from her and moving toward more age-appropriate companionship. This meant that Jenny lost an important part of her sense of self just as she was approaching adolescence.

I've emphasized that adolescence is one of the worst times for real-life disruptions, because these disruptions interfere with the continuity of the self, making the eventual late-adolescent task of character consolidation so much harder. Jenny's loss of her father's physical presence in the home left her feeling bereft and isolated at a particularly vulnerable time in her life. In addition to this significant loss, Jenny also seems to have taken the brunt of her mother's anger and bitterness at the very onset of puberty—the time when a young girl needs her mother's love and approval in order to negotiate the path from girlhood to womanhood. But most important, the dismantling of a family in adolescence calls into question the teenager's entire history of her childhood, shattering her illusions about the continuity and comfort of love, at exactly the time when she will be asked to begin her own love life.

So, for Jenny, the normal tasks of adolescence—*separating from her old ties to her parents, creating new attachments, beginning to establish a sexual life and identity, forming new ideas and ideals,* and *consolidating her character* have been unable to be adequately resolved. Her parents' divorce has intensified her need for her father and heightened her antagonism toward her mother, just at the time when her feelings toward both her parents need to remain steady and shift into the background, leaving her free to develop relationships with her peers. Filled with a sense of hopelessness and helplessness, Jenny has no energy left to form these new attachments nor has she begun to take any pleasure in her newly emerging sexual identity. Overwhelmed and absorbed by her angry thoughts and feelings toward her parents, the tasks of reexamining her own beliefs and values and consolidating her own character and identity have also been subverted. Instead, Jenny's only wish is to give up fighting what she feels is a losing battle. Her depressive responses to the claims of adolescence have virtually shut down all of the areas of Jenny's life—she has no friends, no interests, and no accomplishments to sustain her. Jenny's behavior, in fact, displayed a great many of the early warning signs of clinical depression, if her parents had been aware of them.

The Five Basic Fears

The circumstances of Jennifer's life have heightened her struggles with the five basic fears. First, her parents' decision to separate, just as Jennifer was approaching adolescence, intensified the ordinary *fears of the unknown.* Adolescents ordinarily rely upon their familiar family life to provide them with some sense of firm grounding, as everything else around them shifts, but an adolescent in a divorcing family has no ground to stand on. Not only is her own life shaken by all the new physical and psychological changes she must master, but her family life has been shattered by the divorce. Who knows what lies ahead?

The disruption of both Jennifer's relationship with her younger brother, David, and her relationship with her father intensified her *fears of being alone,* leaving her more needy and more lonely than she had ever been before. In addition, her parents' antagonistic divorce precipitated an *actual* loss of them, at the same time that Jennifer needed to cope with their *symbolic* loss through the dynamics of psychological separation, a normal part of every adolescent's development. Further, because of her depression, Jennifer had little energy or opportunity for creating a new social life among her peers, so her loneliness at home was not mitigated by any secure or supportive relationships with her peers.

Jennifer's *fears about her body*, the third basic fear, are expressed in her physical inactivity, her weight gain, and her lack of interest in her appearance. As she approaches adolescence, when her body should become a new source of pleasure and power, and she should be taking on its care, Jennifer is refusing to take care of herself. In fact, shielding her new female body in a layer of "baby fat" reveals her underlying (and persistent) wishes to still be "babied." Weight gain and/or obesity in adolescence (like its opposite, weight loss or anorexia) can also be a way for a young sexually maturing teenager to "turn back the clock." By continuing to present themselves to the world as *asexual objects*, neither the obese nor the anorectic adolescent is seen as an object of sexual desire. Both are hidden by the childlike changes in their bodies; both unconsciously engage their parents in continuing to care for their bodies, at the same time that they punish their parents by trying to hurt their own bodies.

Jennifer's *fears of the voice of conscience* have become very heightened and extreme, and play an important role in her depression and her recent attempt to kill herself. The voice of conscience is the repository of all of the parental standards, expectations, and admonitions that were laid down in childhood. When a child has felt loved and admired by her parents (particularly her mother), this voice is gentle, flexible, and benevolent. It permits the adolescent leeway to discover and determine what ideas and ideals she wishes to hold as her own. But when the child has felt criticized and abandoned by her parents, then the voice of conscience can be harsh, rigid, and malevolent. The anger she feels toward her parents gets turned against herself and provokes the adolescent into feeling that nothing she ever does will be any good, that nothing she stands for is valuable or worthwhile, and that she would be better off dead. This is often the internal state of mind that permits a teenager like Jennifer to try to kill herself.

Finally, Jennifer's life is riddled with *fears of the self*, the fifth basic fear. She can no longer pride herself on being Davie's "big sister"; she is no longer "Daddy's little precious" (her father has fallen in love with another woman, who herself has a little girl), and she has not developed a new social self that can be admired and respected by her friends. In fact, Jennifer is so afraid of the unknown challenges of adolescence, so worried about being abandoned and alone, so anxious about her changing body, so tormented by the voice of her conscience, and so unable to form a stable and satisfying sense of herself, that she would rather die than live.

Let's take a look at some of the other factors in Jennifer's life that have also contributed to her depressive response to the developmental claims of adolescence.

The Parents' Part

There were some important problems in the Berenson family, right from the beginning of Jennifer's birth. For one thing, neither parent anticipated the effects that quitting her job, moving to the suburbs, and giving birth to a girl baby would have on Ellen. She felt isolated from adult stimulation, deprived of a professional arena in which she could achieve, resentful of giving up her commitment to the business, and angry at her husband for his new attention to the baby and his lack of attention to her. *She had a hard time adjusting to being a full-time mom, and appeared to have a difficult time adequately bonding with and taking pleasure in her baby daughter from the beginning.* Whether this circumstance initially caused Jennifer and her father to seek each other out, or whether Alan and Jennifer's early intense bonding caused Ellen to feel hurt and pull away, is hard to know at this point. But early on, Ellen clearly felt excluded from the warm and adoring relationship Jennifer and her father appeared to share.

It is also likely that this mom may have suffered from unrecognized and untreated postpartum depression. As long as Ellen remained depressed, she had fewer emotional resources to call on in her role as a wife and a mother. She became competitive with the baby and irritable with her husband. She began to hold Alan and the baby responsible for her unhappiness, and her hostility toward both of them began to grow. This increased Alan's protective feelings toward Jenny, so a vicious cycle was implemented in the marriage—the angrier Ellen got, the more distant Alan became, and the more distant he became, the angrier she got.

Interestingly, it was not until David's birth that Ellen felt she had someone she could love, who could love her back, unconditionally. She described David as "my child, all mine." The intensity of her bond with her baby boy shut out both Jennifer and Alan, just as she felt the intensity of her husband's bond to Jennifer had shut her out.

Jennifer, caught between her parents' struggles with each other, came to believe that her mother didn't love her and didn't really care about her. Compelled to put all her emotional eggs in her father's basket, *Jennifer felt emotionally orphaned when her father left home, and moved in with a woman who had another girl child.* (This is often the most bitter aftermath of divorce—a father's own children no longer live with him, while, if he marries a woman with children of her own, they do.) Jennifer terribly resented the fact that Dorrie's young daughter, Rachel, seemed to have it all—a loving mother and *her* loving father.

As the couple began to lead increasingly separate emotional lives, Alan (in the beginning) increased his attachment to his daughter, turning to her for the emotional support he felt he couldn't get from his wife (and offering Jennifer a false emotional promise that he would ultimately be unable to keep). Once Alan found adult love with Dorrie, and moved out of his marriage and out of his home, Jennifer felt completely abandoned by her father. Used to being at the center of her father's emotional existence, she was totally bewildered and unprepared to accept a lesser or shared role in his life. But while she was used to feeling angry at her mother, her anger at her father terrified her. How could she be angry at the only parent who had ever loved her? It was this final dilemma that persuaded her that life was no longer worth living.

What Needs to Change?

A lot of things need to change in the Berenson family if Jennifer is to survive. There are some short-term changes that can immediately relieve some of the pressure on her, but most are long-term changes—changes that must alter the dynamics of Jennifer's relationship to her parents, as well as her sense of herself.

In the short term, Ms. Berenson's competitive and antagonistic relationship to Jennifer is not providing an adequate environment for Jennifer's adolescent development. Further, Jennifer herself is adamant that she wants to live with her father and refuses to live with her mother. *Both parents need to agree that for the time being, Jennifer will reside with her father and visit with her mother.*

But this change in residence cannot address the underlying psychological problems that Jennifer must still face with her own mother—how to address their lack of positive attachment, their chronic antagonism, and the absence of empathy between them. *Ms. Berenson clearly needs her own therapy to help her deal with the ongoing struggles in her life, as well as to address her own undiagnosed and untreated chronic depression.*

It might also be useful for Ellen to return to her career now that David is old enough to manage his afternoons without her, and Jenny will be living during the week at her father's apartment. *This mother's return to the workplace may help her to regain some of her lost self-esteem.*

Mr. Berenson, too, needs to see his role in the history of the decline of his marriage, as well as his own contributions to Jennifer's depression. His previous emotional reliance on Jennifer throughout her childhood has prevented her from appropriately separating from him and seeking out her peers, a crucial developmental step in early adolescence. And his subsequent creation of a new family life for himself has left Jennifer feeling abandoned.

For Jennifer to "beat the blues," get out from under her depression, and commit to living her own life, her mother has to change, her father has to change, but most of all, she herself has to change. *Jennifer must be able to modulate the punitive internal voice that drives her to despair; she must relinquish the centrality of both of her parents to her emotional existence; she must move toward her peers for satisfaction; she must come to terms with herself as a sexually mature young woman; and she must find sources of pleasure and power in her own sense of self—in school, in activities, and in relationships.* Only then will she have developed the psychological strengths necessary to ward off her depression; only then will she be able to face the developmental tasks of adolescence with confidence and competence.

Using the Four C's to Help a Teenager Like Jennifer

Let's take a look at how Jennifer's mother might begin to use the four C's to create a new ongoing dialogue with Jennifer:

Compassion: It's not at all unusual for a parent to feel that his/her marriage went downhill as soon as the baby was born. But instead of blaming the baby, *Ellen needs to accept responsibility for her own feelings.* She could open up a discussion of the past with Jennifer by explaining to her, "I can see now how depressed I was when you were born, and how sad you must have felt when I wasn't able to enjoy you." She can also offer Jennifer compassion for her feelings in the present: "I know you have good reasons for believing that I don't love you, but I hope you'll give me a chance to show you that I really do."

Communication: Even if your adolescent, like Jennifer, is depressed and withdrawn, you can still use communication to open up a window (however small). *Stick to communicating your thoughts and feelings; don't try to talk about your adolescent's feelings and thoughts yet.* "I know you don't feel very much like talking to me right now, when you're so angry with me, but I just wanted to tell you that I'm trying to understand why I did many of the stupid things I did when you were little. I know that I made a lot of mistakes that I'd like to discuss with you when you're ready."

Comprehension: *Even when your adolescent refuses to communicate with you, don't stop trying to understand her, and helping her understand you.* Despite the fact that your teenager doesn't appear to be paying attention, most adolescents listen with some part of their brains to what their parents are saying. "There are things I really need to let you know about, things I realize that I handled very badly before. For instance, I felt really jealous of your relationship with your father. I even felt sometimes that he loved *you* more than he loved *me*. That was our problem. I should have discussed it with him. We should have done something about it. Instead, I took it out on you, as if you were my rival, when you were only a little kid."

Competence: Your adolescent's sense of competence grows when she understands something important about herself, and is strengthened to manage her own life. In the case of a child who has made a suicide attempt, *competence comes from understanding what made her feel so hopeless and helpless, and developing other ways to deal with her feelings.* In Jennifer's case, her parents could tell her, "You must have been very angry with both of us but afraid to let us know. That's why you felt it was no use trying anymore. But we're all in this together now, and we need you to tell us your thoughts and feelings even if they're very angry ones, so we can help."

What Happened to Jennifer and Her Parents?

Jennifer's suicide attempt shocked her parents into recognizing how desperately unhappy she felt. In initial family sessions, Alan and Ellen Berenson were quickly able to agree that Jennifer would go to live with her father on a trial basis for the next six months (a decision that they had been unable to reach in the three prior years of negotiation). While this move immediately eased the ongoing tensions between Jennifer and her mom, of course, it created some new tensions between Jennifer and Dorrie, her father's girlfriend. At first, Jennifer continued to see Dorrie as an adversary who had taken her father away from her. She had a hard time sharing her father with Dorrie, and she tried to snub and exclude Dorrie whenever she could. But while Alan remained attentive and empathic toward Jenny, and arranged to spend time alone with her, he also made it clear that his life included Dorrie, and that wasn't going to change. Luckily, Dorrie herself (raised in a divorced family with a stepmother of her own to deal with as an adolescent) understood Jenny's antagonism, and was able to remain sympathetic to Jenny, and encourage her to express her feelings.

A series of parent guidance sessions were set up with Dorrie and Alan to help prepare them for the shift in Jennifer's custody, and to encourage them to establish ground rules for their new family. Dorrie's willingness to talk about the hard time she had when her own parents divorced and her father remarried helped Jenny to gain perspective on her own situation, and to feel less alone in her plight. *Jennifer's own deep underlying wishes for maternal love and support eventually enabled her to accept Dorrie's friendship,* and she settled into an admiration of Dorrie, describing living with her as "like having a cool older sister."

In the beginning, Jenny remained somewhat envious of her new stepsister, Rachel, but the eight-year difference in their ages gave both girls plenty of room to create their own individual lives within their new, combined family. It didn't hurt that Rachel (an only child for six years) also became quite attached to Jenny, following her around and hanging on her every word. *This new relationship re-created the satisfying role of "big sister" that Jennifer had once enjoyed with her brother, David, and helped her regain some of her good sense of herself.*

Jennifer and her father worked to restore the close and connected relationship they had always had with each other, but this time, with Dorrie in the picture, *Alan was able to main-*

tain better boundaries with Jenny, permitting her to be a teenager and encouraging her to seek emotional attachments among her peers. He also tried hard not to permit Jenny to continue to identify with the role of "the victim" of the family. This opened up the possibility of other healthier roles she could assume.

Freed from her parents' relentless conflicts about their divorce, and kept apart from the daily antagonisms of life with her mom, *Jenny and Ellen were able to be much less angry with and disappointed in each other.* Ellen agreed to go into her own therapy, and was beginning to take responsibility for her own chronic depression and its consequences for Jenny. She was also trying to separate her feelings for Jenny from her feelings for Alan. David benefited, too, from the changes in the family's living arrangements. In Jennifer's absence, he no longer felt as guilty about being his mother's "good" child, while Jenny was clearly the "bad" one. He and his mother felt freer to express the positive aspects of their relationship to each other, and they were both happier to see Jenny when she was around.

Through Alan's help, Ellen was able to get an excellent job as a copywriter at another firm, and her self-esteem and self-confidence began to grow. Somewhat softened by his willingness to help her out (as well as his fairness about other financial matters in their divorce), the Berensons were finally able to resolve their divorce settlement, including their differences about custody. They accepted the court's recommendation that both parents share legal custody of their children, with Alan retaining custodial care of Jenny, while Ellen retained custodial care of David.

Finally, Jennifer was able to accomplish a great deal of psychological work in her own individual treatment. The primary focus of our work was to *modify the harsh and critical internal voice that made Jenny feel worthless* by connecting it with her mother's early conflicts over being a mom, and relieving Jenny of any responsibility for her mother's experience. ("You were only a baby, not a *bad* baby.") The physical separation from Ellen made it possible for both of them to feel better when they were together; her father's love for her and

The Warning Signs of Adolescent Depression

1. Feeling "blue," sad, or irritable almost every day
2. Losing interest or pleasure in most activities
3. A change in eating habits (Jenny had begun to eat all through the day and was rapidly gaining weight)
4. A change in sleeping habits (Jenny had begun to nap during the day and have trouble getting up in the mornings to go to school)
5. Feeling fatigued and enervated a lot of the time
6. Feeling worthless and useless
7. Having trouble concentrating
8. Voicing the thought that life is not worth living, often stating "I wish I were dead"

continued protection of her in his new family did a lot to convince Jenny that he would not abandon her again; and her newly created relationship with her stepmother, Dorrie, helped her to fill in some of the identifications with a supportive maternal figure that had been missing from her life. Once Jenny began to diminish the power and persuasiveness of her harsh critical conscience, suicide was no longer seen as the solution to her problems, and *she was able to be guided by a more tolerant, accepting, benevolent, internalized sense of herself.*

By the end of the year, as she felt less needy and less angry, Jennifer began to take more of an interest in her appearance, and to experiment with her dress and hairstyles. She also got her ears pierced and began making her own earrings. (Her artistic interests were expressions of an old identification with her father's artistic talents and a new identification with Dorrie.) Other girls in her class admired them, and Jenny began to be noticed. As her mood lightened, Jennifer was able to turn more toward the world for satisfaction. Her academic work improved, and she joined a summer bike trip, making two new friends among the kids in her group, one of them a boy. When she returned to school in the fall, Jenny was also eight pounds lighter. Though she still had times when she felt blue, and times when she seemed to lose confidence in herself, she never again completely lost her perspective or her judgment. She described how she felt the weight in her chest had lifted and she no longer "slid down to the bottom." There were new "brakes" on her behavior that she hadn't felt before. She felt stronger and even more optimistic.

One year later, at sixteen, Jennifer was no longer clinically depressed, and she was no longer at risk for suicide. When she thought about how miserable she had been, it felt like someone else—"some unhappy stranger." "The way I feel now is more me," Jenny concluded. She had begun to embark on her normal adolescent journey.

CHAPTER 9

A Withdrawn Response to Adolescence

Why Do Adolescents Withdraw?

The developmental struggles of adolescence take place in the context of new, hormonal changes that fuel sexual feelings, aggressive impulses, and shifting moods. But they also take place in the context of new biochemical changes in the brain that increase your adolescent's capacity for abstract thought and reasoning. In other words, the changes of puberty alter the *mind* as well as the *body*.

We are familiar with those adolescents who can't wait to embark on the new physical adventures that their bodies offer to them. They immerse themselves in their bodily world, with its fascinating wishes, intriguing desires, and challenging activities. This, in fact, is what provides these years with most of their excitement, most of their anxieties, and most of their peril.

But we are less familiar with those adolescents who begin to live inside their minds—who retreat from the demands of the real world, and become completely absorbed by their own thoughts and fantasies. Often, these fantasies offer them sanctuary from painful experiences with others. This may be particularly the case with those children who have always held themselves apart from close attachments—who have never felt at ease in the company of their peers. With the exception of the aged (with whom they also share a high predisposition to suicide), adolescents probably experience more of a sense of loneliness and isolation than any other age group. The normal loosening of ties to one's parents creates an emotional and social void that needs to be filled by an adolescent's peers. Teenagers who have trouble making and keeping friends, who feel inadequate, shy, or disconnected are more at risk during this phase of development than those who have been able to create and maintain close ties to others. *Belonging is crucial in adolescence.* Teenagers who don't feel that they belong—in their homes, in their schools, in their neighborhoods—are likely to move *away* from social experience, withdrawing into a world of their own, instead of moving *toward* the normal social, emotional, and sexual experiences that will help them define their adult lives.

This withdrawal often takes the form of a kind of *asceticism* (a relinquishing of worldly pleasures) and aspects of this *adolescent asceticism* motivate many of the teenage behaviors we find bewildering—the fourteen-year-old who refuses to eat the rare hamburgers that used to be her favorite food, the fifteen-year-old who decides to fast or be celibate in order to "purify" his body, the seventeen-year-old who spends most of her time alone in her room, listening to the sounds of whales, the eighteen-year-old who wants to join a monastic order. All of these can be seen as ascetic gestures that turn the adolescent away from the life of the body and toward the life of the mind.

These ascetic responses may, of course, go on to define some of the real-life choices that your adolescent will make in adulthood. A teenager who fasts or refuses to eat meat may go on to become a vegetarian, a celibate adolescent may go on to become a nun or a priest, a young girl who is moved by the sounds of whales may become a marine biologist, while a young boy who yearns for the serenity of monastic life may simply incorporate meditation into his day.

How can you determine whether your adolescent's withdrawal falls within normal developmental boundaries or indicates the presence of a serious retreat from reality? And how can you figure out if your adolescent's behavior reflects a *choice* (over which she has control) or a *compulsion* (over which she has no control)?

In Chapter 6, I discussed how the ordinary anxieties stimulated by puberty in thirteen-year-old Elisa crossed over to become the extraordinary anxieties of an eating disorder. In Chapter 7, I talked about fourteen-year-old Frankie, whose angry and rebellious responses precipitated delinquent behavior. In Chapter 8, I explored how some of the necessary psychological losses that a fifteen-year-old normally faces are intensified when a family falls apart, resulting in Jennifer's depression and attempted suicide. In this chapter, we're going to look at how a teenager's focus on her inner world (again, a normal focus in the adolescent years) became such an exclusive preoccupation that it produced an abnormal withdrawal from human engagement. We will see how the mental health of this particular sixteen-year-old came to be threatened.

Bethany: Out of Sight, Out of Mind

Paul and Cynthia Marlowe came to see me about their sixteen-year-old daughter, Bethany. She was described as the third child in their family of four youngsters ranging in age from fourteen to nineteen. Always perceived as the quiet one, Bethany tended to get lost among her more voluble and volatile siblings. Since "she was always a good child," and never in trouble, Bethany rarely took center stage in her family. But increasingly, in her adolescent years, Bethany's behavior began to worry her parents.

Reverend Paul Marlowe was a Protestant minister in his mid-forties. An intelligent, reserved man who appeared tired and troubled, he began speaking first. "Beth was always shy and serious. She was the one I felt was the most like *me* as a child—watchful, sober, thoughtful. But in the past two years, she seems to be withdrawing into her own world. She spends more and more time in her room, alone, writing poetry, she doesn't want to do anything with friends, and she's become a vegetarian and refuses to eat any meat or eggs or dairy products. But what troubles me the most is she's become very devout. I know it sounds strange because I'm a minister of the church, but Beth's religious devotion doesn't feel right; it's too intense. She's become obsessed with the lives of the saints, and she spends hours praying. Recently, she told us she wants to convert to Catholicism and become a nun. She said that she needs to be 'cleansed of her sins,' but what sins could she have?" He pulled a sheet of notepaper from his pocket and handed it to me. "Look what is going on inside her head." Bethany had written the following poem:

> *The Virgin*
> I kneel in the snow, falling, falling,
> to touch its white core, to reach its pure center.
> But my thoughts darken its surface,
> and my feelings bleed black, defiling its depths,
> no longer virgin.

"This poem isn't incoherent or bizarre in any way," I point out. "It presents its theme with clarity and cohesion. It seems to be Bethany's way of telling us how dark and dirty her thoughts and feelings seem to her right now. She sees these thoughts as her 'sins' and she wishes to be 'cleansed' of their influence," I observed. "Perhaps she believes that becoming a nun will help her attain this goal."

Bethany's mother, an attractive woman with an easygoing charm and a vivacious manner, who worked as a social worker at a local nursing home, explained, "We're a Christian family, but we're modern Christians. Bethany is attracted to all of these extreme orders, where the nuns take vows of silence, or embrace lives of extreme poverty. She doesn't only want to be a nun; she wants to be a medieval nun! We've been letting her attend mass at the Catholic church in our community but even Father Gruneberg, who's a colleague of

Paul's, is concerned about the fact that religion has become her whole life, and he's a priest."

I asked Bethany's parents to tell me about the rest of her life. "Is she functioning at school? Does she have any friends? Is she eating and sleeping?" I inquired. "She's in eleventh grade at our parish school, where she's always been an excellent student," her mother replied, "but she's never been at ease, socially. There are several girls that she's known since kindergarten, but there's a big gap now between Bethany and her friends. They've moved ahead to boys and dances and parties, and Beth has chosen to stay behind. She doesn't seem interested in teenage life at all. It's so strange, I remember having the time of my life as a teenager! She's so different, sometimes I can't believe she's my daughter. I mean, I guess we should be glad she's not getting high or having sex, but her life isn't normal. What else did you ask about? Oh, yes, eating. Well, Beth's always had a small appetite, but she eats unless she's having one of her fast days. She did have nightmares as a kid. Sometimes, she'd wake up screaming and Paul was the only one who could calm her down. It still takes Bethany a long time to fall asleep. She can lie in her bed for hours. Of course, now we find her on her knees, praying."

Ms. Marlowe described Bethany as a "quiet baby." As a toddler, she never worried about her because "she always played on her own." There were some struggles over bedtimes, but once Bethany began to read (at five years old), they just let her read until she fell asleep. She particularly liked to read fairy tales, and they remembered that in her pretend play, Beth would always enact the role of a princess. The Marlowes had difficulty coming up with many childhood anecdotes about Bethany. Reverend Marlowe explained, "She wasn't a child that jumped out at you, it was more like still waters that ran deep."

In school as well, Beth was perceived as a quiet, serious, industrious little girl. She never drew attention to herself; she never neglected to hand in homework; she never failed tests; she never challenged authority. The only disturbing school incident they recalled was when Bethany was six or seven. She had told some kids in her class that she was *really* a princess, and at recess, they called her a liar and made fun of her. Bethany became so hysterical from their teasing that she had to be sent home. For several days she didn't want to go to school, but then the incident seemed to fade and she never referred to it again.

In early adolescence (twelve to thirteen), Beth began to become more religious. At first, Reverend Marlowe was pleased at her interest, and he offered her the opportunity to teach a children's Bible class in Sunday school. But after a few times, Bethany asked to be relieved of her responsibilities because she felt that the children were "too rowdy." Now Beth began to become absorbed by the lives of the saints and martyrs, and spent hours alone in her room fantasizing about becoming a saint. By the time Bethany was fourteen and fifteen years old, the differences between her interests and those of her peers were striking, and could no longer just be attributed to Beth's being "a late bloomer." Now, in addition to describing her as "quiet" and "shy" and "withdrawn," her family was beginning to feel she was becoming "odd" and "eccentric."

"Does Bethany know you've come to see me?" I ask. "No," her father replied. "I didn't want to upset her unnecessarily. We thought we'd see you first and then, if you decided that we were just overanxious parents, or that Beth was just going through a phase, no harm would be done." "It's not unusual for teenagers to produce extreme behaviors like Beth's," I responded. "Adolescence is an extreme time of life, but I do understand your concerns about some of Bethany's thoughts and feelings, and your worries about how far off-track she seems to have gone. I think you were wise to consult someone. But I need to see Beth myself to evaluate what's going on, so she'll have to be told about this consultation."

"How should we raise it with Bethany?" Reverend Marlowe asked. "We don't want her to feel as if we don't trust her." "This isn't a matter of trust," I replied, "it's a matter of her emotional health. The best way to approach Bethany is tell her the truth, what you've just told me. You're very worried about her spending so much time alone; you're concerned about the fact that her religious devotion is causing her to retreat from her life, and you're anxious about her emotional and social isolation. You can tell her that you weren't sure if you were overreacting, so you went to talk to someone who's a specialist in adolescence. Tell her that I asked to speak with her, directly." Paul and Cynthia later reported that when they approached Bethany about coming to see me, her response had been to look at them and reply in a flat, detached voice, "I'll go, but I'm not crazy, you know."

Indeed, when Bethany came into my office, she didn't look crazy. She looked like an ordinary, pale-skinned teenager with wire-rimmed glasses, short dark blonde hair, and no makeup. Her demeanor was quiet and composed and there was an ethereal quality to her presentation of herself, as if she were already in training to be a nun. Her eyes, however, were alert and wary and she avoided my glance. I asked Bethany if she knew why she was coming to see me, and she replied, "Yes, my parents think there is something wrong with me, because Father Gruneberg told my father that I wanted to be a nun." "Were you upset that he spoke to your parents without letting you know?" I asked. "I didn't tell him in confession," Bethany replied, "and besides, I don't get upset at anyone." "Oh?" I asked. "That sounds pretty hard to do—there are so many things that are annoying." Bethany smiled a pale, superior smile. "I try not to let those sort of things get to me," she replied. "Is it an effort?" I asked. "Sometimes," Beth answered, reluctantly. "Well," I replied, "I'd like to know how you manage. I've always felt that feelings can get a little out of hand, particularly when you feel strongly about something." Beth replied, "I try to rise above my feelings." "It sounds like you're taking turning the other cheek very seriously," I observed. Suddenly Beth asked sharply, "Why did my parents *really* come to you? What did they tell you about me?" "You must have some ideas about

that," I reply. Beth retorted, "They think I'm going crazy."
"And what do you think?" I ask. "Why can't she be an ordinary teenager like I was?" Beth replied, mocking her mother's voice, "I had such fun when I was a teenager!" "Why
doesn't anyone get it?" Bethany continued bitterly. "I hate
the way teenagers are. I hate their stupid music and their
stupid clothes and their stupid lives! Why can't everyone
leave me alone?" "Well," I replied, "if the life you're sup-
posed to lead is so stupid, I can see why you'd want to try to
find another sort of life. And it certainly sounds as if adolescence seems gruesome to you. But you're right. Your parents
are really worried about your emotional withdrawal, and
they're concerned not so much about your becoming a
nun—but *why* you've chosen to become a nun. What are you
running away from?" "They're such hypocrites!" Bethany exclaimed, "*I* want to live a true spiritual life, and *they* think
I'm crazy!" (She pulled a rosary out of her pocket and agi-
tatedly began running the beads through her hands.) "Are
you praying for forgiveness because you're so angry?" I asked.
Bethany didn't answer. I waited for her to finish her litany.

"Are you a Christian?" Bethany asked. "Are you worried
that I won't be able to understand your feelings if I'm not?"
I answered. "How could you possibly understand, if you're
not a Christian?" "What are you afraid I won't understand?"
I replied. "Your wish to live the life of a nun?" "Yes," Bethany
answered. "You can't imagine how I feel." "Maybe you could
tell me about it." Bethany replied, "It's the same way the
saints felt—ecstasy. When I imagine myself as a bride of
Christ, I feel ecstasy." "I can hear how thrilling it must be to
feel so special," I replied. "But, you're right, I'd need to hear
much more to really understand, because it's such a deep
and complex feeling. Would you be willing to give me that
chance?" "If I'm not crazy, why should I see a doctor?" Bethany replied. "Do you think that coming to see me would just
be confirming to your parents that you're crazy?" I replied.
"There are better ways to think about therapy. If we think
about someone like St. Augustine, for instance, you remem-

ber the high regard he had for self-knowledge. Therapy can be a private path to self-knowledge. That might be very useful to you when you're facing this important decision about becoming a nun. If you're going to live a spiritual life, maybe it would be a good idea to know as much as possible about your inner world. Think about it, and we'll talk again."

History of the Family

Reverend Paul Marlowe was the eldest of two brothers, born a year apart. His father abandoned the family when Paul was only five years old, and his mother moved in with Paul's grandmother and worked as an elementary school teacher to support them. Paul was very close to his grandmother and she to him. He took on a lot of responsibility for her welfare after she was blinded by glaucoma, including reading to her in the evenings. Her death, when Paul was twelve, left him bereft, as he felt closer to her than he did to his mother.

Paul Marlowe described himself as the "good" son in his family; his younger brother, Peter, was the "bad" son. Reverend Marlowe related that Peter barely graduated from high school, had several near brushes with the law, and eventually settled in Canada, where he now runs a car dealership. He's been married and divorced three times. Paul, on the other hand, was an honor student, graduated magna cum laude from college, and went on to train for the ministry. But Paul has always felt that his mother loved his charming, irresponsible brother better. He explained, "It's like the old parable about the prodigal son. I was always there, always doing what I should. He was never there when you needed him. But the less my mother saw of Peter, the more she seemed to love him."

Paul met Cynthia, his wife-to-be, while he was studying at the theological seminary. She was working as an executive secretary to the dean. They fell in love and married within the year. Paul was twenty-four and Cynthia was twenty-two. Paul remembers how attracted he was to Cynthia's charm and vitality. He also remembers being happy that she hadn't ever met his brother, Peter, because he was sure that she would have preferred him.

Cynthia was the middle child in a family of three and the only daughter. She was born to a first-generation Irish Protestant religious family and raised in Boston. She remembers her mother and father as "Dubliners who drank when they were happy, and drank when they were sad." A bright and bouncy child and her father's favorite, she had a turbulent adolescence that included a lot of drinking and sexual experimentation that filled her with guilt and remorse. As she moved into her twenties, her life seemed to become more focused, though she still struggled with the idea that she was really "wicked deep down." When Cynthia first applied for a job at the theological seminary, she remembers feeling a sense of calm and control, "surrounded by all that goodness." Similarly, she describes being drawn to her husband, Paul, because he seemed "so good" and she felt that he would protect her from her worst impulses.

Paul and Cynthia had both always wanted a large family and thought it would be a good idea to start early and have babies while they were young enough to take care of them. Cynthia quit her job once their first child, Judith, was born. Three other babies (Calvin, Bethany, and Margaret) were born in the next five years. Cynthia soon felt overwhelmed by how much work her large family actually required. Also, once her husband graduated from the seminary and began to take on responsibilities for his parish, she was left on her own to assume full-time care for their home and their children. She remembers feeling "old and exhausted" by the children's needs. She also felt like she had to be "on her best behavior," because she was the minister's wife. She resented the scrutiny of Paul's parishioners, and yearned for some time to herself. It was at this time that Cynthia secretly began to return to her adolescent alcohol abuse.

At first, there would be long periods between her "binges," when Cynthia didn't drink at all. Cynthia would use these dry periods as evidence to convince herself that she wasn't "addicted to alcohol," since addicts can't stop. But soon Cynthia became less and less capable of controlling her drinking, and she was not able to keep it a secret from Paul. She tried to maintain that drinking was a natural part of her Irish heritage, but once Paul became aware of her excesses, he refused to accept this explanation. As things got worse, and her behavior got more blatant, Paul began to be distant and withdrawn. He expressed a great deal of concern about her ability to be emotionally available to the children, and worried about her judgment. He tried to stay home as much as he could, assumed more responsibility for the children, and relied on their eldest daughter, Judith, to help with the little ones. On two occasions, Paul asked Cynthia to go into a rehabilitation program or leave their home. Each time she decided to leave, but within a few weeks, she returned, repentent and remorseful. Both times, Paul forgave her and took her back, hoping that this time, she'd really changed. Then the whole cycle of binge drinking would begin again.

The turning point in their lives came when Cynthia's father died of the consequences of chronic alcoholism (cirrhosis of the liver). For the first time, Cynthia was finally able to face up to her alcoholism, and she made the decision to join AA (Bethany was five years old at this time). For several years, staying sober absorbed all of Cynthia's energies and she needed to go to several AA meetings a day to bolster her resolution. AA's reliance on placing your faith in God was a comfort to her, and made her feel closer to Paul as well. Their relationship to each other deepened.

When Bethany was eight years old, Ms. Marlowe (now sober for three years) decided to apply to graduate school for social work training. This, too, claimed a lot of her energies and occupied a great deal of her time, but, she said, "At least when I was with the children, I was really with them, not off somewhere, in an alcoholic daze."

The Five Tasks of Adolescence

Bethany is an example of a shy, quiet child whose character-istic traits deepened and broadened in adolescence, inhibit-ing and constraining her development. As she turned inward, she was drawn to asceticism as a radical solution to her strug-gles with the ordinary tasks of adolescence. Bethany's asceti-cism, for example, has enabled her to *separate from old ties* (she has changed from her parents' religion to Catholicism); *create new attachments* (to God and to the Catholic church); adopt *new ideas and new ideals* that will shape her adult life (her spirituality and her devotion). Her acceptance of celibacy as a life goal, of course, *obviates the necessity of ever having to develop a mature sexual identity or sexual life.* In essence, through her withdrawal, Bethany has managed to ward off her develop-mental progress. But she has paid a high price for this solution—her emotional life has shriveled; her intellectual life has narrowed; her social life has been stunted; and her sexual life has been suppressed.

The Five Basic Fears

Though Bethany presents herself as "above it all" and ap-pears strong and determined to pursue her chosen course, a great deal of her behavior actually reveals a young girl rid-dled with fears about herself and her life.

For one thing, her *fears of the unknown challenges of ado-lescence* with its bewildering hormonal surges and bodily changes has caused her to withdraw completely from the world of her peers, and to set herself apart from their ado-lescent preoccupations. She has not retreated back to child-hood (as Elisa attempted) nor has she given up on life altogether (as Jennifer did). Rather, she has absented herself from the demands of the real world and instead created a spiritual world that she can more happily occupy. In this spir-itual world, she is absorbed by her fantasies of being special (not dissimilar from her early childhood fantasies of being a princess).

Second, Bethany's deep wishes to live a communal life may also reveal some of her underlying *fears of being alone*. Her mother's alcoholism, coupled with her father's preoccupations with his work and retreat from his marriage, added to Bethany's quiet temperament, conspired to leave her on her own a lot of the time in her childhood. Now, as an adolescent, she is still leading a solitary (and probably lonely) life. But as a nun, Bethany would never be alone again.

Third, Bethany has embraced a commitment to celibacy. Her contempt for adolescent life ("I hate the way teenagers are") also reveals her disgust with sexuality, exposing her *underlying bodily fears*. Bethany appears to be relying on her religious devotion to help her relinquish her normal (but disturbing) adolescent impulses and desires.

Bethany's *fears of the voice of her conscience* are particularly heightened. As her poem indicated, she is struggling, above all, to become "good" and "pure," revealing that she must feel she is "bad" and "impure" on some deeper level. These "impure" thoughts may be *aggressive* as well as *sexual*. Her anger at her mother (revealed in her mockery) seems to simmer right beneath the surface of her consciousness.

And as far as the fifth fear is concerned, *fears about the self*, Bethany may seem to have everything under control and even consolidated, but she is actually tormented by questions about herself. Is she good or evil? Clean or dirty? Protestant or Catholic? Sane or crazy? Her attempts to surrender her individual needs to a life of religious discipline indicate how fervently she feels her unruly self needs to be disciplined.

The Parents' Part

There are significant tears in the fabric of the Marlowes' family life that have had profound effects on Bethany's development. *The most serious is Ms. Marlowe's alcoholism and its influence on both her marriage and her motherhood.* While she has remained sober now for ten years, Ms. Marlowe was a serious binge drinker for most of Bethany's early childhood, leaving Bethany exposed to an emotionally unpredictable mother who was unable to pay consistent attention to her children's needs. Cynthia described "getting her act together" when Beth was about six or seven, but acknowledged that even then, she and Paul were still very preoccupied with her rehabilitation for the next two or three years. Meanwhile, Beth's increasing emotional withdrawal, and her deepening reliance on her *fantasy* life to console her against the losses in her *real* life, were overlooked by both parents.

Bethany (of all the children) may have been particularly neglected because she appeared to demand so little from her parents. But in addition, *other children in the family absorbed their parents' diminished emotional energies,* particularly Bethany's older brother, Calvin. Reverend and Ms. Marlowe explained that Calvin had always been "up to mischief" as a child, but by the time he was an adolescent, he was "wild and reckless." Things reached a crisis two years ago when Calvin (sixteen years old) got his girlfriend pregnant. Both families were in terrible upheaval for months, until the young girl miscarried.

Reverend Marlowe observed wryly that they seem to have two "good" children in their family (Bethany, sixteen, and her sister Judith, nineteen, who wants to be a missionary doctor), and two "bad" children, Calvin, eighteen, and Bethany's sister Margaret, fourteen, who was described as "a pistol and a heartbreaker"). Reverend Marlowe explained that he has always been more in sympathy with the two "good" ones, and noted that he has always felt that Cynthia was more in sympathy with Calvin and Margaret. Ms. Marlowe did not contradict him. She added that she thought Bethany was "a hard child to love." "Even as a baby," she explained, "she wasn't cuddly; she was solemn—like an old soul in a young body." Ms. Marlowe described that she used to feel that Bethany was "watching me with her big eyes" during the years that she was drinking. "I know this sounds crazy," she continued, "but even now, sometimes I feel that Bethany's become devout to show me that she's better than I am. I feel she's making me feel guilty all the time, in her own quiet way."

The initial lack of emotional warmth between this mother and daughter has created and maintained the sense of disconnection that Cynthia and Bethany continue to feel toward each other, and contributed to Bethany's underlying sense of distrust of others. The unpredictability of Ms. Marlowe's maternal responses under the influence of alcohol has exacerbated this distrust. In addition, Ms. Marlowe's own guilty feelings have made her particularly sensitive to Bethany's disapproval, which she keenly feels. This disapproval makes her reluctant to engage Bethany. And while Reverend Marlowe seems to favor Bethany and is concerned about her, *his own helplessness in the face of his wife's alcoholism offered Bethany no sense of safety, while his emotional retreat during these years left her feeling very much alone.*

What Needs to Change?

Bethany's parents have begun to take notice of her, an essential first step in helping her to deal with her conflicts. But more than just their attention will be needed, since Bethany's problems have a long and complicated history.

The description of the Marlowe family dynamics helps us to understand much more about Bethany's ascetic withdrawal from adolescence. As a child, she was exposed to all of the "messy" aspects of her mother's alcoholism as well as angry confrontations between her parents. Then, just as Bethany approached adolescence, her brother, Calvin, gets a girl pregnant, resulting in another "mess" with its accompanying painful confrontations, to which Bethany is again exposed. Old enough to understand, at fourteen years, that the trouble lies in people's impulses, but not old enough to have any useful perspective on the management of these impulses, Bethany seems to have sought out a drastic solution in early adolescence—get rid of all desires and impulses (particularly sexual and aggressive ones), get rid of all entanglements (particularly with people who can hurt or disappoint and abandon you), and get rid of all actions in the real world (particularly any actions that involve you with another). This massive withdrawal, while it completely paralyzed her adolescent growth and development, offers her the only possibility of protecting her self-esteem—she will identify with her father's "goodness," and disidentify with her mother's "badness." *But Bethany's black-white version of her childhood and her all-or-nothing solution to her sexual and aggressive impulses needs to be modulated.*

Cynthia Marlowe's observation about Bethany's criticality toward her is probably correct. Bethany's religious devotion and her choice to become a nun may express her wishes to become "the saint" in her family, reminding her mother (by contrast) that she is "the sinner." By demonstrating her moral superiority, Bethany both competes with her mother and connects with her father. Her decision to become a nun (a bride of Christ), in fact, can be seen as a symbolic enactment of her wish to embrace her father (a man of Christ) and have him all to herself. *This connection between Bethany's desire to be a nun and her loving and protective feelings toward her father and rivalrous, angry feelings toward her mother needs to be understood,* if Bethany is to be able to make informed choices for her future. Reverend Marlowe's emotional containment has left Bethany yearning for an intense connection to him that he has never been able to provide for her. *Bethany's development will be better served in the future if her relationship to her father can be deepened and sustained now.*

Using the Four C's to Help a Teenager Like Bethany

Bethany's parents need to reach out to Bethany as quickly as possible in order to deflect her from her isolated path. They also need to ensure that Bethany gets professional help to safeguard her emotional development. They could use the four C's to construct a dialogue with Bethany that helps motivate her to commit to therapy.

Compassion: *They need to let Bethany know they understand and respect her thoughts and feelings.* "Beth, you know that Daddy and I have committed our lives to God and we respect your right to do the same. We know how important your decision to be a nun is to you."

Communication: *But Bethany's parents also need to be clear about their concerns about her emotional well-being.* "We'd like you to take this time to consult with a psychologist who can help you understand a lot more about your own thoughts and feelings. This is a big decision, and you need to know as much as possible about yourself to make sure you're doing the right thing. We have concerns about your withdrawal from life and your seeking sanctuary as a nun."

Comprehension: *Her parents also need to make sure that Bethany understands that her decision could have many developmental meanings.* "We're worried that your withdrawal from secular life may not be going *toward* something, but rather *running away* from something. We don't want you to choose to be a nun because you feel hurt or frightened or angry or disappointed by life, and the church wouldn't want that either. Your decision may have a lot to do with the hard times our family has gone through with Mom's drinking and Calvin's troubles, or maybe other things we don't even know about. That's the part we don't understand yet, and we need more information."

Competence: Lastly, Bethany's parents also need to let her know that *they will respect her decision if it turns out to be a real choice.* "Once we know more, and you understand more about your reasons, if you still want to become a nun when you have graduated from high school and have turned eighteen years old, then your mother and I will not oppose your decision, though we would still prefer that you went away to college and *then* made your decision."

What Happened to Bethany and Her Parents?

By not presenting therapy as a process to subvert her decision to become a nun, but rather as a process that would help her to understand the meanings of her decision, Bethany was able to agree to remain in treatment until she graduated from high school. This gave us about one and a half years to work together until she turned eighteen. Confidentiality and trust were significant issues for Bethany. She absolutely refused to admit either of her parents into her sessions, and because of her high level of distrust I often had to reassure Bethany that I would never speak to her parents without her express permission.

Even though Bethany seemed closed off from so much of ordinary life, her therapy soon confirmed my initial sense that she was not as devoid of feelings as she wanted to be. Indeed, some of her underlying feelings had already leaked through. (For example, in Bethany's initial interview, both her admiration of her father and her criticism of her mother were revealed.) As Bethany began to trace her own childhood history, her underlying anger at her mother surfaced and intensified. Bethany saw her mother as the *aggressor* in the marriage, and her father as the *victim*. She remembered that she had always felt "on her father's side" as a child, and that there were lots of times she felt she hated her mother. She also recalled how guilty these strong hostile feelings made her feel. But Bethany also harbored some anger toward her father for his passivity in the face of her mother's drinking. "Why did he always forgive her?" Bethany asked. "She didn't deserve his forgiveness." Acknowledging her anger at both of her parents was not easy for Bethany, as it rudely disturbed her ideal vision of herself as "pure" and "good," and compromised her own wishes to be "forgiving." We came to understand that Bethany's wish to be a nun was a way of fortifying her ideal vision of herself; it would help her be all the things she wasn't yet—but wanted to be—kind, gentle, uncritical, and accepting.

In her therapy, Bethany began to recapture her memories

of a lost part of her childhood—her close early relationship to her older sister, Judith (which neither of her parents had mentioned). In fact, of all the people in her life, Bethany felt that Judith (almost five years older) had actually given her the most emotional support. It was clear that Bethany had felt rejected by her mother throughout her childhood, and somewhat neglected by her overwhelmed and emotionally distant father. But she had many warm early memories of being taken care of by Judith, who had often assumed the role of surrogate mother for Beth. It was Judith who baked her birthday cakes with her name in colored M & M's, Judith who took her into her bed at night when Beth couldn't fall asleep, and Judith who taught her how to read when she was only five years old. It appeared to be Judith's influence that kept Bethany emotionally nourished at critical points in her development.

Surprisingly, Bethany remembered feeling angrier at her mother once she was sober than she had been while she was abusing alcohol. She particularly resented her mother's attempt at that time to reclaim many of her maternal responsibilities. ("I felt like *now*, you want to be my mother? Who needs you?") Bethany recalled how she would deliberately ignore her mom, and choose Judith to read to her every night. She felt gratified knowing her mother's feelings were hurt, but she also felt very guilty about hurting her mother's feelings. Bethany believed that only an "evil" child would be so cruel.

Because of her sole reliance on Judith in her childhood, Bethany was particularly devastated when Judith herself became a teenager and began to want to go to parties and date boys her own age. Bethany hated these boys, whom she saw as rivals for Judith's love and attention. But the more she tried to cling to Judith, the more Judith tried to get her to become less dependent on her. It was at this point that Bethany began her withdrawal into fantasy. Her withdrawal coincided with a developmental phase in childhood (seven to ten years) that encourages the *internalization* of thoughts and feelings, and emphasizes the use of fantasy as "symbolic action." Ordinarily this transformation from action to thought is *adaptive* because it helps the child gain better self-control and prepare for eventualities in the real world. But Bethany's use of fantasy was *not* adaptive because her reliance on her inner world became so profound and pervasive, and served to disengage her from real life.

Nine months into her treatment, Bethany asked if Judith could join her in her sessions. These sister sessions (which took up one of Bethany's two weekly sessions for three months) proved to be the most compelling moments in Bethany's treatment. With Judith's participation, the two sisters were able to reconstruct a fuller and more vital picture of Bethany as a child. She was not just a quiet "goody-goody" when she was little. She was shy, but she also had a sense of humor, and she had been connected and affectionate toward Judith. Through her new renewed contact with Judith, Bethany was freed to identify consciously with her sister. Judith's interests in medical missionary work, and her attendance at a small Quaker college in the area, permitted Bethany to see another kind of life in which she could gain self-esteem without cutting herself off so completely from the real world. Bethany was able to make the observation that *Judith was interested in "doing good" by participating in the world, while she was interested in "being good" by leaving the world.*

Meanwhile, over the summer, Bethany began to keep a diary to chart her self-exploration. She brought her written perceptions of herself and her life into her therapy in the fall. Surprisingly, her writings revealed a sharp and satiric edge, and a keen wit. For the first time we began to laugh together at Bethany's sarcastic observations of others. Bethany was still keeping her distance from both her parents, toward whom she felt cold and critical. While it was painful for Reverend and Ms. Marlowe to recognize Bethany's separation from them, they were able to recognize that Bethany's willingness to show *any* feelings to them was a form of engagement that she had never risked before. They were able to keep trying to talk with Bethany despite her continual rejections of their efforts.

Warning Signs of an Adolescent Retreat from Reality

1. Does not appear to be motivated to seek out or maintain friendships
2. When given a choice, will almost always choose solitary activities; could be described as a "loner"
3. Seems to be detached, emotionally cold or distant, unreachable, or in her/his own world
4. Keeps thoughts and feelings "under wraps"; has no confidant
5. Feels uncomfortable in social situations and avoids them
6. Has no interest in romantic or sexual experiences that would be age appropriate
7. Is attracted to extreme religious or philosophical ideas (cults, ESP, telepathy, clairvoyance, etc.)

In the spring break of Bethany's senior year, she took on her first social challenge—a weekend Catholic retreat with boys and girls her own age. While the invitation to participate filled her with anxiety and dread, Bethany made herself go through with the plan as part of her agenda to "face her fears." She later reported that the event was "no big deal," and she'd kept mainly to herself. Nevertheless, for Bethany, this weekend was a developmental triumph, and was followed by other religious occasions in which she read some of her poetry, planned a special children's mass, and organized meals for the homeless.

Despite the urgings of her parents, her school, and even her sister Judith, Bethany remained steadfast in her refusal to apply to college. Instead, in her senior year, she visited with several Catholic orders to discuss her plans to become a nun. She was particularly impressed by the mother superior of an order of working nuns who actively devoted themselves to the community. She urged Bethany to "get out in the world a bit more" before she made her final decision to take her vows. Toward that end, Bethany decided to join a Christian program that was sending young men and women to build a church in a small village in the Peruvian Andes. She would be living with a Peruvian family for six months, and working on construction with other members of the team.

While Bethany was still a long way from the kinds of relationships that most late adolescents have already experienced in their lives, and while she was not yet able to create either a social or a sexual life, Bethany had begun her adolescent journey. She continued to remain close to her sister Judith, and still felt drawn to the idea of a spiritual community of women, but she was now actively engaged in searching for a more complete way to use herself in the world. Whatever her final destination, Bethany was on the way toward consolidating a fuller, richer, and less restricted life.

CHAPTER 10

An Overattached Response to Adolescence

What Keeps Adolescents Overattached?

We're familiar with the idea that adolescence is an "age of rebellion," and we all know (or have) adolescents who can't wait to lead independent lives. But not all adolescents are anxious to break the ties that bind them. Some, in fact, are quite reluctant to grow up and grow away. They may be afraid to face life on their own; they may see any move toward independence as a betrayal of their parents' love and care; or they may feel responsible for their parents and guilty about taking any steps toward separation.

In addition, some teenagers continue to remain enmeshed with their families for cultural reasons (the Italian daughter, for example, who is expected to share a two-family home with her parents after she's married), or for economic reasons (the Iranian son who is expected to work in his family's jewelry business), or for medical reasons (the unfortunate teenager who is crippled in a motorcycle accident and remains dependent on his parents' physical care).

We've already seen some of the ways in which an anxious, rebellious, depressed, or withdrawn response can shape a youngster's entry into adolescence and influence the eventual resolution of his/her conflicts. But of course, an overattached response to the developmental tasks of these years can also compromise emotional growth, and erode an adolescent's ability to construct a life of his/her own. Overattached adolescents resist the necessary losses they must face, and are unable to use their psychological resources to help them separate out from their primary connection to their families, or to seek out meaningful relationships with members of their own generation. Instead, these youngsters continue to cling.

Often their parents give them a great deal of implicit and even explicit support for their attachment. This support may be presented as a financial consideration ("Why spend good money on an apartment when you could live at home?") or an anxious consideration ("I feel better when I know you're home with us, living in a safe neighborhood."). Many overly attached adolescents have enjoyed a particular childhood closeness with one of their parents—a father, for instance, who cushions all disappointments. ("Don't worry, baby, Daddy will always take care of you.") Or they've come to assume a powerful role in their family that provides them with an important source of self-esteem. ("Now that Daddy's had a stroke, you'll have to be the man in the house.")

We can easily understand how an adolescent and a parent can become dependent on one another during a family crisis. In fact, we would hope that a teenager could "rise to the occasion," and be a source of strength and support for his family when they hit hard times. But often this interdependence continues long past the crisis, making it difficult for the adolescent to disengage later on.

In this last real-life story, I'll be talking about how a young man in late adolescence struggled with an overly attached response to his mother throughout the years of his adolescence—a response that was generated not only from his own psychological needs, but also from the special circumstances that prevailed in his particular family. Alex is an adopted child; he is of a different ethnic and racial background than his adoptive family; and his father has recently died. He is trying to find a comfortable place for his complicated feelings about his father's death, his wishes to know more about his own biological heritage and cultural history, his protectiveness and loyalty toward his mother, and his normal developmental needs, in order to get on with his own life. That's a lot for an adolescent to address all at once.

Alex: Too Close for Comfort?

Alex Cahill was seventeen years old when he made an appointment to see me in the spring. A slim, slight young man of Asian background, he was poised, articulate, and organized. He got straight to the point of his visit. "There are some things you need to know about me to understand my problem. I'm an adopted child. My mother had five miscarriages before they found me in Hong Kong when I was only a few weeks old, so she's always been worried that something could happen to me. My biological parents were both young Chinese university students who couldn't take care of me. My adoptive parents are American and they've been great parents, but my father died suddenly of a brain tumor three years ago, when he was only fifty-six, so now, there's just me and my mom." Alex continued, "Now, I'll tell you my problem. I love my mom a lot, and I don't want to do anything to hurt her, but lately I've had this strong wish to find out more about my background, maybe even go to China to study. But how could I do that? How could I leave her? Every time I think about it, I get this terrible feeling about myself." "What sort of feeling?" I ask. "Like something bad is going to happen, like I'm going to do something bad." "What's bad about this wish?" I say. "Your history is a part of who you are, and it makes sense that you'd like to have more information about this missing part of you." "You can understand," Alex continues, "because you're a psychologist, but I don't think my mother will understand. I'm afraid that she's going to be really, really upset if I start to try to track down more information about my biological parents." "So," I continue, "the sense of dread is about your mom. You're afraid that she'll see your search as a betrayal of her adoption of you. Is that what would cause her pain?" "Yes," Alex states empathically. "You see, we've always been close ever since I was little, and now, more than ever, she depends on me a lot." "You mean since your father died," I note. "That's put more pressure on you. What will happen when you leave after next year for college?" "I'm entering college this fall," Alex continues. "I was skipped a grade, so I'll be graduating in June. I'm going to a university near here, so I can still live at home." "So you've already made some important decisions based on your wishes not to hurt your mom," I note. "Well," Alex continues, "it was one of the best schools for me anyway." (He mentions a top Ivy League university in his city.) "I'm good at math, I did really well on my SAT's, so they gave me a big scholarship, and my father used to teach there."

"What are your worst worries about your mom?" I ask Alex. "I'm all she has," he replies. "She's an only child and so was my dad, and none of my grandparents are alive." "So, you feel it's really up to you to take care of her; you feel really responsible for her." "Yeah," Alex states, "but it's not just a duty thing. I *like* to spend time with her. She's a writer for a science magazine and we like a lot of the same things. We go to movies and museums and out to dinner together. We're, like, good friends." "Do you have any other close friends your own age?" I ask. Alex replies, "Kids my age can be really boring and immature, and my mom is really interesting." "Uh-huh," I mumble. "I don't have much time for a complicated social life anyway," Alex continues. "I have a lot of work at school, I have a lot of projects to do, and I'm writing a science fiction novel." "You have a lot on your mind," I reply. "And then there are all these new thoughts about your biological parents." "I want to know how to find out more about my biological parents, so it won't hurt," Alex replies. "Hurt your mom or hurt you? It sounds to me as if you're trying to work out how you feel about a lot of things at once—your own history, your dad's death, your feelings for your mom, your worries about separating from her. I'm not sure we can get *all* of those or even *any* of those not to hurt." "I don't mind my stuff," Alex explains. "I'm sort of interested in the human mind, anyway. You know, brain behavior, from the neurobiological side, cognitive science, not all that Freud stuff about childhood and sexuality."

"How did you decide to see me?" I ask. (Keep in mind that I'm professionally committed to the study of childhood and sexuality.) "I remember when you came to our high school two years ago to talk to us about that kid that killed himself in our class, and you seemed okay, I mean you sounded normal, so I looked you up in the phone book." "Well," I replied, "I'm glad you remembered me. I think it was a good idea to come here, and I'm very interested in your dilemma. One thing I can hear right away. There's a lot of guilt underneath the surface of your thoughts—and conflict about attachment and separation. We need to find out more about those feelings. And of course, your dad's death has made all of this much more complicated for you. And then, there are the crosscultural issues here that you've raised but you haven't commented on." I smile. "It's a good thing you're good at math because I guess we could say there are a lot of unknown factors in this equation that we need to solve.

"But let's start with the person who's at the center of all your feelings—your mom. What's she like?" Alex replies: "She's smart and pretty and a good cook." "No wonder it's hard to leave home," I note. "Do the two of you ever tangle over anything, or is she easygoing and sweet-tempered, too?" Alex laughs. "Well, she's not perfect. She has her cranky moments, but even then, we don't really fight. Besides, my parents have always treated me more like an adult than like a kid, so there isn't much to fight about. I mean, I always called them by their first names, Phillip and Louisa; I never had a curfew; I don't smoke or drink; I do all my work." "So your mom isn't the only perfect one in the family," I say, teasing Alex a bit. "I don't have any reason to be a rebel," Alex replies. "I don't want anything that I can't have, and I can have pretty much anything that I want." "So, this wish to know more about your biological parents is the first time you've ever wanted anything that you couldn't just get from your mom," I reply. "Yes," Alex replies, "and I feel bad even talking to you about it. It's like I'm keeping a secret from her or something." "It's hard to have a secret life," I reply, "when you and your mom have been so close to each other. That's part of that guilty feeling that I was talking about before. Whenever you have private thoughts of your own, it may feel as if you're doing something wrong."

I asked Alex how he wanted to use his therapy. Did he want to come to see me *with* his mom? Were these issues he wanted to work on alone? And how was he going to pay me, without involving his mom? He promptly replied, "Alone. I don't want my mom to know anything about this, until I know how I'm going to handle things." "I can see you're used to taking charge of things and protecting your mom," I answer. "Is this one of those things that has a lot to do with your dad's death?" I ask. "My dad was a great guy," Alex says, his eyes filling with tears, "but he was a mathematics professor, and his head was always in the clouds. Mom and I always had to take care of the practical things. He'd even forget to eat, if she didn't remind him." "So, you and your mom have been a team for a long time," I note. "Even while your dad was alive." Alex quickly replies, "I don't mind. Anyway, I've got my own money to pay for this. She doesn't have to be involved at all. My dad left me some money, and I'm a computer hacker, and I make lots of money consulting." "That sounds good," I reply, "and you're old enough to be in therapy without your mom's permission. So, let's set up some appointments."

History of the Family

Alex began his treatment talking about his parents and his life with them: "I know people say they had a happy childhood, and then there's all this bad stuff that really happened to them, but I think I *really* had a happy childhood. My dad grew up in Ohio and went to MIT on scholarship. My mom grew up in Oregon and met my dad at a scientific conference. They loved each other, but they couldn't have kids, so they adopted me. My dad taught mathematics at the graduate school of the university I'm attending. He was usually home in between classes working on his computer. He was brilliant. I can't even understand his papers. And my mom wrote for this magazine, so she was always home, too. We always did a lot of things together. In the summers, we'd usually switch houses with another professor, you know, so we didn't have to pay for hotels. I've been to England and Germany and Sweden and Italy and Ireland, and before I was born, my dad was a visiting professor for a year in China. That's how they adopted me. A student of my dad's was pregnant and she didn't want to interrupt her studies. So there they were in China for the summer, and suddenly there was this baby that nobody wanted. It wasn't easy because there was a lot of red tape, but they were finally able to take me out of the country. My dad always used the story of my adoption to teach me about probability theory. He thought the chances of getting me were neat, mathematically. We lived in California for about four years and then we moved east when Dad was appointed to the graduate mathematics department here."

Alex described his parents as a quiet, reserved, scholarly couple. They spent a lot of time reading and writing, and had a lot of professional colleagues with whom they corresponded, but not many close friends. Alex described himself as a "nerd" as a child. He was small for his age and somewhat timid with other children. He remembered that he frequently refused to go to places where other children played (like parks and playgrounds), preferring to stay in his room and work on his own projects. His mother never urged or insisted that he engage with other kids, and if he was teased in school, she comforted him by assuring him that the other children were envious of his intelligence, and they weren't worth his time and trouble. Alex attended a prestigious private boys' school on scholarship, and was always at the top of his class.

As his therapy progressed, Alex began to realize that his

parents had always fostered a sense that he was separate and different from his peers. When he was about four or five years old, his father told him about his adoption. Alex made his father tell him the story over and over again every night before he went to bed. He was fascinated by it, but he does not remember asking any questions at the time about his biological parents. The only part that upset him was that he wanted to look more like his parents and he realized that his features were different. He recalled that when he was about three years old, he had asked his mother, "Why aren't my eyes like yours?" and he remembers the look of pain that crossed her face. He was worried that he'd hurt his mother, but he didn't know what he did. He never asked about their differences again.

Alex described his mother as his "playmate" when he was growing up. When he was seven or eight years old, he remembers trying to read his father's mathematical papers, "so I could be inside his head with him." He recognized that his father's absorption with his work must have made him feel "shut out" at times.

Early in Alex's life, he displayed his mechanical skills, and he reports that his family totally relied on him to take care of most household things, from unstopping drains to fixing the computer to talking with the mechanic about the family car. He remembers being proud of his particular competence in his family because no one else had it. (Poignantly, it was Alex, at fourteen years old, who first noticed the neurological signs of the brain tumor that would eventually claim his father's life.)

Alex's father's illness coincided with his entry into adolescence. While other kids his age were going to parties, hanging out, and beginning to experiment with love and romance, Alex was coping with his father's increasing deterioration and his mother's increasing depression. By mid-adolescence, Alex was trying to deal with his father's death, which propelled him into the role of his mother's comfort and support, a role that he has continued to fill for the past three years. Unfortunately, Alex's prior relationship to his mother (and hers to him) far *exceeded* the ordinary attachment between a parent and a teenager, so that after his father's death, it easily became transformed into an *overattachment* that interfered considerably with Alex's normal development. By the time he reached late adolescence, Alex's emotional and social world was *shrinking*, at the very time that it needed to be *expanding*.

The Five Tasks of Adolescence

Alex is an example of a child who was always encouraged to feel that he was an important part of the adult world his parents inhabited. An only child, he was deeply attached to his parents, who placed him at the center of their emotional and intellectual lives. Set apart from friends and classmates in childhood by his superior intelligence, Alex has not been able to develop much capacity for the give and take of ordinary social relationships. On the rare occasions when he did try to participate with his peers (school trips, graduation parties, and so on), he was usually disappointed, concluding that they were "boring and immature." This had the effect of reconfirming his primary attachment to his family. While Alex's constant exposure to his parents' interests and occupations has helped him to be motivated and devoted to learning, his intellectual life seems to have developed at the expense of both his emotional and social life.

Alex's *overattachment* has left him unprepared to live a full life on his own, and has delayed his ability to master early and mid-adolescent tasks; *he is still seeking most of his emotional satisfactions within his family, he has not formed new attachments, he has not developed a mature sexual identity or embarked upon a sexual or romantic life.* Only Alex's wish to know more about his own history and his decision to seek out therapy independently of his mother testify to the adolescent urges to *develop new ideas and ideals.* With so many of the normal tasks left unaddressed, *Alex has still been unable to consolidate a character structure* that adequately integrates his emotional and social life with his intellectual life, despite the fact that he is seventeen years old and about to attend college. Let's take a look at how the five basic fears have conspired to keep Alex emotionally stunted.

The Five Basic Fears

On the one hand, Alex's parents were skilled at providing him with a "safe sanctuary" in childhood, and adept at providing him with "an emotional cushion" against the world's intrusions, but on the other, Alex was not helped to develop the psychological skills that could help him face the *unknown*—particularly the unknown dimensions of his biological heritage, and his understandable questions about his adoption.

Alex's fears of hurting or alienating his mother reflect his underlying realization that not only is she alone in the world without him, but he would be alone in the world without her. The *fears that an adolescent would normally have of being alone* have been exacerbated by his father's death, and by his profound lack of connection to his peers. In addition, Alex's memories of his childhood make it clear that he has always felt small and somewhat helpless physically. His avoidance of social contact with others (particularly other young men) may be linked as well to underlying *bodily fears* that he has yet to address.

Alex's *fears of the voice of conscience*, the fourth basic fear, dominate his inner world. He is riddled with guilt and conscience-stricken about his wishes to separate from his mother. (You often see heightened worry about parents in youngsters who harbor underlying wishes to separate from them.)

Finally, Alex is expressing many fears about his *sense of self and identity*. He has questions about his biological parents and his cultural identity, he is worried about what role he should play in his mother's life, and he has yet to fully participate in the world of his peers.

The Parents' Part

There are unique conditions in Alex's family life that have clearly contributed to his overattached response to the developmental claims of adolescence:

His mother's inability to hold and nourish a fetus, and her painful experience of repeated failure, may have increased her need to keep Alex close to her. This experience of profound loss, which so many women share as they try to conceive and bear a child, often predisposes both parents to overprotect the child they are finally able to keep and raise. As a child, this unusual closeness to his parents provided Alex with safety, security, and a strong sense of his own worth and value. But in adolescence, particularly without his father's presence to dilute the intensity of his relationship to his mother, this same closeness has begun to obstruct Alex's development.

The dynamics of adoption itself exert a special influence on adolescent development. Adopted children often face particular conflicts about attachment as they move toward this phase of development. Since adolescence is the time of life when identity is shaped and character is consolidated, an adopted teenager can feel particularly torn between his attachment to his nurturing adoptive family, and his curiosity about his abandoning biological family. Parents who leave no room for this curiosity or clearly convey the sense that such an inquiry would cause them conflict, disrupt the adolescent's attempt to come to terms with his own history.

In addition, when adopted children become adolescents, they must come to terms with the fact that they possess two sets of parents, one known to them in *fact* (their adoptive parents), and the other known to them only through their *fantasies* (the biological parents). This can lead to some complicated thoughts and feelings as the adolescent begins to try to deidealize his adoptive parents and to see them in a new, more realistic way. Often the biological parents then take on the lost idealizations, heightening the teenager's yearning to search for and find the biological parents, which can be extremely dismaying to the adoptive parents.

When parents accept or seek out a crosscultural adoption, and the baby cannot be easily perceived as their biological child, the adoptive dynamics become more complicated. Because Alex was clearly Asian, while his parents were not, they tried to make special efforts throughout his childhood to make him feel that he was as much a part of them as a biological child would have been. While these attempts were well intentioned, they also had the effect of ignoring and even obliterating the real ethnic and racial differences that were constantly being acknowledged (often insensitively) by others: "Oh, what a sweet baby. Is he Japanese?" "Isn't he adorable. Where did you get him?" Alex's parents' avoidance of this issue made Alex feel that these cultural and racial differences were "taboo" and should not be recognized or discussed.

Finally, *Alex's development was profoundly affected by the illness and death of his father.* Adolescence is a particularly difficult time to sustain the death of a parent, because it is the time when the teenager would normally be *moving out of the family circle.* Instead, with the death of a parent, an adolescent is often compelled to *move back into the family,* delaying and sometimes even destroying his chances to develop and build a life of his own. What starts out as a normal, healthy response to a family crisis can become rigidified into an abnormal, chronic sense of duty and obligation.

In addition, when the *actual* loss of a parent replaces the *symbolic* loss of the parent, the process of normal *deidealization* (which aids an adolescent's separation from his parents) is interrupted by the *reidealizations* that are an inevitable part of the mourning process. You can get angry at a healthy father without too much guilt because he's strong enough to "take it," but getting angry at a sick father is much harder to do, and maintaining anger at a father who has died is really difficult.

Finally, an adolescent's *identification* with a parent who is lost to him usually intensifies when a parent dies (because through this identification, the adolescent can internalize the lost parent and symbolically keep him alive). It's not unusual, for example, for a teenager who always hated playing tennis to take up the game after his tennis-playing father suddenly dies of a heart attack. Or for a daughter who never liked to garden to take over the care of her mother's flowerbeds after she's died of breast cancer (or for Alex, for that matter, to want to become a mathematician like his father).

What Needs to Change?

The tie that binds Alex to his mother is too close for his own comfort. He is in danger of staying home for the rest of his life, stepping into his father's shoes, and continuing to turn toward his mother (and she toward him) for nurturance and companionship and love. This resolution would prevent both Alex and his mother from pursuing more appropriate loving relationships with members of their own generation.

Alex's own wish to travel and study in China reveals his understanding, on some level, of the depth of his present emotional entrapment. He realizes that he needs to get far, far away from his mom, in order to give himself enough space to lead a more mature life. *This wish to separate (which is also making Alex feel guilty) needs to be clarified and strengthened in his therapy.* Currently his wishes for automomy have been paralyzed by conflict. This means that Alex must begin to deal with his overattachment to his mother, his overdeveloped sense of responsibility for her, and his ambivalent feelings about replacing his father in his mother's affections (a place he seems to have occupied even when his father was alive). As long as Alex remains so emotionally entwined with his mother, the possibility of romantic encounters with his peers is thwarted.

Both the absence of Alex's father (psychologically, when Alex was younger, and actually, through his death) as well as his fantasies about his adoption have made it possible for Alex to entertain more romantic feelings toward his mother than are useful or healthy for him. *In other words, in order for things to change in his life, Alex will have to begin to deal with "all that Freudian stuff"* (including his feelings that his mother is his "best playmate").

Alex will also need to work hard to develop some social skills and to take some social risks to counteract his mother's overprotection of him, which has served to alienate him from his peers. ("They're just envious of you.") He will need to permit himself to develop both emotional and sexual connections to others and to place his trust in strangers. His spending an extended time in China may go a long way toward freeing up the inhibitions that have prevented him from pursuing these normal connections.

And finally, Alex's mother needs help to permit and encourage her son to separate from her. She also needs support to reach out to men and women her own age who can help her to cope with the grief of losing a spouse, and encourage her to build a new life for herself. In the past, Ms. Cahill has relied on her relationship with her son to fulfill most of her emotional needs. This has prevented her (as well as Alex) from forming other appropriate attachments.

Using the Four C's to Help a Teenager Like Alex

Compassion: Alex's mom, Louisa, needs to *talk directly to Alex about his dad's death and acknowledge its impact on both of them.* "Dad died three years ago, and I know we both still miss him a lot. I've lost my partner in life and you've lost your dad. Because we're such a small family, Dad's death leaves a big empty place in our lives. But we've both got to try to fill it."

Communication: She also needs to *communicate her thoughts about the future, acknowledging the inevitability of separation as a part of that future.* "You're almost an adult, and you're going to need to make choices and reach for things in your life that may take you away from me. I love you very much and it's going to be hard for both of us to separate from each other, but we both need to try if we're going to move on and get what we need."

Comprehension: Through compassion and communication, *Alex's mom has got to make sure that he really understands that she is aware of his worry and sense of guilt and responsibility for her and that it's time to relinquish these feelings.* "I know that my depression has made both of us feel bad, and that it's increased your worries about me, but I need to learn how to live my life on my own, and I want you to have a real life too—with friends and fun, without having to think about me all the time. Nothing would make me sadder than to think that you were holding yourself back from doing things because of me."

Competence: Louisa can help Alex to see that *the more he moves out in the world, the richer both their lives will be.* "I hope that one day, you'll have your own family and your own career. Dad and I always talked about how happy we would be when you had a chance to find work you love and a girl you love, and maybe even a family of your own. When you were little you used to tell me you were going to have ten children, so that they'd never be lonely. That was a wonderful idea!"

What Happened to Alex and His Parent?

Six months into Alex's treatment, he was ready to ask his mother to join us. Louisa Cahill was a delicate-looking woman whose intelligence and thoughtfulness were evident, despite the fact that she was obviously depressed. I was able to observe how diminished Alex's energy immediately became in the face of his mother's emotional heaviness. After just a few sessions in which we explored the developmental dilemma Alex was facing, I noted that it would be easier for Alex to pursue his own development if he could be assured that his mother was feeling better. I asked Ms. Cahill if she would be willing to see a bereavement counselor for a while. For several months, she declined the offer, but she finally agreed "for Alex's sake," as we continued to emphasize how his sense of responsibility for her was paralyzing him. Through her counselor, Louisa began to participate in a bereavement group, which she reported was "a surprising comfort." At the urging of another woman in her group, Louisa began to play bridge (a game that she had played before she was married) and she soon accumulated master points and began to play seriously in tournaments. These tournaments required her to travel, opening up more opportunities for social encounters with a community of people who shared some of her interests, and providing her with more of an adult life. Alex, interestingly, initially showed some jealousy about his mother's social activities, and he worried and fussed over her traveling in an overprotective way that probably mimicked her earlier overprotection of him.

Gradually, as Louisa's grief and mourning for her husband abated, and she began to permit herself to live more in the world, Alex, too, began to be more capable of leading a fuller life. The joint therapy sessions with his mom had given them both a chance to discuss his adoption directly for the first time. Louisa was able to reveal her fears that he would prefer his biological parents because they were Chinese, and that he would resent her, a white woman, for taking him away from them. Alex's reassurances to his mother permitted her to tell him his biological mother's name as well as the name of the small village where she had been born and raised— the first key to Alex's biological heritage.

The following year Alex was able to make the decision to spend the summer in China. He decided to study tai chi with a famous teacher, and visit the university in Hong Kong where his father had been a professor and his biological parents had been students. Interestingly, he ultimately made the decision *not* to try to meet his birth mother or birth father. When he returned, Alex explained that he discovered he wasn't as interested in his *past* as he was in his *future*. In addition, he realized that he had considerable anger toward his biological parents that he'd never acknowledged. "They were as old as I am now," he exclaimed, "and I would never give a son away if I got someone pregnant, never!"

Alex continued with his studies of tai chi after he returned to the United States, and he began to make friends with a young man from Thailand who had been in this country for only two years. Invited back to his new friend's home for dinner, Alex was captivated by his friend's sixteen-year-old sister, and she with him. Her family did not permit her to date as she was too young, but Alex was clearly welcome in their home, and her father (who had been an engineer in his own country) obviously approved of him.

So, in late adolescence, Alex was beginning to take up some of the developmental tasks that he had been unable previously to approach. He was able to *begin to separate from his mother* (aided by her increasing ability to separate from him) and to *form some new attachments.* In addition, Alex was beginning to be less compromised by guilt. He was starting to *develop his own ideas* and pursue his own path. Most important, he was beginning to expand his emotional horizons and *his sense of himself was beginning to become both more complicated and more consolidated.* The only adolescent task that Alex had yet to address was the *development of a sexual life and a mature sexual identity.* Locked into his long-term overattachment to his mother, and constrained by his guilt and conflict over his father's death, Alex's sexual life had been developmentally delayed. While he had recently begun to feel more confidence in his body, he was still quite shy and inhibited. His choice of a younger girl, whose family kept careful watch over her, was a wise one for Alex. He could be comfortable with his newly emerging attraction to the opposite sex, without feeling that he had to act on his emotions.

Alex's psychotherapy had helped him to understand his overattachment to his mother and the developmental price he paid for this mutual devotion. Until late adolescence, the unusual comforts of his family protected Alex from having to encounter the outside world, but now Alex seems ready and able to move on. As he wryly commented, "I'm a late bloomer, but I hope to catch up." Alex has embarked on his rightful adolescent journey, with every hope of crossing over into a satisfying adult life.

Are You and Your Adolescent Overattached?

1. Does your adolescent have any friends his/her own age?
2. Does your adolescent prefer to spend time with you rather than with his/her peers?
3. Does your adolescent worry about you a lot?
4. Do you find yourself wondering how you'll manage without your adolescent?
5. Do you find you rely on your adolescent's advice more than your partner's advice?
6. Sometimes, do you feel like your adolescent is the parent and you're the child?

Coda: Journey's End

Crossing Over

In this book, I've tried to help you think about what it means to become an adolescent, and what it means to become the parent of an adolescent in today's times. I've explained the enormous physiological and psychological changes that all adolescents must integrate, and I've described the new, more perilous environment in which these changes take place. I've outlined the five basic developmental tasks that each and every adolescent must solve, and talked about how to use the four C's to enhance communication with your adolescent. I've explored the five basic fears that can erode and compromise your adolescent's growth, and finally, I've told you the stories of five different teenagers who, for a time, lost their way on the adolescent journey, and eventually found their way back.

But as your adolescent's journey nears its end, you will also need to think about what it means to be a "grown-up," and what it will mean to become the parent of a grown-up child. This is particularly confusing in today's times, because it no longer seems clear exactly when an adolescent crosses over into the adult world, or even what criteria can be used to mark her arrival at this destination. What is adulthood, anyway? Is it the age at which you can drive or vote or leave school? Are you an adult once you have served in the armed forces or become self-supporting or married? Our present inability to determine when one becomes an adult and is held responsible for one's actions can produce some odd discrepancies. For example, thousands of teenagers in this country marry before they are eighteen, which means they get to *have* sex before they are permitted to *watch* sex in an X-rated movie. There are some inconsistencies. The age of consent, for instance, varies considerably, so that sexual behavior that might be perfectly *legal* in one state can become *illegal* once you cross the state line. There are even some absurdities, such as the misguided prosecution of a six-year-old boy for sexual harassment of a five-year-old girl.

Just a generation ago, the parameters of adult life seemed familiar and predictable. We all knew who the adults were. Adults were those people who graduated from school, found jobs, fell in love, got married, had children, advanced in their careers, made money, and looked forward to retirement. Alas, nowadays, none of these developmental milestones is necessarily sequential or even inevitable. Immature, unmarried teenagers have babies and so do mature, unmarried women. Heterosexual couples raise children, and so do homosexual couples. Older men and women continue to work with no plans to retire, and younger men and women "strike it rich" and retire in their thirties. And it's hard these days to tell if a sixty-year-old man is the grandfather of the baby he's wheeling in that stroller, or the father.

Just as we've discussed how adolescence has become a more diffuse, prolonged, and extended phase of development, reaching way into the "thirty-something" generation, so, too, young adulthood has been pushed further into the forties, middle age now spans the fifties and sixties, and even people in their seventies and eighties prefer to describe themselves as "mature," rather than "elderly."

Most of you reading this book will live longer and lead healthier lives than your parents. You will also look and feel younger. (A quick peek at your parents' old photo album will confirm this observation!) And there's more good news, because the lengthening of your life span also means that you and your soon-to-be-adult child are likely to have many more years together than ever before. This will offer you more opportunities to keep transforming your relationship to each other in surprising and wonderful ways.

Lasting Impressions

Adolescence gives your son or daughter a chance to revise the first childhood draft of her life—a chance to work on a later edition of herself that is yet to come. This book has outlined many of the ways and means of this revision. Most particularly, in the five stories I have told, you can trace how Elisa, Jennifer, Frankie, Bethany, and Alex first *formed* the conflicts and constraints of their childhood years, and then *transformed* them through adopting new adolescent resolutions to their old problems.

But what happens after adolescence? Luckily, for all of us, development continues; it never ends. Adulthood, too, will afford your adolescent another and another and yet another chance to *create* and *re-create* the dimensions of his or her life. And as each new layer of experience is laid down, it will shift the meaning of everything that has gone before. A tense relationship with an overanxious adolescent (like Elisa) can become more relaxed once she becomes an adult and falls in love; a confrontational relationship with an angry adolescent (like Frankie) can become more cooperative once he becomes an adult and starts his own business; a stormy relationship with a moody adolescent (like Jennifer) can become calmer once she marries and bears her own child; a distant relationship to a withdrawn adolescent can become closer after an illness or a separation; and an enmeshed relationship to a dependent adolescent can become more autonomous as he grows up, builds his career, and begins to feel his own adult strength. It is in these ways that development gives us time and time again to rewrite the history of our lives, without having to reach a final version.

Some closing thoughts about the meaning of the adoles-

cent passage: I have been trying in this book to help parents
raise emotionally healthy teenagers in today's troubled times,
so I have been focusing on the problems that today's teens
and today's parents must face. But it is equally important to
recognize that adolescence is not all storm and stress and
struggle. There are very special pleasures to these years as
well.

Adolescence is a time of reckless action, but it is also a
time of focused commitment. It is a time of terrifying experimentation, but it is also a time of exciting adventure. It is a
time of separation and sadness, but it it also a time of attachment and joy. Most important, many of the qualities that I
have described as characteristic of adolescence can go on to
enrich your children's adult lives. Adolescent *energy*, for example, will enliven their work and sustain their adult accomplishments; adolescent *passion* may deepen their relationships
and intensify their devotion; adolescent *assertion* can help
them confront difficult situations and make necessary
changes; and adolescent *enthusiasm* enables them, as adults,
to enjoy themselves and to feel optimistic about the future.
The years of adolescence leave a lasting impression on all
of us.

APPENDIX
When You or Your Adolescent Need Help

Parents face a lot of difficulties in their daily attempts to determine whether their adolescents are "on track" or are derailed in their development. For example, suppose your thirteen-year-old daughter seems tired and listless most of the time. Is she getting enough sleep? Does she have mononucleosis? Or is she clinically depressed? Without knowing what your adolescent is thinking and feeling, it's impossible to decide what's needed. Should you insist on an earlier bedtime? Have her blood tested? Or take her to a psychologist?

Or, suppose your fifteen-year-old son has trouble concentrating and seems disoriented and disorganized most of the time. Is he abusing drugs? Is he suffering with learning disabilities? Or is he overwhelmed and agitated? Should you send him for drug rehabilitation? Have him evaluated by a neuropsychologist? Or encourage him to talk about his anxieties?

And what about an adolescent who is unhappy at her new high school? Is the work too hard? Is she shy and unable to make friends? Or is her unhappiness temporary, reflecting a normal process of adjustment? Should you explore other schools? Encourage her to have a pajama party? Or just remain compassionate and assure her things will feel better in

a few months? How can a parent tell when to leave well
enough alone, and when to consult with a professional?

Most of us are aware of how to get the right kind of professional help for *physical* symptoms, and are comfortable
about medical consultation. If your daughter has acne, you
whisk her off to the dermatologist; if your son has a fever,
you immediately contact the internist; if your teenager breaks
out in hives, an allergist is called. But we are not so alert or
informed about *emotional* symptoms, nor are we as comfortable seeking out a psychological consultation. Sometimes the
source of the problem may lie within you, and you may be
the one who needs some *psychotherapy*. Sometimes the problem may lie between you and your partner, and *couples therapy*
may be indicated to ease the tensions, and sometimes *parent
guidance* is needed—special professional support to help you
find a way to become a more effective parent. There are situations where the problem seems to be embedded within the
dynamics of the entire family, and *family therapy* (where every
member participates) may be the best solution. And of
course, when your adolescent is floundering in his life, or
suffering with internalized conflicts, *adolescent psychotherapy*
may be the most direct and effective way to help him work
on problems that are blocking his psychological growth.

Parents can have a particularly hard time in adolescence
deciding when a child's problem is a *normal* part of the ups
and downs of development, and when it is an *abnormal* reaction that requires professional intervention. In this last section of this book I want to help you understand and respond
to the special needs that you and your adolescent may have,
and to recognize when problems in your life exceed your
ability to cope with them.

Every relationship can hit some hard times, and the relationship between parents and their children is no exception.
Your teenager's *external* behavioral symptoms (losing weight,
failing tests, fighting with friends, abusing alcohol, and so on)
are signals that her *internal* emotional resources are overwhelmed. A teenager's symptoms should be understood as a
cry for help, and that help needs to come from you. *Effective*

*parents pay attention to their adolescent's behavior and recognize the
early warning signs of psychic distress.*

But it's remarkable how often parents will collude with a
teenager's attempts to remain *hidden from view.* One parent
of a fourteen-year-old girl described how she remained "totally unaware" of the fact that her teenager was five months'
pregnant. She ignored her daughter's missed periods, morning bouts with nausea, and obviously swollen breasts and
stomach—unable to imagine the possibility of pregnancy. Another father recalled seeing his teenage son holding his hunting rifle on his lap for hours at a time, just staring out the
window, but attached no significance to the scene until his
son tried to kill himself. In another family, two well-educated
and perceptive parents repeatedly ignored the fact that sums
of money were missing from their home, unable to believe
their daughter was a serious cocaine addict until they saw her
selling their stereo on a street corner.

After the fact, parents frequently say, "If only I had
known," but often teenagers are desperately trying to give
their parents clues. They *reveal* the very problems they are
trying to *conceal.* It's up to us to get these messages before
it's too late.

The Five Mental Health Myths

Parents who would fly to the ends of the earth to track down
the most skilled doctor for a physical problem will think nothing of delaying or avoiding consultation with a mental health
professional about an emotional problem. Why? I have found
that there are five major myths about mental health consultation that usually prevent parents (even relatively sophisticated, effective parents) from seeking out such help when it
is needed.

She'll Outgrow It!

There is so much emphasis on adolescence as a *normal phase of development* that it's easy, when things aren't going well, for us to tell ourselves that if we do nothing, our adolescent will simply "outgrow" the problem. Some of the time, this attitude, in fact, may be appropriate to the situation, particularly if your teenager's disturbed behavior is a *reaction* to a recent event (like the death of a grandparent, or a mugging, or a divorce). But (and here's the important distinction) if your adolescent's behavioral reactions seem to have *"hardened"* (become brittle) and if her reactions have *persisted over time* (remained unchanged), then she is demonstrating that she does not have the internal resources to master this recent experience, nor to move on in her life. When this happens, your adolescent's reactions have created an obstacle to her ongoing development. In these cases, she is no more likely to "outgrow" this emotional fracture than she would be to "outgrow" a physical fracture of her arm. Seeking out a mental health professional to help her heal is as essential as seeking out an orthopedist would be. An orthopedist will set your teenager's fractured bone so that it will grow in the right direction, reducing interference with the arm's function as your adolescent develops. Similarly, a mental health professional can help your adolescent heal the fractures in her mind. An adolescent therapist can help reduce the obstacles to growth, diminishing the abnormal interferences with the mind's natural course of development.

You Have to Be Really Crazy to Wind Up in Therapy!

Just as the practice of pediatrics is often referred to as "well-,,baby care," so the practice of adolescent therapy is primarily work with youngsters who are *not* severely disturbed, but rather, have come up against a developmental obstacle, either internally (conflicts within their own minds) or externally (conflicts within the dynamics of their relationship to

their parents, their family, their friends, or their school).*
Most of these adolescents are struggling with psychological
issues that can be effectively eased by psychotherapeutic
treatment—issues like the ones I have addressed in the stories of Elisa, Frankie, Jennifer, Bethany, and Alex (anxieties,
eating disorders, angry, rebellious, manipulative, or oppositional behavior, low self-esteem, lack of self-confidence, depression, shyness, distrust, withdrawal, asceticism, etc.). Many
of the parents of these adolescents can also be helped to alter
both their understanding and their approach, in order to
lighten the emotional burden their adolescents have shoul-
dered. Most important, seeking out psychological support
early in the onset of the problem prevents it from worsening,
and permits new patterns of behavior for both you and your
adolescent to take hold, easing his entry into adult life.

Therapy Is Only a Crutch!

Very often, when parents first consult with me, one of their
greatest fears is that their teenager will become *dependent* on
the very process that they are hoping will make them *independent.* Parents like this often unwittingly sabotage their
teenager's treatment by continuously giving her the ongoing
message that "it's time you stood on your own two feet." The
parents of one of my teenage patients repeatedly required
her to assess her own mental health, asking her every few
months, "Don't you think you can manage by yourself
now?" or "You've gotten so much better, isn't it time to
stop?" No matter how many times I held special family meetings with them to point out that these questions only produced a panic reaction in their daughter (which then

* There is, of course, a small, constant percentage of adolescents who suffer
with severe mental disabilities, just as there are a small percentage of adolescents who suffer with severe physical disabilities. An understanding of
and approach to these disabilities (which appear to have their origin in
abnormal brain behavior) lies outside of the scope of this book.

dismantled her fragile growth and reawakened her old conflicts), it was still hard for them to control their own wishes
to terminate their daughter's treatment so they could feel less
threatened.

Sometimes parents will say, "I don't want therapy to become a crutch." And I often reply, "Why not? A crutch, after
all, is something you use to lean on when you're not yet
strong enough to support your own weight. As your body
heals, you naturally use your crutch less and less until, one
day, you throw your crutch away and are ready to walk."
When you make the decision to take your teenager to a therapist, it is because she is dealing with something that she is
not strong enough to master on her own. She needs the support of a therapist. Through therapy, the adolescent's mind
is strengthened, and as she is strengthened, she takes over
more and more of the therapeutic process on her own. One
day, when she is strong enough and has understood enough,
treatment will no longer be necessary to her development,
and her therapy will stop. She will now be ready to throw
away her crutch and stand on her own two feet. What's wrong
with that?

Therapy Will Open Up a Can of Worms!

Every family has its struggles. Sometimes one of the members
of a family becomes emotionally overwhelmed and can no
longer manage. When this happens to an adult, sometimes
we say that she has suffered a "nervous breakdown." This has
become a socially acceptable way of indicating that things
have gotten to be too much to handle. *But so-called "nervous
breakdowns" can happen to adolescents, too.* As we've seen, they
can begin to have trouble eating or sleeping, or listening or
learning, or making friends. They can become anxious, rebellious, depressed, obsessed, preoccupied, or withdrawn.
They can be unable to function at school, or be unable to
leave their home, their room, or even their bed.

When this happens to your adolescent, you had better

"open up the can of worms," because that's the only way to let them out. Otherwise, both you and your adolescent are trapped inside. Every family has its wormy side, but keeping things in the dark only encourages more worms to grow. Shedding some light on the issue enables you to see things as they are. (After all, it's only worms, anyway!) The most important thing the effective parent of an adolescent can do when things go wrong, is to get help to get better. Translate the four C's into effective action:

Let your teenager know you understand what she's feeling. (Compassion)
Recognize the warning signs of trouble and acknowledge them. (Communication)
Address your teenager's problems directly with him and explain your concerns. (Comprehension)
Introduce psychotherapy as a way to address your adolescent's problems. Insist upon his/her participation (at least for a trial run). (Competence)

It's All My Fault!

Bringing your adolescent to a therapist is much harder than bringing your adolescent to any other kind of doctor. That's because if a teenager gets a virus, you don't think it's your fault. But, because you are so intimately connected to and responsible for your adolescent's life, you feel responsible if something goes wrong. Many parents are reluctant to "bare their souls" to a professional who (they're afraid) will judge them and (they're sure) find them lacking.

This is not to say that parents aren't often part of their teenagers' problems (just as teenagers are certainly part of their parents' problems!). But even with the most devoted, attuned, sensitive, and effective parents, and even with the strongest, most resilient, and adaptable teenagers, all kinds of unexpected psychological difficulties can arise that may require special attention. If you feel that the therapist you consult is *judging you* rather than *helping you* explore and understand, find another therapist!

Choosing a Therapist

Picking a professional who can work with you and your adolescent is understandably confusing to most parents—first, because mental health practitioners come from many different professional backgrounds. Adolescent therapists, for example, may be drawn from psychiatry, psychology, social work, nursing, or education. But whatever the therapist's background, what's most important is whether the therapist has had *specialized training to work with adolescents and their parents*. Without this training, you are much less likely to find a practitioner who is aware of and alert to the special developmental needs of teenagers, and you are much less likely to find a therapist who is able to address those needs effectively. You are also less likely to get the kind of empathic parent guidance that will help you understand and improve your ongoing relationship with your adolescent.

Each of the mental health disciplines brings its own unique perspective to the treatment of teenagers. For example, psychiatry is the only discipline at this point licensed to prescribe drugs, and psychiatrists are therefore most familiar with the extensive advances in psychopharmacology and with the effects of psychotropic medications. (Nonmedical therapists consult with a psychopharmacologist if they wish to add medication to their treatment plan.)

On the other hand, many psychologists and clinical social workers with advanced adolescent training have extensive experience with the kinds of psychological difficulties that enmesh teenagers and their parents, and both of these disciplines may be able to offer the understanding and therapeutic interventions that will effectively address these issues. In addition, psychologists are specially trained in the administering of psychological tests, which can be crucial to the evaluation and diagnosis of many psychological disturbances in adolescence, while social workers are usually familiar with the special resources in your particular community, including psychiatric and rehabilitation centers, hospitals, special camps and schools, group homes for adolescents, etc. Psychiatric nurse practitioners (nurses with special psychiatric training) are also licensed to provide adolescent therapy in some states, and may be particularly sensitive to the problems of teenagers with chronic physical illnesses (epilepsy, diabetes, cerebral palsy, etc.). And both art therapists and dance therapists are licensed to work with patients in some states.

As with all professional referrals, a satisified customer is your best resource. Ask your friends and relatives if they've had any good personal experiences with mental health practitioners, or if they've heard of anyone excellent "through the grapevine." Schools are often a fine source of professional referrals as well, since they often maintain a referral list. Your pediatrician or family doctor may also be a good person to ask for a referral, but keep in mind that you are more likely to be sent to a psychiatrist by your doctor, since doctors often feel most comfortable recommending colleagues who share their medical background. In most cities and large towns, there may also be local mental health organizations or hospitals that you can call for referrals, or you may be able to find a training institute that specializes in adolescence and can provide you with a listing of its graduates. National organizations for each discipline (American Psychiatric Association, American Psychological Association, National Association for Social Workers, for example) maintain lists of their members who treat adolescents.

Over and above the standard discipline training for a Ph.D., C.S.W., D.S.W., M.D., R.N., and so on, some mental health practitioners go on for *postdegree specialty training* in psychoanalytic therapy, family therapy, behavioral therapy, cognitive therapy, and other specialties. All of these represent different approaches to psychological problems, and many of these approaches can help you and your adolescent. The approach used in this book is *developmentally based* and *psycho-*

analytically informed. It is an approach that I have practiced with confidence for more than twenty-five years. It empha-sizes change through understanding, and attempts to help you and your adolescent dismantle old, destructive patterns of behavior while building new, more effective responses. It is not a "quick fix," but it does produce lasting results.

Don't be afraid to ask any therapist you interview to tell you about her education, her training, and her approach. Don't be afraid to ask about the therapist's clinical expe-rience, either. Has she treated many adolescents? Many adolescents the same age as your son or daughter? Many ad-olescents with problems similar to your son's or daughter's problems?

Remember, therapy, above all, is a relationship—a special kind of relationship that makes the expression, exploration, and understanding of your adolescent's emotional struggles possible. It is also an extended relationship, very different from "Take two aspirin and call me in the morning." So, you need to ask yourself, "Do I like and trust this therapist? Is this someone that I would want my teenager to get to know? Do I think she's smart and thoughtful? Can I talk easily and in depth to her? Do I think she has the capacity to help me and my adolescent?" *You should be able to have a positive feeling about the therapist you select, before you entrust your son or daughter to her care.*

Find out, too, if your adolescent's therapist will meet pe-riodically or regularly with *you.* Often adolescents need the privacy of seeing their own treating professional, and you may not be a part of your teenager's treatment. Will there be periodic opportunities for you to meet with your adolescent's therapist? If not, will you (and/or your partner) be seeing another therapist?

While your adolescent has the absolute right to *approve* of the selection of his/her therapist, a younger adolescent (ten to fifteen) cannot be expected (or permitted) to *choose* his/her own mental health professional. (You wouldn't let her select her own orthopedic surgeon, would you?) This is too great a burden for an adolescent to assume, and further, a youngster this age does not have any sense of the appropriate criteria for making this decision. It's best to interview several therapists yourself and choose the one *you* like best. If your adolescent is particularly oppositional, a choice between two previously screened (and approved) therapists can be offered to him, giving him some options.

On the other hand, it is appropriate for an older adolescent (sixteen to nineteen) to be involved in the selection of his/her therapist (if they wish). Older adolescents can be given two or three names of competent therapists and make appointments to meet with them, choosing the one with whom they feel most comfortable. *Again, make sure you're confident about the choices before you present them to your adolescent.*

Of course, a late-adolescent or postadolescent who is living outside of your home will probably be making their own inquiries and choosing their own therapist (though, of course, you may still be "footing the bill"). This is an appropriate task for an "almost adult," and your input or opinion may (or may not) be solicited. (Interestingly, even most young adults still seek out parental recommendations.)

Talking About Therapy

So now you've realized that your adolescent needs help above and beyond what you can provide. And you understand that in today's times, seeking out the help of a professional adolescent therapist to address emotional problems is no more (and no less) appropriate than seeking out the help of an ophthalmologist to address your adolescent's problems with vision. You're also aware that the earlier you recognize and help your teenager, the greater your chances will be of avoiding more serious consequences for both of you. Now you are ready to approach your adolescent about treatment. But what should you say? There are three important elements to include as you create your dialogue.

Discuss your adolescent's symptoms directly. (Communication)

Empathize with your adolescent's conflicts. (Compassion/ Comprehension)

Describe what therapy is and how it will help your adolescent to feel stronger. (Competence)

Here's a dialogue between a father and an early adolescent (twelve to fourteen years old) about therapy:

Compassion: This dad opens the conversation by *expressing compassion* for his son's unhappiness.

"Mom and I have been really worried about you lately. You've been down in the dumps, and there doesn't seem to be anything we can do to help you feel better."

Communication: He also lets his adolescent know *the problem is real,* and he's been observing and thinking about it for some time.

"First, we thought it was just changing schools, and you needed some time to get adjusted, but things don't really seem to be getting any better. I know it's been hard to make friends in your new school and I think you feel lonely."

Comprehension: He's linking his son's feelings (depression) with his behavior (writing a sucide note), reassuring him that *he's gotten the message.*

"I found this note you wrote, in your wastebasket, where you said you wished you could die, and you drew a boy with a noose around his neck. I know you didn't intend me to see your private note, but I'm glad I found it, because it helped us to know how unhappy you really are."

Competence: Now, this dad supports his son and offers him a better way to deal with these feelings.

"We wouldn't be taking good care of you, if we let you suffer without doing something about it. When kids feel really depressed, like you do, there are special therapists that they can go to."

More Competence: This discussion lets his son know that his parents are already trying to help. Therapy is presented positively as a course of action that offers *hope for the future.*

"We went to see a few therapists last week to pick someone we feel you could really trust with your problems. We liked this guy Bob Morris best. He's young but he's smart and really nice and easy to talk to. He helps kids with problems like yours by talking to them. We've made an appointment for you to see him next week, so you can get to the bottom of these bad feelings and get rid of them."

But suppose you've said all of that, and instead of your adolescent eagerly awaiting his appointment, he protests and refuses to go. What if, instead of a cooperative, compliant, relieved adolescent, you wind up with a sullen, oppositional, rebellious one?

Once you've decided that your adolescent needs professional help, you must stick to your decision. This is part of what being an effective parent means. You wouldn't give your adolescent the *option* to take an antibiotic for her strep throat—or let her decide *whether* she wanted to get her appendix taken out. Similarly, you can't give your adolescent the *option* to decide whether or not she'll go to therapy for her depression, or *whether* she should be evaluated for her academic failures. *This decision is up to you.* It's best if she understands that therapy is in her best interest, but treatment is not impossible if she doesn't. (In fact, part of every adolescent therapist's training deals with handling resistant adolescents as well as resistant parents!)

Most of the time, it will be your adolescent's anxiety, fear, or humiliation that stands in the way of treatment. When that's addressed, the resistance falls away. Here's a possible way of handling an adolescent's protest that again combines compassion with communication, comprehension, and competence.

(ANGRY) ADOLESCENT: "Forget it, No way! I'm not crazy and I'm not going to see any stupid shrink!"

MOM: "Of course you're not crazy, but you *are* sad and upset, and maybe even angry about things that you can't talk to us about. Lots of kids and lots of adults talk to shrinks when they're having problems, just like they go to doctors. Remember when Adam's parents were divorcing and he told us that he was seeing a therapist? And what about last year, when your cousin Julia was doing so poorly in school, and she was tested and then went to see that psychologist who helped her with her learning problems? You know and I know that these feelings aren't going away or get-

ting better. You need help and you
owe it to yourself to at least try it.
We'll meet with a therapist next
week. You can either see her on
your own, or with us, and then
we'll discuss it again."

Remember, you're not alone in helping your adolescent
to accept therapy. The therapist is there to provide you with
support as well. If you are having a particularly difficult time
persuading your adolescent to come for an appointment, and
none of the approaches that I've outlined in this chapter
seem to help, call your new therapist. Now, it's his/her problem, too! Engaging an adolescent in treatment, helping
him/her to understand the nature of the problem, awaken-
ing an interest and investment in a richer more complex life,
and creating a trusting therapeutic relationship in which the
adolescent feels free to be his/her fullest self, is the job of a
skilled adolescent therapist.

In order to help you get a sense about *when* you or your
adolescent might need to seek out professional attention, I've
created the following Psychological Checklists.

A PSYCHOLOGICAL CHECKLIST FOR YOU

1. Do you and your partner disagree or fight a lot in front of
   the kids? Do the fights get abusive or even violent?
2. Are you and your partner contemplating a separation or
   have you just separated or divorced your partner?
3. Do you find yourself feeling depleted and exhausted most
   of the time?
4. Do you often feel that being a mother, or being a father, is
   a joyless or thankless task?
5. Do you find yourself losing your temper when you're around
   your adolescent? Do you scream or hit him/her?
6. Do you have a major drug or alcohol problem? Does your
   partner?
7. Do you look for every opportunity to spend time *away* from
   your kids?

8. Do you feel your adolescent is not living up to your expectations or not turning out the way you imagined?
9. Do you feel very anxious when you're not with your adolescent, and imagine all the terrible things that could happen to him/her?
10. Are you or your partner seriously ill, or are most of your emotional and physical energies mobilized by the serious illness of someone close to you?
11. Has there been a significant death in the family?
12. Do you wish you could just escape from your life? Do you sometimes wish you could give up or die?

A PSYCHOLOGICAL CHECKLIST FOR YOUR ADOLESCENT

1. Has there been any sharp or substantial change for the worse in your adolescent's behavior?
2. Has your adolescent's school performance consistently deteriorated? Does your adolescent appear to be struggling and/or frustrated or is she/he cutting school or not turning in assignments?
3. Does your adolescent have a serious and consistent problem with eating? (Gaining weight/losing weight?)
4. Does your adolescent have difficulty getting to sleep or staying asleep or does she/he sleep too much?
5. Has your adolescent's mood seemed consistently sad, blue, or melancholy?
6. Has your adolescent seemed anxious, nervous, fearful, or phobic for some time? Is she/he afraid to go out or leave the house?
7. Has your adolescent been steadily lying or stealing? (Are money or possessions missing from the house?)
8. Has your adolescent repeatedly gotten into aggressive fights at home, in school, or in his/her neighborhood?
9. Does your adolescent seem unusually volatile and unpredictable? Have you smelled marijuana, noticed drug paraphernalia, or seen powder or pills in his/her room?
10. Is your adolescent consistently reporting that she/he has no friends, and that no one likes him/her? Would you describe your adolescent as very shy socially, or a "loner"?
11. Does your adolescent seem precociously interested in or overinvested in sexuality? Does she/he trade sex for love?

12. Has your adolescent ever reported that he/she doesn't want to live, wishes he/she were dead, or imagined his/her own death in specific detail?

If you've answered *yes* to any of these questions, then a professional consultation may be useful or even essential to both you and your adolescent. You've just spent a lot of time carefully reading these chapters; now it may be necessary to get the help you need—beyond this book. Good luck!

INDEX

· A NOTE ON THE TYPE ·

The typeface used in this book is a version of Baskerville, originally designed by John Baskerville (1706–1775) and considered to be one of the first "transitional" typefaces between the "old style" of the continental humanist printers and the "modern style" of the nineteenth century. With a determination bordering on the eccentric to produce the finest possible printing, Baskerville set out at age forty-five and with no previous experience to become a typefounder and printer (his first fourteen letters took him two years). Besides the letter forms, his innovations included an improved printing press, smoother paper, and better inks, all of which made Baskerville decidedly uncompetitive as a businessman. Franklin, Beaumarchais, and Bodoni were among his admirers, but his typeface had to wait for the twentieth century to achieve its due.